A STORY *of* DUBLIN

The people and events that shaped the city

John McCormack

MENTOR BOOKS

First Published in 2000 by

MENTOR BOOKS
43 Furze Road,
Sandyford Industrial Estate,
Dublin 18,
Republic of Ireland.

Tel: +353-1-295 2112 / 3   Fax: +353-1-295 2114
e-mail: admin@mentorbooks.ie
www.mentorbooks.ie

ISBN 1-84210-072-6

A catalogue record for this book
is available from the British Library

Cover Photograph courtesy of The Gorry Gallery

Illustrations by: Nicola Sedgwick
                   George Kavanagh

Printed in Ireland by ColourBooks Ltd.

3 5 7 9 10 8 6 4 2

CONTENTS

1 In the Beginning 5000BC – 837AD 1

2 The Coming of the Vikings 837 – 1169AD 8

3 Enter the Normans! 1169 – 1210 19

4 A Scottish Army Besieges Dublin 1210 – 1367 37

5 Dublin Welcomes Pretenders to the English Throne;
  Silken Thomas Rebels 1394 – 1537 43

6 The Reformation Brings Turmoil 1532 – 1556 51

7 The Prisoner in the Castle 1556 – 1603 57

8 The Scourge of Oliver Cromwell Hits Ireland 1607 – 1654 63

9 King James II and the Battle of the Boyne 1660 – 1690 76

10 From Penal Laws to United Irishmen 1690 – 1782 87

11 From Rebellion to Union 1798 – 1801 113

12 Ireland and Great Britain become the United Kingdom 1800 125

13 Robert Emmet, 'The Darling of Ireland' 1778 – 1803 132

14 Daniel O'Connell, The Great Liberator 1775 – 1848 139

15 The Great Hunger Stalks the Land 1845 – 1848 155

16 The Fenian Chief 1824 – 1901 161

17 'The Blackbird of Avondale' 1846 – 1891 172

18 The Dawn of the Twentieth Century 1890 – 1916 197

19 'A Terrible Beauty is Born' 1916 225

20 After the Rising 1916 – 1922 243

21 The Civil War and the Hungry Thirties 1922 – 1939 255

22 From the Emergency to the Haughey Era 1939 – 1990 271

23 The End of the Second Millennium 1991 – 1999 288

To my wife
Monica
for all her help
and encouragement

1

◎

IN THE BEGINNING
5000 BC – 837 AD

lthough no town as such existed at Dublin prior to the arrival of the Vikings in the ninth century AD it is known that man had occupied the area long before this. Traces of human habitation from 5000 BC have been found on Dalkey Island, stone axes from 4000 BC were unearthed at Sutton, portal graves from 3500 BC exist at Kilternan, Larch Hill, Mount Venus and Brennanstown and Dublin's first dolmen from 3000 BC was found on the Hill of Howth. Other prehistoric remains in the area include the gallery graves at Ballyedmonduff and Kilmashogue (2000 BC), burial cists at St Mary's Hospital in the Phoenix Park (1800 BC) and a tumulus at Drimnagh (1500 BC).

About the year 300 BC the first Gaelic settlers came to Ireland and are believed to have arrived in the Dublin area around the year 250 BC. As well as erecting countless ring forts (*raths*) and forts (*dún*) throughout Ireland they have left place names such as Rathfarnham, Rathmines and Raheny.

The River Liffey has always played an important part in the story of Dublin. The river rises east of the Sally Gap in the Wicklow Mountains, about 550 metres above sea level. In Celtic times the wide mouth of the river was just east of the present Capel Street Bridge. The River Poddle entered the estuary at this point and tidal action is believed to have created a large pool where the present-day gardens of Dublin Castle are situated. The pool was known as the *Linn Dubh*, or Black Pool, from which the town eventually got its name.

The Liffey itself was shallow and tidal. An earlier name for it was *Ruirtheach*, meaning turbulent or flooding. In fact it was not until the twentieth century that the danger of flooding was brought

———— ◎ ————

It is interesting to note that the Gaelic version of the name Dublin today is *Baile Átha Cliath* (Town of the Hurdle Ford) and not *Dubh Linn* (Black Pool) from which its name really derives.

———— ◎ ————

An unusual feature of the River Liffey is the fact that while the river is 110 kilometres long from source to finish it is only 23 kilometres long between the same two points as the crow flies.

———— ◎ ————

The early monasteries were mostly wooden structures enclosed inside ramparts for protection. They resembled small villages rather than the imposing buildings we associate with monasteries today.

———— ◎ ————

The Celts were a warlike people, their main weapons being iron swords and spears. They often rode into battle on light two-wheeled chariots, which carried two men – the warrior and his charioteer. Their favourite form of fighting was single combat where the best warrior from each side settled the issue. According to the historians they sometimes fought completely naked.

———— ◎ ————

They were fond of food and drink and great feasts feature largely in their sagas. The greatest warrior present at the feast would be given 'The Hero's Portion' but this could lead to trouble. There was often a fight to the death to decide who would receive the honour.

———— ◎ ————

under control by the building of dams at Pollaphuca, Golden Falls and Leixlip. Normally the river would flow through a fairly narrow channel with sandbanks and sloblands on each side but during flooding and at high tides the river would spread over vast areas. At its mouth it was about three hundred metres wide when the tide was out. When Essex Bridge, at the end of Capel Street, was built in 1676 it was the nearest bridge to the mouth of the river. All of Dublin which now lies between O'Connell Bridge and Sandymount, except for a narrow neck of land at Ringsend, was covered by the sea twice daily

In those early times the land was covered in vast forests, bogs and marshes. Wolves, wild boar, bear and the gigantic Irish elk roamed the land. Over time, however, man gradually began to cut down sections of the forest and by the time of St Patrick much of the forest north of the Liffey would have been cleared away. In the more mountainous areas south of the river, forest clearance would be confined to areas around the monasteries and other small settlements.

As mentioned above, the Gaels came to Ireland sometime around 300 BC and they brought with them a tribal form of society, the Irish language and the use of iron. Historians generally agree that Gaelic Dublin consisted of two settlements, *Áth Cliath*, (from the Gaelic *áth*, a ford and *cliath*, a hurdle) and *Dubh Linn*, (from the Gaelic *dubh*, black and *linn* a pool). The Hurdle Ford, *Áth Cliath*, across the Liffey, was probably just upstream from where Fr Mathew Bridge joins Church Street and Bridge Street today. The hurdle ford itself may have consisted of a sort of mat of branches laid at right angles on lines of saplings bound together and stretching across at the bottom of the river. At low tide it would be possible to cross the river on the pathway thus provided, but not without some danger. (In 770 AD a large party of raiders from the Boyne valley were drowned there as they made their way home from a successful expedition.)

The *Áth Cliath* settlement was ideally positioned where four of the major 'roads' or pathways of ancient Ireland met at the Liffey, the *Slighe Midluachra* from Ulster, the *Slighe Mór* from Connaught, the *Slighe Chualann* from South Leinster and Waterford and the *Slighe Dála* from Munster. One can only guess why the four roads should meet in the Dublin area but it does

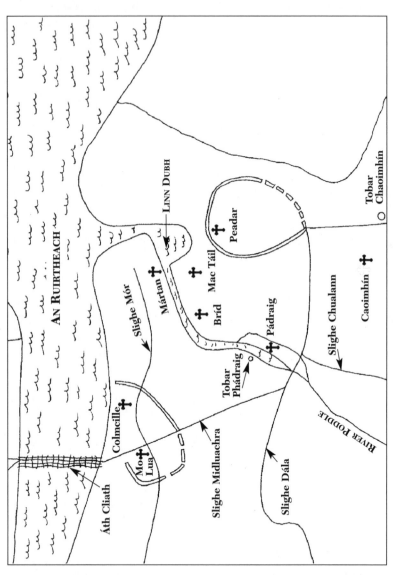

Ancient roads and religious centres of Gaelic Dublin.

suggest that the area was of some importance even then.

The first three of these roads are believed to have met where present day Thomas Street, Francis Street and St Augustine Street meet at Cornmarket. The *Slighe Mór* probably followed the Inchicore, Kilmainham, James Street route; the *Slighe Chualann* came in by Harold's Cross and the *Slighe Midluachra* along the Drumcondra, Dorset Street route. The fourth road, the *Slighe Dála* from Munster, came in by present-day Crumlin Road and ended in the area of St Patrick's Cathedral. This was the site of the large monastic settlement, called *Dubh Linn*, during early Christian times. The last abbot of *Dubh Linn* died five years before the arrival of the Vikings.

From around 430 AD onwards Ireland gradually became converted to Christianity, mainly through the efforts of St Patrick. With Christianity came reading and writing and for the first time written annals came into existence. In the *Áth Cliath* area two churches dedicated to St Colum Cille and St Mo Lua are thought to date from the early Christian period. Other early monasteries and hermit cells were established at Howth Head (St Fintan) and Dalkey Island (St Begnet). Along the Poddle, churches dedicated to St Martin, St Mac Táil, St Brigid and St Patrick were established.

As the centuries passed, the Irish monasteries became centres of learning and were filled with wonderful works of art such as illustrated manuscripts, chalices, shrines and crosses. The monasteries, therefore, were to prove an irresistible target for the next race of invaders. These were the Vikings.

St Patrick's Cathedral was first built sometime in the fifth century on an island created where the River Poddle divided in two. It was originally a wooden structure and was rebuilt a number of times over the centuries. (Today the Poddle flows in a culvert underneath the church and enters the Liffey through an opening in the south wall at Wellington Quay. An iron grating was placed over the opening in the nineteenth century during the 'Fenian' era to prevent an underground attack on Dublin Castle.)

   Tradition has it that St Patrick baptised Christian converts at a spot marked today with a Celtic cross at the west end of the nave of the cathedral. He is also credited with causing three miraculous springs to gush forth, one near the cathedral, another in the grounds of Trinity College, and the third in Nassau Place, between Frederick Street South and Kildare Street. Each of these wells was supposed to have great healing powers, while in later years one of the many myths about Guinness stout was that water from the well at the cathedral was responsible for its excellent quality!

St Patrick's Cathedral. Jonathan Swift, author of *Gulliver's Travels* was Dean of St Patrick's in the early eighteenth century.

The church dedicated to St Colm Cille stood where St Audoen's now stands. It had a 'lucky stone' to which Dubliners flocked when they needed favours. It is still to be seen in the porch of St Audoen's.

The Lucky Stone in St Audoen's Church where Dubliners flocked to ask for favours.

One of the most famous Irish relics in early Christian times was the *Bachall Íosa* (the Staff of Jesus). The staff was believed to have been presented to St Patrick by Jesus Himself on an island in the Mediterranean. St Bernard of Clairvaux describes it as 'covered with gold and adorned with the most costly gems' but in all probability he was describing the case which St Patrick had made for it by his favourite goldsmith and companion, St Tassach. The Annals of Ulster and the Annals of the Four Masters mention the staff as being one of the symbols of St Patrick's authority. During disputes between Irish chieftains, peace treaties were made and signed over it and the most solemn vows were made in its presence. The staff was originally kept in Armagh but in the eleventh century it was brought for safekeeping to *Baile Bachaill* (Ballyboghill), north of Dublin.

2

◎

THE COMING OF THE VIKINGS
837 – 1169 AD

(Note: The raiders from the Scandinavian countries are variously known as Danes, Norsemen, Ostmen and Vikings. For purposes of convenience the term Viking is used throughout this book.)

Early in the ninth century the first Viking raids occurred on the coasts of Ireland. The raiders came from the valleys and fjords of Norway and were excellent seamen. Although highly skilled in many crafts, they excelled particularly in the design and construction of ships. The typical Viking ship had low raking lines, a high curved prow and was of such shallow draught that it could operate equally well on the high seas and in estuaries, lakes and rivers.

The Viking ship. Because of its shallow draught it was equally at home on the high seas and rivers and lakes.

Sporadic hit-and-run attacks occurred all around the coasts of Ireland, where the raiders showed no mercy, looting the monasteries and carrying off booty and slaves back to their homelands. Then in 837, according to the Annals of Ulster, a fleet of sixty-five ships sailed from Scotland and Orkney and entered Dublin Bay. From then on the character of the Viking attacks changed. Monasteries continued to be targeted but the seizure of land for settlement became their chief objective. Four years later the Dublin Vikings built a permanent ship enclosure called a *longphort*, where they could draw up their ships above the tide. The exact location of this *longphort* is not known but archaeological remains discovered at Islandbridge, when workmen were digging a railway cutting in the nineteenth century, seem to confirm that the settlement was in that area. The site there was enclosed by the junction of the Camac with the Liffey and would be an ideal location for an easily defended stockade.

In 902 the settlement at Islandbridge was destroyed by the native Irish and the Vikings apparently abandoned the whole area for fifteen years. When they returned in 917, they established a new settlement two miles downstream from Islandbridge. The new settlement then established was located on a natural ridge about sixteen metres above the river and running parallel to it from present day High Street to Castle Street. (It is difficult nowadays to observe contours and elevations in built-up areas but if one stands at the junction of High Street with Christchurch Place one can see the steep slope down Winetavern Street to the Liffey and the gentler slope down Nicholas Street to St Patrick's Cathedral.) Side streets such as Winetavern Street and Fishamble Street running down to the Liffey were included inside the defences. The sites of Dublin Castle, Christchurch and the new Civic Offices at Wood Quay also mark areas within the boundaries. To protect the settlement the Vikings built a ditch and an earthen bank with a fence of stakes at the top all around it.

The people lived in rectangular wooden houses, with mud-and-wattle walls and thatched roofs. Such houses never lasted very long and when one collapsed another was built on the remains. (During excavations at Wood Quay layers of such houses have been found on top of each other like a pack of cards.) In most cases they had only one room, with an open fire in the middle for cooking and

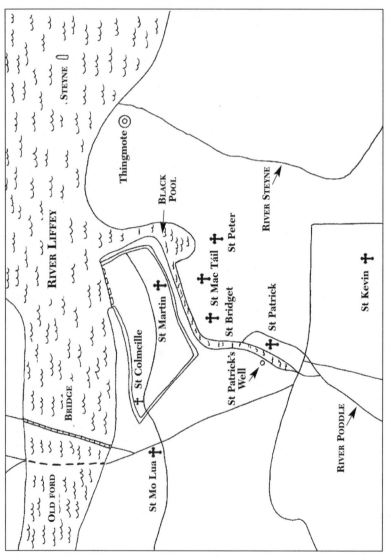

Viking Dublin

warmth. There was no chimney, simply a hole in the roof to let the smoke escape. Fire was a constant hazard and the many burned remains discovered in archaeological digs bear witness to this.

Gradually the settlement became the most important one on the eastern part of the country. The new settlers generally got on well with many of their new neighbours and engaged in trade and commerce. The increasing importance of the settlement was shown by the establishment of the Thingmote (or Thingmount) at Hoggen Green (later called College Green). It was located where Suffolk Street meets Church Lane today and was therefore outside the settlement. The 'Thing' was an assembly place widely used by Scandinavians as a sort of parliament. The Thingmote in Hoggen Green was a specially built flat-topped hill about thirteen metres high and eighty metres in circumference at the base. The king would have the seat of honour at the top and his sons and other noblemen would be arranged in tiers of seats below him. Apart from political decisions being made at the Thingmote, it is believed that the Vikings used to sacrifice prisoners there to appease their gods.

The Thingmote also served as a lookout post; because of the flat land all around, it afforded an uninterrupted view of the bay and the mouth of the Liffey. Games and contests were also held around the base of the hill.

With the passing of time the Vikings engaged more and more in trade and commerce. They depended a great deal on the native Irish population for food, clothing and other materials. Most of the Gaelic monasteries still survived, such as those at Clondalkin, Swords, Crumlin, Shankill, Kilmainham, Glasnevin and Tallaght. Some historians have regarded the years 876–915 as 'the forty years of peace' when Viking raids outside Dublin greatly reduced. Soon afterwards new waves of invaders, mostly Danes, began invading the Dublin area. Again the Irish resisted but were decisively defeated in the Battle of Dublin which was fought at Islandbridge on 17 December 919. The presence of the Vikings was now to be a permanent feature.

The Viking victory at Islandbridge did not bring peace, however, as during the following years the Irish outside the settlement began to attack and plunder Dublin. Constant battles continued between the Vikings and the native Irish for the rest of the century,

———— ◎ ————

When the Vikings first landed in Dublin they erected a pillar of stone, about four metres high, to mark the spot. It is thought to have been erected where College Street, Pearse Street, Townsend Street, Hawkins Street and D'Olier Street meet today. It is believed to have stood there for 850 years before it was removed and its whereabouts forgotten. In 1986 a granite pillar, sculpted by Cliodhna Cussen, was erected to commemorate the original Long Stone, or Steyne, as it was called.

The granite pillar at the junction of Pearse Street and D'Olier Street represents the original Long Stone (Steyne) which the Vikings erected.

———— ◎ ————

Even though the Vikings were the first to mint coins in Dublin, it seems that generally they did not have much use for them. They did not carry purses and are supposed to have concealed coins in times of danger by sticking them to armpit hair with beeswax.

———— ◎ ————

culminating in the Battle of Clontarf in 1014. (It must be said however that Viking chieftains formed many alliances with native Irish leaders.)

In 1002 Brian Boru, leader of the Dalcassians of North Munster, declared himself High King of Ireland. The Vikings, who retained the kingship of Dublin, sided with Maolmordha, King of Leinster, in his refusal to acknowledge Brian as High King. So when Malachy, King of Tara, asked for his assistance against Maolmordha and the Vikings, Brian marched on Dublin. His route was through east Leinster, and around the Wicklow Mountains until he reached Kilmainham. (At that time Kilmainham included the district north and south of the Liffey covering present day Phoenix Park, Inchicore, Kilmainham and Chapelizod.) Here he encamped overlooking the Viking settlement. Meanwhile the Dublin Vikings appealed for help from their countrymen all around northern Europe and consequently a large Viking fleet sailed into Dublin Bay on Palm Sunday, 18 April 1014. There they found Brian's army waiting for them.

At that time all of Dublin lay south of the Liffey. The district on the north side of the river was open country, with a natural forest called Tomar's Wood (named in honour of the Norse god Thor) stretching from the neighbourhood of Drumcondra, on by Phibsborough, towards the Liffey. The only way to cross the river was by Dubhghall's Bridge, a wooden structure, which is thought to have been built in 1000 by the Vikings, on, or close by, the site of the ancient ford (*Áth Cliath*).

The main battleground for the Battle of Clontarf extended from about the present Upper O'Connell Street, Dorset Street and Drumcondra Road to the River Tolka, and down to Ballybough and the North Strand. The Vikings stood with their backs to the sea; the Irish on the land side facing them. Malachy and his men stood on the high ground, probably somewhere about Cabra and Phibsborough. The fiercest fighting appears to have taken place round the fishing weir on the Tolka, at, or perhaps a little above, the present Ballybough Bridge: and indeed the battle is known in some Irish histories as 'The Battle of the Weir of Clontarf'.

At the end of the day (Good Friday, 23 April 1014) seven thousand on the Viking side were dead, of whom four thousand are said to have been 'foreigners' that is, they had not been living in

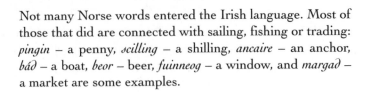

Not many Norse words entered the Irish language. Most of those that did are connected with sailing, fishing or trading: *pingin* – a penny, *scilling* – a shilling, *ancaire* – an anchor, *bád* – a boat, *beor* – beer, *fuinneog* – a window, and *margad* – a market are some examples.

The Viking word for island was Ey or Eyland and from this we get the names Lamb Ey (Lambay Island), Dalk Ey (Dalkey) and Ireland's Ey (Ireland's Eye)

Strangely enough in view of the description of the Viking army which fought the Normans, no body armour from Viking times has been discovered in Dublin archaeological digs but iron swords, spearheads, axeheads, and large numbers of decorated bronze pins and combs made from bone or the antlers of red deer, have been found.

Among items discovered in archaeological digs in Dublin in 1970 were finely woven hair nets. They also discovered that the diet of the inhabitants included beef, pork, grain, wild nuts, berries and figs.

During excavations at Copper Alley in Temple Bar West an extraordinary discovery was made when the archaeologists came across the remains of a 'strange house' which seemed to pre-date the arrival of the Vikings. The house appeared to have measured seven metres by four metres, with a hearth and a side entrance. The walls were of a type not used by the Vikings.

The house was found at the lowest level of the dig, under the Viking buildings and a comb found in it could only have come from Roman-Britain. The experts are convinced that the site was occupied by Anglo-Saxons before the arrival of the Vikings in the ninth century.

Ireland before the battle. Most of the leaders on both sides were killed, including Maolmordha, the chief inciter of the battle. Brian Boru, himself, being too old to take part in the battle, was slain in his tent by Brodir, one of the Danish leaders.

In spite of the fact that the Battle of Clontarf is given a prominent place in romantic Irish history in reality it was of no real political significance. It is true however that it marked the end of the Viking wars. There were some later raids but they had little effect on the internal political struggles which followed the death of Brian Boru. Sitric Silkenbeard, the Viking king of Dublin, remained in control until 1036 and far from being the pagan ogre of legend, he was in fact a devout Christian. Coins minted in Dublin during his reign (the first coins ever to be minted in Ireland) bore his image on one side and the Sign of the Cross on the other. He also went on pilgrimage to Rome and is credited with the foundation of Christchurch Cathedral (originally called the Church of the Holy Trinity). He ended his days as a monk on the island of Iona.

Sitric Silkenbeard's coins were the first to be manufactured in Ireland.

———— ◎ ————

The first stone wall defence around Dublin was built about 1100. Around 1030 the defences of the town were extended to the west to protect the newly built Church of the Holy Trinity (Christchurch).

Christchurch Cathedral was founded by Sitric Silkenbeard and was originally called the Church of the Holy Trinity.

———— ◎ ————

The Vikings who raided Ireland came mostly from the coasts of Norway and Denmark. Early Irish writers called those who came from Norway *Fionnghaill* (White Foreigners), and those from Denmark *Dubhghaill* (Black Foreigners). In popular language in Ireland they were referred to as Danes, while in England they were called Norsemen, Vikings or Ostmen.

———— ◎ ————

St Michan's Church was founded by the Vikings in 1095 but the present church dates from 1685.

———— ◎ ————

With the passing of the years more foreigners intermarried with the native Irish. Both the Vikings and the native Irish practised bigamy. It was considered a status symbol to have more than one wife. When young Viking men were seeking a wife they grew their beards long and used make-up on their eyes.

———— ◎ ————

Legend has it that when Brodir was captured he was executed by disembowelling. His intestine was tied to a tree around which he was then led until he died. However another account tells how Brian cut off both of Brodir's legs with one blow of his heavy sword before he himself was killed. In all probability there is no truth in either legend.

———— ◎ ————

———— ◎ ————

Brian Boru married Gormflaith, sister of Maolmordha, King of Leinster, and mother of King Sitric of Dublin. King Sitric in turn married Brian's daughter.

———— ◎ ————

In 917 the Vikings built a wood-and-timber rampart around their settlement. Present century excavations have discovered Viking artefacts, such as combs, footwear and necklaces, from the period. Many of these are now on display in the National Museum

———— ◎ ————

Harold's Cross in Dublin gets its name from a Viking tribe called Harold which owned land in that area.

———— ◎ ————

Gradually the foreigners became converted to Christianity, so much so that in 948 the Vikings are believed to have founded St Mary's Abbey near the bottom of present day Capel Street. This abbey was said to be run by the Benedictines. (The existing abbey of the same name was founded on this site in 1139 by the Normans and was run by the Cistercians.)

———— ◎ ————

Vegetables commonly used by the Vikings were onions, cabbages, parsnips, peas, beans and leeks.

———— ◎ ————

3
◎
ENTER THE NORMANS!
1169 – 1210

In 1166 Rory O'Connor of Connacht was formally crowned High King of Ireland in Dublin, the only King of Ireland ever crowned there. The leading families from the rest of the country paid homage and gave him hostages but in reality the power of the High King was extremely limited. Dermot Mac Murrough, King of Leinster, who was actually born in Dublin, was among those who submitted to O'Connor.

Mac Murrough's career was extraordinary. He was responsible for the establishment of the Priory of All Hallows on the site of present day Trinity College and also of the Augustinian Convent at nearby Hoggen Green. One of the nuns there was his own ex-wife,

Dermott Mac Murrough hated the Vikings because they had thrown the body of a dog into his father's grave. As it was he who invited the Normans to Ireland he is forever known as Diarmaid na nGall (Dermot of the Foreigners).

———— ◎ ————

Dublin expanded a good deal in the fifty years which followed the Norman invasion. The areas of expansion were along Thomas Street, Francis Street and Church Street. The most unusual expansion, however, was along the Liffey wall area. The river was shallow here and the Normans decided to reclaim the land by building wooden stockades out from the water's edge and filling in the area between with refuse and rubble. By constantly repeating the process the area between the city walls and the Liffey was reclaimed.Thus when Prince John, Lord of Ireland, granted Dublin a charter he addressed its citizens 'dwelling without the walls and within'.

———— ◎ ————

Although the Vikings were the first to introduce coinage to Dublin it was the Normans who set up mints to issue an official coinage accepted by all. An idea of prices at the time is given by the wages paid to workers at the manor at Clonkeen, Co. Dublin; labourers got one penny a day, carpenters and blacksmiths got two pennies, and thatchers got one-and-a half-pence a day.

———— ◎ ————

During Norman times oxen were very important as they were used for ploughing – their tails were tied to the plough. This practice was to last for many more centuries.

———— ◎ ————

The Normans were the first to introduce rabbits to Ireland. At first they were regarded as a luxury but by the fourteenth century they had become a regular part of the people's diet.

———— ◎ ————

Because of the tendency of the Liffey to silt up during Norman times, large boats were unable to navigate its waters and were obliged to anchor at Clontarf, Howth or Dalkey.

———— ◎ ————

the sister of Archbishop Laurence O'Toole. On one occasion he attacked the town of Kildare where he dragged the abbess from her convent and married her off to one of his officers. In 1142 he attacked some of his opponents, killed two of the nobles, gouged out the eyes of another and blinded seventeen lesser chieftains. In 1152 he carried off Devorgilla, the wife of Tiernan O'Rourke of Breifne, while O'Rourke was absent from home and she took away all she had brought to her husband as a dowry, including 140 cows. Some historians say she arranged the whole thing! Mac Murrough was later forced to restore Devorgilla and all her dowry to her husband. She later retired to Mellifont Abbey in Co. Louth where she died in 1193 at the age of eighty-five.

Finally in 1166 Mac Murrough's behaviour became unbearable and he was banished by O'Connor, O'Rourke and others. He fled to Bristol to seek help from the King of England. On learning that the king, Henry II, was in France at the time, Dermot went there and presented himself before him.

Henry was a fierce, determined man with great energy and ability but so given to violent rages that he was said to be possessed by the devil. He was more French than English; of his thirty-five years as King of England, he only spent thirteen years there and never spoke any of the language. While the Normans, (descendants of Vikings who had settled in northern France), had easily conquered England, they got much stiffer resistance from the Welsh chieftains. Henry had placed some of his toughest barons, together with their Flemish mercenaries, on the Welsh 'marches', with the liberty to keep any land they could wrest from the Welsh. It was to these tough barons that Henry sent Mac Murrough for help.

Chief among the Norman barons in Wales was Richard de Clare, Earl of Pembroke – better known as 'Strongbow' – who had recently lost back to their rightful owners the lands his father had won. Strongbow was, therefore, only too willing to jump at the chance of a new conquest in Ireland. Another group of Norman families, known in Irish history as the 'Geraldines', were also on the Welsh marches. They were closely related and had names like FitzGerald, FitzHenry and de Barri. They were more or less in the same position as Strongbow. They too lent a willing ear to Mac Murrough.

———— ◎ ————

During Norman times there was only the most basic water supply in the town and a complete lack of sanitary facilities. The finding of bundles of moss in excavated cesspits seems to indicate that moss was used as we would use toilet paper today. Streets were filthy and stinking from offal, carcasses and dung. Herds of scavenging pigs roamed the streets and the smells must have been horrendous. Animals grazed on the grass of Hoggen Green and other sites.

In 1224 a rudimentary water supply was provided for the city. Water was diverted from the Poddle and the Dodder along a conduit to large tanks along the High Street-Thomas Street ridge. Some pipes extended the supply from there. St Saviour's Priory, just across the Liffey to the east of the Old Bridge, had water supplied to it through a 125mm pipe. Because of the scarcity of the water supply it was decreed that 'within [the priory] the pipe is to be so narrowed that its opening may be stopped by the insertion of a man's little finger'. (In houses, if they had a water supply, the pipes were to be 'no thicker than a goose quill'.)

———— ◎ ————

The first fortified castles built by the Normans consisted of earthen and wooden defences called motte-and-baileys. First they built up huge circular mounds of earth over ten metres high with steep sides. On the flat top of this mound they built a wooden tower for living quarters. The whole area was then protected by a wooden palisade around the edges. A sloping ladder-like bridge connected this part (the motte) to a lower area called the bailey. This was another circular area protected by a palisade, inside which, soldiers, workers, cattle, horses and provisions were kept in safety. If the castle was attacked, the people in the bailey could retire to the motte and destroy the connecting bridge. The remains of many of these motte-and-baileys can still be seen around the country in the form of grassy mounds, without the wooden buildings of course.

Among the castles built by the Normans were those at Castleknock, Drimnagh, Dalkey and Clondalkin. From about 1200 onwards, because the Normans were more in control in Ireland they started to build more substantial castles of stone. Many of these imposing buildings are still standing to this day.

———— ◎ ————

Strongbow's tomb in Christchurch Cathedral

What is sometimes called the 'English' invasion of Ireland was, therefore, carried out by the subjects of a French king, the leaders were French-speaking Normans, many were half-Welsh, and many of their followers were Flemish mercenaries.

The most outstanding thing about the Normans was their military prowess. Like their ancestors the Vikings, the Norman barons and knights looked upon fighting as their only profession. Their arms and armour were the best available at the time. The knights, clad completely from head to toe in armour, and carrying long lances, fought on horseback. Their archers, no less formidable, armed with the famous long bow or the cross-bow, supported them on foot. The Normans had perfect discipline in battle, and they never allowed the fierce jealousies which otherwise prevailed among them to interfere with their effectiveness on the field of battle. They were also expert in the building of castles and fortifications.

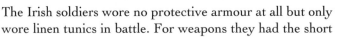

The Norman soldier was a formidable fighting man; fighting was his trade. From the age of thirteen he was specially trained for war. The most important soldiers were the mounted knights who charged the enemy in tight groups. Each knight wore a coat of mail consisting of thousands of rings of steel linked together. The head was protected by a steel helmet, which at first was cone-shaped with a narrow strip to act as a nose guard. Later helmets covered the head completely, with slits for the eyes. Each knight carried a kite-shaped shield, usually bearing his coat of arms. For weapons they used a combination of long lances, swords, battle-axes or maces with fearsome cutting edges.

The Norman infantry did not wear armour but they did have helmets and padded tunics. The most feared of all were the archers. Mostly they used the long bow, which was about 1.8 metres in length and generally made of yew. The bowstring was made of hemp.

The arrows were made of ash or oak, tipped with a steel arrowhead. A good archer could pierce chain mail at a distance of about 370 metres.

The Irish soldiers wore no protective armour at all but only wore linen tunics in battle. For weapons they had the short sword, the sling and the battle-axe.

It was extremely difficult to qualify as a freeman of the city of Dublin if one was of Irish stock. A roll of the free citizens of Dublin at this time lists only one citizen as being Irish (Hiberniensis).

When Mac Murrough arrived in Bristol he secured an agreement that Strongbow would come to Ireland on condition that Mac Murrough would give him his daughter Aoife in marriage and that Strongbow would become King of Leinster on Mac Murrough's death. Mac Murrough also got a number of Geraldines, among them Robert Fitzstephen and Maurice Fitzgerald, to agree to help him on the promise of the gift of the town of Wexford and surrounding districts. He then returned to Ferns in Co. Wexford where he spent the winter of 1168 in the monastery founded by himself.

In May 1169 the first body of Normans landed at Bannow Bay and proceeded to capture the town of Wexford. In August the following year Strongbow arrived in Waterford Harbour with an army of 3,000 men and together with Mac Murrough's army and earlier Norman arrivals they attacked the town. After a fierce battle they were successful and 'while the streets ran red with blood', Strongbow and Aoife were married.

Immediately after the wedding the combined army set out for Dublin. The Vikings of Dublin had a special reason for fearing Mac Murrough, for they had murdered his father and insultingly buried him with the body of a dog. Accordingly, when Mac Murrough sent messengers demanding their submission, their king, Asculph Mac Torkill, defied him, and at the same time, asked for help from the High King.

Rory O'Connor had a far larger army than the five thousand Normans who were coming to attack Dublin, while the Wicklow Mountains presented a natural barrier to their progress. When O'Connor arrived at the city he established his main army on a plain at Clondalkin and set up defences at the Scalp above Enniskerry and at Windgates on the coast road just south of Bray. But he had not reckoned with the local knowledge of Mac Murrough, who simply bypassed the defences and came across the mountains by way of Glendalough, Glencree and down through Rathfarnham. From there his army made its way through the woods which reached to the very walls of the city.

The defenders were taken by surprise and sent out Archbishop Laurence O'Toole to mediate. But while he listened to the demands of his brother-in-law, Mac Murrough (that the town give him hostages and recognise him as High King) two Norman

———— ◎ ————

When the Normans took control of Dublin they set about organising it like a typical European town. Strong surrounding stone walls, strengthened by towers at strategic points, were started about 1204. The walls were about five metres high and two metres thick. Elaborate gateways were built at various points in the walls to allow access to the town by approved persons. St Audoen's Arch is the sole surviving example today. Other gates were known as Pole Gate, Dames Gate, St Nicholas Gate, and New Gate. The River Poddle was diverted to run around the walls on the south and east, while the Liffey flowed along the northern side, so that Dublin was surrounded by water on three sides. On the fourth side, the west, large ditches were used for defence. The wall which had been built by the Vikings was kept as another line of defence in case the outer wall was breached.

St Audoen's Arch is the last surviving gateway from the city walls of the thirteenth century. Its demolition was prevented in 1880 but its renovation was poorly done.

———— ◎ ————

knights, Raymond le Gros and Milo de Cogan, led a small party of knights on a raid and forced their way into the town. They then commenced slaughtering the townspeople. King Asculph and many of his followers, seeing the town was lost, ran to some ships they had moored in the Liffey for just such an emergency, and sailed away. And so, on 21 September 1170, Dublin fell into the hands of the Normans. This date, therefore, marks the start of the 'English' occupation of Ireland. (When Dublin fell to the Normans, O'Connor's army withdrew, each unit going back to its own territory.)

Early the following year, when Mac Murrough died at Ferns Strongbow declared himself King of Leinster, a decision that was bound to annoy King Henry II, among others. In the meantime the ousted king of Dublin, Asculph Mac Torkill, had gathered a large force of Viking allies, amounting to about a thousand men, and returned to attempt the recapture of the town. The Norman historian, Geraldus Cambrensis, describes the Vikings thus:

> They were warlike figures, clad in mail in every part of their body after the Danish manner. Some wore long coats of mail, others iron plates skilfully knitted together, and they had round, red shields protected by iron round the edge.

After they landed the Vikings attacked the eastern gate of Dublin, armed with that ferocious weapon, the battle-axe. Norman knights on horseback charged out to meet them and after a final fierce fight at Hoggen Green, the Vikings were routed. Asculph was taken prisoner and tried in the hall of his own palace in Dublin. He was defiant to the end and was beheaded forthwith.

By this time Rory O'Connor had assembled a large army to attack Dublin. When he reached the town he set up his camp at Castleknock and sealed off all approaches in order to force the Normans into surrender by starvation. For two months he cut off all supplies until the Normans were in a desperate state. Not only could they get no assistance from their other Norman strongholds at Wexford and Waterford, but also they had no hope of getting help from King Henry II who was afraid that Strongbow might set up an independent kingdom in Ireland.

The following is a contemporary description of Strongbow:
He had reddish hair and freckles, grey eyes, a
feminine face, a weak voice and a short neck,
though in almost all other respects he was of a tall
build. He was a generous and easy-going man.
What he could not accomplish by deed he settled
by the persuasiveness of his words. When he took
up his position in the midst of battle, he stood firm
as an immovable standard round which his men
could re-group and take refuge. In war he
remained steadfast and reliable in good fortune
and bad alike. In adversity no feelings of despair
caused him to waver, while lack of self-restraint
did not make him run amok when successful.

When Strongbow died, he was buried with great ceremony
by Raymond le Gros in Christchurch Cathedral, with
Archbishop Laurence O'Toole conducting the ceremonies.
In 1562 Strongbow's tomb was badly damaged when the
roof of the cathedral collapsed. The tomb was repaired by
Sir Henry Sidney in 1670. (The coat of arms displayed on
the tomb today is that of another Norman knight called
FitzOsmund. This knight may have been substituted for
Strongbow after the roof collapse.) A small statue by the
side of Strongbow is believed to contain either part of the
body of his wife or the body of his son, whom he cut in half
with his sword for cowardice in the face of the enemy.

Up until the middle of the eighteenth century Strongbow's
tomb was a regularly used meeting point for the payment of
bonds, rents and bills of exchange.

Apart from Strongbow's tomb in Christchurch Cathedral,
two other Norman tombs can be seen in Dublin churches.
St Werburgh's has the double tomb of a knight and his lady
from the thirteenth century, while St Audoen's houses a
similar tomb dating from 1482. (St Audoen's, which was
called after the Norman Saint Ouen of Rouen, is the only
medieval church still surviving in Dublin.)

So the Normans inside the town decided to make one final effort. They assembled three experienced units, each consisting of about forty knights on horseback, sixty bowmen and a hundred foot soldiers. Commanded by Milo de Cogan, Raymond le Gros and Strongbow (who had hurried back from Wexford), they set out to attack O'Connor's main army at Castleknock. The Irish were taken completely by surprise and O'Connor, who was in his bath at the time (other accounts have him bathing in the Liffey), was lucky to escape half-naked from the field. The rest of his army fled in panic, while the Normans returned in triumph to the city with enough provisions for a whole year. After that the Norman presence in Dublin went unchallenged.

In the meantime King Henry II was becoming more and more alarmed at the successes of his knights. He was afraid that Strongbow might make himself King of Ireland. So he decided to come to Ireland himself, taking with him *Laudabiliter*, a papal bull issued many years before by Pope Adrian IV, an Englishman. This authorised the king to take possession of the country. It was also convenient for Henry to be out of England at this time because of the murder of Thomas a' Becket, Archbishop of Canterbury, by four of the king's knights. Henry was accused of the murder and was threatened with excommunication by the Pope. By coming to Ireland at this time he would avoid meeting the Papal Legate who was on his way to England. In October 1171 Henry landed in Waterford Harbour, bringing with him an enormous fleet of 400 ships and a fully equipped army of about 10,000 men. Most of the local chiefs submitted and Henry set out for Dublin where many more of the chiefs surrendered.

King Henry II and his court spent the winter of 1171 in Dublin. A special palace in the Irish style of polished wickerwork was built beside the Thingmote in Hoggen Green. Here Henry gave lavish feasts for the local princes and included such delicacies as roast peacock, wild geese and cranes (the latter a food the Irish hated).

During his stay King Henry II issued a charter presenting the town of 'Duvelina' to the city of Bristol. This ensured that Strongbow would not have control over it, while it also conferred certain economic benefits on the town. In 1172 before Henry left Ireland he confirmed Strongbow as King of Leinster and appointed William de Burgo as his viceroy.

———— ◎ ————

Christchurch Cathedral was rebuilt by the Normans in 1172. For many years afterwards parliament was held in the building.

———— ◎ ————

In 1173 Strongbow captured Ballyboghill and granted the town and the *Bachall Íosa* to Holy Trinity Church (Christchurch Cathedral). Both the Normans and the Irish regarded the *Bachall Íosa* as the most important relic in the cathedral. The ancient practice of having oaths and treaties sealed over it was continued by the Anglo-Normans. The *Bachall Íosa* had a special shrine in the cathedral where both Normans and Irish could come to pray and make their offerings of lights, etc. During a great storm in 1461 the *Bachall Íosa* miraculously survived when the great east window of the cathedral was blown in and other relics of the shrine were destroyed.

———— ◎ ————

In 1192 the reconstruction of St Patrick's Cathedral was begun. It was modelled on the cathedral at Salisbury in England and was built by Archbishop John Comyn as a rival to Christchurch Cathedral.

———— ◎ ————

Although the body of St Laurence O'Toole is buried in Normandy his heart is enshrined in an elaborate casket in the chapel of St Laud in Christchurch Cathedral.

———— ◎ ————

The mummified bodies in St Michan's Church are those of seventeenth-century inhabitants of the city and not those of Norman crusaders as is popularly claimed.

———— ◎ ————

The Vikings in Dublin were in a very weak position at this time. Their king had been beheaded, many of their number had been slaughtered by the Normans and their best men had emigrated. Soon after Henry's visit the majority of the Vikings (Ostmen) still in the city crossed to the north of the river and went to live in an area which became known as Ostmantown (and later Oxmantown). Here they set up their own community. Gradually from this time on, the Vikings of Dublin declined in importance and no longer existed as a separate race. (Stoneybatter in this area of the city still has an individual style and culture to the present day.)

———— ◎ ————

In 1210 the first real bridge to be built over the Liffey was constructed by the Normans. It was where Fr Mathew Bridge is today, linking Church Street and Bridge Street.

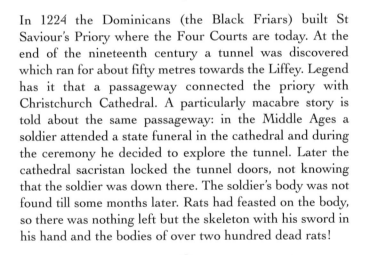

Whitworth (now Fr Mathew) Bridge is on the site of the first bridge across the Liffey. This was the only bridge on the river until the late seventeenth century.

———— ◎ ————

In 1224 the Dominicans (the Black Friars) built St Saviour's Priory where the Four Courts are today. At the end of the nineteenth century a tunnel was discovered which ran for about fifty metres towards the Liffey. Legend has it that a passageway connected the priory with Christchurch Cathedral. A particularly macabre story is told about the same passageway: in the Middle Ages a soldier attended a state funeral in the cathedral and during the ceremony he decided to explore the tunnel. Later the cathedral sacristan locked the tunnel doors, not knowing that the soldier was down there. The soldier's body was not found till some months later. Rats had feasted on the body, so there was nothing left but the skeleton with his sword in his hand and the bodies of over two hundred dead rats!

———— ◎ ————

The office of Mayor of Dublin was first created in 1229 by Henry III. In 1665 the title became the 'Lord' Mayor.

———— ◎ ————

Dublin Castle was constructed on the orders of King John, son of Henry II, who gave the following mandate to his deputy, Meiler Fitzhenry, in Dublin in 1204:

> You have given us to understand that you have no safe place for the custody of our treasure, and because of this reason and many others, we are in need of a strong fortress in Dublin. We command you to build a castle there, making it as strong as you can with good dykes and strong walls. But you are first to build a tower, to which a castle and bailey and other requirements may be conveniently added: for all of these you have our authority.

The first tower to be erected by Meiler Fitzhenry was the Gunpowder Tower. The city wall joined the castle at that point. Boats from the Liffey could reach the castle by means of the Poddle and land provisions at a small gate beside this tower. The construction work was continued by Henry de Londres, Archbishop of Dublin, who was appointed justicier (the king's representative) in 1213 and the task was completed by 1230. The completed castle consisted of a rectangular wall enclosing an open courtyard. The wall was extremely thick and incorporated a tower at each corner and various gates. The main entrance to the castle, which was flanked by two large towers with a drawbridge between them, was in the north wall facing present day Castle Street. The two towers continued in existence up to the middle of the eighteenth century.

Henry III, who never came to Ireland, ordered the construction of a great hall, to be modelled on that in Canterbury. The hall was built between 1243 and 1245 and was to be the centre for many great occasions in the following centuries. It was also the first building in Dublin to get a piped water supply. The finished castle covered an area corresponding fairly closely to that of the present Upper Castle Yard.

The construction of Dublin Castle was ordered by King John and completed around 1215. The most outstanding remains today are the Bermingham and Record Towers. During extensive reconstruction in the twentieth century, Viking town defences were uncovered and are now on view to the public.

———— ◎ ————

In 1209 one of the greatest tragedies to hit the Normans occurred. On Easter Monday of that year a hurling match was played on a pitch located at Cullenswood, beside present-day Sandford Road in Ranelagh. A large number of Dublin citizens were present as spectators at the match when local Irish clans attacked the proceedings. Up to five hundred men were killed. This terrible tragedy, on what was called Black Monday, was commemorated annually in Dublin for six hundred years. Every anniversary, the colonists, fully armed and headed by a black banner, would march out to the scene of the tragedy. There they would hold a feast and formally challenge the mountain tribes to combat.

———— ◎ ————

———— ◎ ————

The Church of St Mary del Dam was built where the Dublin City Hall now stands on Cork Hill. An old tomb from St Mary's is now on view inside the entrance to St Werburgh's Church in Werburgh Street

———— ◎ ————

The immense power and wealth of the monasteries can be gauged from the fact that the Cistercians' St Mary's Abbey had more than five thousand acres north of the Liffey, one hundred and thirty-four houses inside the city and all of Monkstown comprising the area from Blackrock to Dun Laoire. It also owned Bullock Harbour.

———— ◎ ————

Charters of Liberties granted to towns assured freemen that they could only be tried for murder and other crimes, in their own court and by their fellow freemen. The Liberties in Dublin had such a charter.

———— ◎ ————

A Liberty gave great privileges to the recipients in terms of freedom from tolls and taxes of all kinds. The first ever hospital built in Ireland was St John's Hospital, which stood opposite the present-day Augustinian church (John's Lane) in Thomas Street. It was built in 1180 and eight years later Pope Clement III conferred the 'Liberty of Ailred' on the hospital. This was Dublin's first 'Liberty'.

———— ◎ ————

Wine was imported from France, particularly from the La Rochelle region. In fact Back Lane in the Coombe area was once known as Rochelle Street. Other types of drink such as ale, beer and whiskey were popular with the people, both men and women. Brewing was largely carried out in the home and consequently most brewers were female. When Prince John granted a charter to Dublin in 1192 he protected the wine merchants by making it illegal for foreign wine merchants to have a tavern or to sell wine in the city. They could sell wine from a ship, however.

———— ◎ ————

---◎---

The Christian religion seems to have been universally accepted in Ireland. There is only one case of heresy recorded. In 1327 a man named O'Toole was burned at the stake in Hoggen Green. He was charged with denying the incarnation of Christ and saying the bible was a fairytale.

---◎---

In 1204 the famous (or infamous!) Donnybrook Fair was established by Royal Charter to compensate the citizens of Dublin for having to pay for the construction of Dublin Castle. The fair was held on low-lying fields just outside the old village of Donnybrook on the road to Bray where Bective Rangers Rugby Grounds and the CIÉ bus garage now stand. The fair played an important part in the commerce of the city particularly as regards horse trading.

All activity in the city was suspended during those weeks in August on which the fair was held. The fair took place annually for over six hundred years and was famous for merriment, fighting, drunkenness and debauchery of all kinds. This eventually led to a campaign by the local priest, Father Nolan, to have the fair abolished. Public subscriptions were collected and in 1855 the patent was bought from the owners and the fair was allowed to lapse.

---◎---

4

◎

A SCOTTISH ARMY
BESIEGES DUBLIN
1210 – 1367

Whoever was governor of Ireland was also the king's deputy and was supposed to stand in place of the king. He usually resided in Dublin but seldom had an army large enough to enforce his authority. The kings of England made sure that the governors never became too powerful in case one of them might sometime make himself the independent king of Ireland. The fact that the central English government in Dublin never became very strong meant that the great barons in other parts of the country generally cared little enough for the king's authority. The king was too far away from them and generally unaware of what was going on. The barons ruled as independent princes, raising armies, imposing taxes and making war when it suited them. The native chiefs were no better; they too continued to wrangle and fight among themselves.

In the first years of King John's reign the country was in such turmoil that he decided to visit Ireland to impose some order. He landed in 1210 at Waterford with a strong army. From the very beginning the country settled down and he met with little or no opposition. King John returned to England after two months and things remained relatively quiet until his death and the accession of Henry III in 1216. The century that followed saw great turmoil again in the country with the barons and chiefs constantly feuding.

When the Scottish king, Robert Bruce, had a glorious victory over King Edward II at Bannockburn in 1314 the Irish chieftains were hopeful that something similar could be accomplished in Ireland. Some Ulster chieftains sent messengers to Bruce requesting him to send his brother Edward to be King of Ireland.

———————— ◎ ————————

Fire was a constant hazard. In 1190 it destroyed a large section of the city; in 1283 the High Street area including half of Christchurch Cathedral went up in flames; in 1302 St Mary's Abbey on the northside of the Liffey fell victim; in 1362 it was the turn of St Patrick's Cathedral to suffer severe damage to the northwest corner including the tower. The tower was replaced in 1370 by the present magnificent structure which is forty-nine metres high.

———————— ◎ ————————

In 1306 a ship, the *Nicholas of Down,* was shipwrecked on Portmarnock Strand and among the wreckage thrown up on the strand were barrels of spice, coffins, wax, jewels, copper pots, lambs' fur and 'a hood of green'.

———————— ◎ ————————

In 1325 a Tholsel was built opposite Christchurch to act as a town hall in which were located the mayor's office, a prison and a gallows. Over the centuries it fell into decay but was rebuilt in 1680. In 1806 it again became neglected and was pulled down. The figures of Charles II and James II which stood on the facade of the building are now in the crypt of Christchurch Cathedral.

The Tholsel

———————— ◎ ————————

Edward Bruce was only too willing and landed at Larne in May 1315 with an army of 6,000 soldiers. He was immediately joined by some of the Ulster chiefs and together they moved south, destroying all before them. From the beginning the campaign was carried on with great cruelty and with reckless waste of life and property. Everything not required by the army was destroyed, even though famine was widespread and the people were starving.

In 1317 King Robert Bruce came to Ireland to join his brother Edward and together they marched on Dublin with an army of 20,000 men, destroying everything in their path. They encamped at Castleknock outside Dublin before attacking the city. The citizens and authorities in Dublin were greatly alarmed. The Scottish army was so close that the campfires of the soldiers could be seen by the citizens on the walls. The preceding years in Dublin had been relatively peaceful so that the city walls had been largely neglected. Now they were in such a state that they would offer little resistance to a determined army. One of the towers had already collapsed, others were in a poor condition. The authorities decided on drastic action – any structure that could hinder the defence of the city were removed. Houses built against the walls were torn down, towers and gaps were repaired. St John's Hospital and even the bridge over the Liffey were torn down. The belfry of the Church of St Mary del Dam was demolished to strengthen the walls. St Saviour's Priory was also pulled down and the stones were used to build a wall at Merchant's Quay and Wood Quay.

The most drastic step of all, however, was the decision of the Mayor to order that the suburbs be set on fire. The fire got out of control and four-fifths of the suburbs and a part of Christchurch Cathedral were destroyed by the time it died down. The Scottish army were so impressed by the determination of the inhabitants to defend their town that they gave up the siege.

The Bruce army then proceeded to Limerick but again found this city too well defended. So they returned northwards again, losing vast numbers from cold, hunger and disease – scourged by the famine for which they, themselves, were largely responsible.

Shortly afterwards Robert Bruce returned to Scotland and Edward was defeated and killed near Dundalk in 1318. His body was cut into pieces to be hung up in Dublin and other towns in the colony. His head was brought in a salted box to King Edward II.

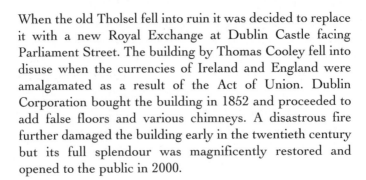

When the old Tholsel fell into ruin it was decided to replace it with a new Royal Exchange at Dublin Castle facing Parliament Street. The building by Thomas Cooley fell into disuse when the currencies of Ireland and England were amalgamated as a result of the Act of Union. Dublin Corporation bought the building in 1852 and proceeded to add false floors and various chimneys. A disastrous fire further damaged the building early in the twentieth century but its full splendour was magnificently restored and opened to the public in 2000.

It is thought that the area in the Coombe just off Clanbrassil Street, known as Blackpitts, got its name from the numbers of victims of the Black Death buried there. Another theory is that the name comes from the black vats used by Huguenot tanners in the area in the eighteenth century.

In the winter of 1338 the weather was so severe that the Liffey froze solid for all of January and February. The citizens of Dublin had a great time, playing football and holding 'barbecues' on the ice.

In 1329 the first attempt was made to pave the streets of Dublin. Many cities in England and elsewhere did not have paved streets until much later.

Certain bakers who were found guilty of using false weights for their bread around this period were publicly punished. They were drawn through the streets of Dublin on hurdles tied to horses' tails.

Even though Bruce's invasion was a dismal failure the Anglo-Irish government forces grew progressively weaker. The Irish, taking advantage of their condition, attacked them at every turn. Moreover, more and more of the English were becoming absorbed into the native population and culture. They adopted the Irish language, dress and customs. The government gave an added impetus to the process by favouring the New English over the Old English, putting them into positions of trust over the older colonists. These were so incensed that many of them – Geraldines, Butlers, de Burgos and others, turned against the government and became as the phrase has it, 'more Irish than the Irish themselves'.

Almost the only part of the settlement to remain loyal to the Crown was the district in the east of the country, with Dublin at its centre. The area of this district varied from time to time but was about 48 kilometres long and 32 kilometres wide. In 1494 a parliament held in Drogheda by the Lord Deputy, Edward Poynings, ordered that the area was to be surrounded with a double ditch, two metres high on the part 'which mereth next into Irishmen'. What this meant was that two ditches, with a high bank between them, were to be constructed. It was not meant to be a very formidable defence but was mainly to hinder the theft of cattle from within the area. It seems the double ditch was never entirely completed and large sections of the area were still open to attack. This is the area that became known as the 'Pale'. (The word 'pale' is from the Latin word for a stake.)

The land within the Pale was entirely under the control of the English settlers. The boundaries were defined as stretching from Dalkey to Merrion, on to the Dodder and from there to Saggart, Rathcoole, Kilkeel, Rathmore, Ballymore Eustace, Naas, Clane, Kilcock and Dundalk.

Not only were the inhabitants of the Pale constantly subject to pillage and war but to add to their miseries they were scourged by terrible plagues. It is estimated that between the years 1000 and 1500 up to fifteen epidemics or plagues were suffered by the unfortunate inhabitants of Dublin. The most serious by far was the bubonic plague, also known as the Black Death, which hit the city sometime in 1348. The first places in Ireland to be affected were Dalkey, Howth and Drogheda.

The fleas of the black rat carried the deadly bacilli from person to person, infecting everyone they bit. The plague was given the name 'Black' because the most obvious symptoms of the disease were black inflamed swellings in the armpits and groin of the victim. The swellings are known as buboes, hence the name 'bubonic'. The terrible epidemic killed huge numbers of the inhabitants of Dublin in the following months. There is no way of verifying the numbers who died. It is estimated that about one-third of the population perished – about four thousand out of twelve thousand inhabitants at the time. People living in close proximity to each other seemed to be particularly at risk. Consequently, the monasteries were badly affected. After 1348 no new entries were made in the annals of the Priory of the Holy Trinity, which was attached to Christchurch Cathedral, which implies that there was no one left to write the annals.

The plague seems to have had a much greater effect on the colonists in the Pale than the native Irish, particularly those who lived in the more remote areas. The loss of so many of the colonists greatly alarmed the authorities because the survival of the colony depended on their numbers.

5

◉

DUBLIN WELCOMES PRETENDERS TO THE ENGLISH THRONE; SILKEN THOMAS REBELS 1394 – 1537

The Irish chieftain who gave most trouble to the Castle authorities towards the end of the fourteenth century was Art Mac Murrough Kavanagh, King of Leinster. He forced the Dublin authorities to pay him 'black rent' – a form of protection money. The growing threat to the English government by leaders like Mac Murrough caused King Richard II to come to Ireland in 1394 with a huge army to force the whole country to submit to English rule.

Mac Murrough at first attacked and harassed Richard's army but finally, along with about seventy other chiefs, offered his submission to the king. They were invited to Dublin where they were feted and feasted by the king for three days in Dublin Castle. Richard knighted the four provincial kings, O'Neill of Ulster, O'Connor of Connacht, O'Brien of Munster and Mac Murrough of Leinster at a ceremony in St Patrick's Cathedral.

After nine months of lavish display, Richard returned to England. No sooner had he gone than the Irish chiefs again resumed their old ways. In 1399 Richard again returned to Ireland, this time landing in Waterford with a somewhat smaller army. Again Mac Murrough attacked and harassed the English army and it was with great difficulty that it reached Dublin.

Shortly afterwards news reached Richard that his throne was under threat in England. He returned there immediately, but his

———— ◎ ————

In 1454 a decree was issued by Dublin Corporation to the effect that all men and women of Irish blood, including 'nuns, clerics, journeymen, apprentices, servants, beggars' had to leave the city within four weeks and anyone found inside the city walls after that time would have all their possessions taken from them and they would be thrown into prison or otherwise punished. It is obvious that the decree had not the desired effect because only three years later, in 1457, Irishmen were again banished from the city. No Irishmen, 'no men with beards above the mouth nor their horses nor their horseboys' were to be allowed inside the city walls. Most of those evicted settled at Irishtown.

———— ◎ ————

Many Dublin place names date back to this period. The names were a mixture of Irish and English. Examples are Booterstown and Stonybatter (where 'booter' and 'batter' come from the Irish word *bóthar*, a road), and Ringsend (*Deire*, the end, and *na Rinne*, of the spit of land).

———— ◎ ————

In 1385 the makeshift Liffey Bridge, which replaced the one destroyed during the Bruce invasion, collapsed. It was not rebuilt until 1428 when the Dominicans needed it for access to their priory. In the meantime people crossed the river by ferry or ford, as the river was still quite shallow at the time. In 1394 King Richard II imposed a tax of one penny per house in Dublin to help to repair the bridge.

———— ◎ ————

great enemy Henry of Lancaster seized the throne as Henry IV. The famous War of the Roses, which lasted for thirty years, broke out in 1454 between the House of York and the House of Lancaster. During this lengthy period the authorities in England were too occupied to pay much attention to the plight of the settlers in the Pale. In Ireland the Geraldines sided with the House of York, while the Butlers sided with the Lancastrians. When the Yorkists were victorious in 1461 and Edward IV was crowned king the Geraldines were in high favour, while the Butlers were in disgrace.

The accession of Henry VII of Lancaster to the throne in 1485, after the death of Richard III of York at the Battle of Bosworth, marked an important change in English policy towards Ireland. The Tudors now paid more attention to Irish affairs and succeeded in recovering all that had been lost by neglect and mismanagement. Up to this time all the state offices were in the hands of the Geraldines, supporters of the Yorkist cause. Henry VII wisely decided to allow the Earl of Kildare to continue as Lord Deputy as it would cause too much trouble to remove him.

Despite the ascendancy of the Lancastrians, the Anglo-Irish retained their affection for the House of York, so that when a young boy called Lambert Simnel, arrived in Ireland in 1486, accompanied by supporters who claimed he was the Yorkist prince, Edward, Earl of Warwick, he was warmly received by most of the Anglo-Irish nobles, clergy and people.

Simnel was actually the son of a tradesman at Oxford. He was eleven years old when rumours spread that the two sons of Edward IV, the 'Princes in the Tower' reported to have been murdered, were still alive. A young Oxford priest first decided to pass Simnel off as one of the sons but later decided he would have a better chance as the son of the Earl of Warwick who was also rumoured to have died in the Tower of London.

Shortly after Simnel's arrival in Ireland, an army of 2,000 Germans came to Ireland to support his claims and he was actually crowned as Edward VI, King of England, in Christchurch Cathedral in the presence of the Earl of Kildare. (The crown placed on his head had been taken from the statue of the Virgin of Dublin in the church of Saint Mary del Dam. This church was inside the city walls beside Dames Gate.) Later he was borne

——— ◎ ———

The intense rivalry between the Butlers, Earls of Ormond and the Fitzgeralds, Earls of Kildare, led to frequent clashes between the followers of both sides. In 1512 one of the worst disturbances occurred when a fierce row developed between the two factions. The Earl of Ormond was forced to flee from his pursuers and to take refuge in the chapter house of St Patrick's Cathedral. He barricaded himself behind a large wooden door and refused to come out until he got assurances from the Geraldines that he would not be harmed. Eventually it was agreed to shake hands on the deal and a hole was chopped in the door through which the two leaders could do so. The expression 'to chance your arm' is believed to have originated from this event and the hole in the door can still be seen to this day.

——— ◎ ———

A book published in the sixteenth century gave some pointers on how to behave at mealtimes:

> Do not spread your butter and cheese on your bread with your thumb. It is very uncivil to lick your fingers or wipe them on your jacket, it is more decent to wipe them on the tablecloth or napkin. A guest at dinner should not spit on or over the table and when in the presence of a man of God should take special care where he spits.

——— ◎ ———

The custom of taking oaths and making contracts at the *Bachall Íosa* continued for more than 350 years after it was placed in Christchurch. As late as 1529 the trial for treason of Sir Gerald Mackshayne, Knight, took place 'upon the Holie Masebooke, and the great relike of Erlonde (Ireland), callid Baculum Christi, in the presence of the Kynge's Deputie, Chauncelour, Treseror, and Justice'.

——— ◎ ———

through the streets of Dublin on the shoulders of a gigantic Anglo-Irishman named Darcy, to the cheers of the city inhabitants.

The so-called 'Edward VI' then went to England where he was defeated and he and his priest mentor were taken prisoner. Simnel's life was spared when Henry recognised that he had been a tool in hands of the Yorkists. The Earl of Kildare and others humbly asked for pardon from Henry and were forgiven for tactical reasons. The following year they were invited to a banquet in England by the king and no doubt were greatly embarrassed to be served at the table by none other than the 'prince' Lambert Simnel! The king loved a good joke.

In 1492 another pretender named Perkin Warbeck landed in Cork and declared himself to be Richard, Duke of York, the other son of Edward IV, who was supposed to have perished in the Tower. Again the pretender was supported by the English colonists, including Garrett Mór, the Earl of Kildare. The rest of Warbeck's career belongs more to English history than to Irish but after causing a lot of disturbance in Ireland he ended up being incarcerated in the Tower of London and later hanged at Tyburn for attempting to escape.

King Henry was becoming increasingly annoyed with the activities of his colonists in Ireland, so he sent Sir Edward Poynings 'to reduce the Lordship of Ireland to whole and perfect submission'. (It was Poynings who ordered the digging of a ditch around the Pale in 1492.) The powers of the Lord Deputy were greatly reduced by Poynings, who also diminished the importance of Dublin as the capital of the Anglo-Irish area. No parliament could meet without the express approval of the king and control of all civic and military administration was taken over by the Crown.

Garrett Mór died in 1513 and was succeeded by his son Garrett Óg. It was not long before the Earl of Kildare's foes, particularly the Earl of Ormond, accused him of making alliances with the enemies of Henry VIII, who came to the throne in 1509. The king summoned him to England but the charges against him could not be proved. However the king kept him in England for four years as part of his retinue. Garrett Óg then returned to Dublin where there were riots in the streets between his followers and supporters of his rival, the Earl of Ormond, who had been appointed Lord Deputy in his absence in 1521.

Sometime later Ormond was dismissed and Kildare again was made deputy. Then Ormond once more accused Kildare of aiding the king's enemies and Kildare was called to London where he was imprisoned in the Tower. In the end, however, the charges against him were dismissed and again he was allowed to return to Ireland. This time, however, he was accompanied by Sir William Skeffington who was appointed Lord Deputy in 1530. Because the rule of Skeffington was so disastrous he was recalled in 1532 and Kildare was made Lord Deputy once more! He immediately returned to his own independent ways and in 1533 a formal complaint was drawn up by his enemies on the council and sent to the king. They said that the citizens of the Pale had no protection from the Irish enemy, that life for the citizens of Dublin was intolerable and the public revenue was ruined.

Henry VIII was greatly angered and immediately summoned Kildare to London to answer these charges. The earl was allowed to appoint a vice-deputy before he left, so he chose his eldest son, Thomas, not yet twenty years old. Thomas was dashing and headstrong and so noted for his gorgeous garments that he was known as Silken Thomas. (Another explanation of the name is that he and his followers wore silken fringes on their helmets.)

Soon after the earl had arrived in London in February it was known in Ireland that he had been imprisoned in the Tower. Early in June it was contrived by his enemies that a letter falsely reporting his execution should fall into Silken Thomas' hands. (The story goes that a priest carrying the letter lodged in the house of a soldier in Dublin and left the letter for the soldier to find. He used it to block a hole in his shoe but opened it later and spread the news immediately.)

Without waiting for confirmation of the report, the headstrong Thomas, saying 'I am none of Henry's deputy but his foe', declared war on all English by birth. (Some historians maintain that Thomas and his father had planned the whole thing in advance and that Thomas was glad of the excuse to act.)

With 140 horsemen Thomas galloped through the streets of Dublin to the Council Chamber in St Mary's Abbey which was outside the city on the northside of the Liffey, just off present day Capel Street. He flung down the sword of state in front of the assembled council and renounced his allegiance to the king.

Archbishop Cromer begged him with tears not to do so but at that moment an Irish harper (Niall O'Kennedy) started chanting the praises of the young leader and the wrongs suffered by his father. Thomas would not reconsider. He roughly silenced the archbishop and before the council could react he and his followers mounted their horses and rode away.

Silken Thomas immediately set about gathering support for his cause. The Irish chiefs of Leinster agreed to join him but the Anglo-Irish nobility in the Pale took a neutral stand. In July 1534 Thomas and his army marched on Dublin and the citizens. Fearing they were not strong enough to resist him, they allowed his troops into the city and to lay siege to the Castle. Among those who had taken refuge in the Castle was Archbishop Allen, one of Garrett Óg's greatest enemies. Before Thomas could get his army into position the archbishop managed to slip out of the Castle and make his escape that night in a ship, which was moored on the Poddle at Dames Gate. Whether by accident or design, the ship became stranded at Clontarf and the archbishop was captured and brought before Thomas in Artane. He is supposed to have told his men, '*Beir uaim an bodach*' ('Take the clown away from me') but, wilfully misunderstanding the order, they 'brained and hanged him in gobbets'. Later they were all excommunicated for their actions.

The murder of the archbishop had a devastating effect on Thomas' cause. It alienated the sympathy of his supporters at home and abroad, and most fatal of all, led to his excommunication by the Pope. All that summer and autumn fighting went on, in and around the Pale. Then the citizens of Dublin rose against the besiegers of the Castle and drove them outside the city walls. The Geraldines then besieged the city itself but when the inhabitants found that the attackers were shooting headless arrows at them they rushed out and scattered them.

In October an English army again under Sir William Skeffington arrived from England. He landed at Merchant's Quay, bringing with him several artillery pieces but after several useless marches through the country he took up quarters in Dublin and spent the winter of 1534 there.

The following spring Skeffington marched from Dublin to the Fitzgerald castle at Maynooth which was defended by 100 men. This castle was supposed to be too strong to be taken by any method but a lengthy blockade, but Skeffington, using cannon guns, battered the castle into submission in nine days. (This was not the first time that cannon had been used in Ireland but it was the first time that their effectiveness was so clearly demonstrated.) When the garrison surrendered there were only 37 defenders left alive but all of them were executed.

However, Skeffington decided to do no more and in July a new Marshal of the Forces, Lord Leonard Grey, arrived in Ireland. He immediately marched against the rebels and was so successful that Thomas surrendered in August 1535. He was brought to London and imprisoned in the Tower. His five uncles, some of whom had not taken part in the rebellion, were invited by Grey to a sumptuous banquet in Kilmainham. He then treacherously had them arrested when they arrived and they too ended up in the Tower of London. All five, and Silken Thomas, were hanged at Tyburn on 3 February 1537.

6

◎

THE REFORMATION
BRINGS TURMOIL
1532 – 1556

In 1532 Henry VIII had begun his quarrel with the Pope by declaring himself Supreme Head of the Church in England. To the end of his life, however, he upheld the religious beliefs of the Catholic Church and he dealt equally harshly with those who denied her doctrines and his own supremacy. In Ireland there was little or no move towards religious innovation. Some complaints were made from time to time about religious appointments and greediness on the part of various lay patrons and monasteries but there were no great scandals and the attachment of the ordinary people to the Church was undiminished.

Henry VIII quarrelled with Rome but always considered himself a Catholic.

During the Reformation the Archbishop of Dublin, George Browne, who was appointed by Henry VIII, was ordered by Henry to gather all the precious jewels and metals from the statues and shrines of the archdiocese and to send them to England for his treasury. Browne enthusiastically carried out the order and went further by ordering the destruction of the relics themselves.

In 1538 the relics of Christchurch Cathedral, including the irreplaceable *Bachall Íosa*, were taken out and burned in a fire in Skinners' Row (now Christchurch Place) in front of the cathedral.

Another of the relics removed and melted down by Archbishop Browne was the golden crown from the statue of the Virgin of Dublin in the Church of Mary del Dam which had been used as a crown for Lambert Simnel.

Even though the destruction of the relics and the confiscation of the monasteries was bitterly resented by the citizens of Dublin the proclamation of Henry as King of Ireland and Head of the Church was celebrated by them with bonfires and drinking in the streets. There was also a general amnesty for all prisoners, except those guilty of very serious crimes such as treason and murder.

Among the monasteries to be taken over was the Priory of Friars Preachers on the north side of the Liffey. It became a place for lawyers to stay and much later became the site for the present day Four Courts.

Archbishop Browne continued to serve Henry VIII and his son Edward for fifteen more years and then, when Queen Mary came to the throne, he repented and was reconciled to the Catholic Church. He was then appointed as a canon in St Patrick's Cathedral, with revenue from an estate beside Ballyboghill where the *Bachall Íosa* had been kept for so long!

The upper classes of the Pale, nobles, gentry, clergy and commercial classes, were not inclined to accept the king's supremacy as head of the Church, while the ordinary people knew little, and understood less, about the matter. Because so few of the Irish clergy had conformed, Henry found it necessary to appoint an Englishman as Archbishop of Dublin in 1535. The new archbishop, George Browne, was tactless and domineering and achieved little success in his efforts. Only one bishop, Staples of Meath, supported him and generally the clergy refused to hand over their churches to him.

Due to the lack of success in his efforts, Browne encouraged Lord Deputy Grey to call a parliament in Dublin in 1536. An act was passed in which King Henry was declared Supreme Head of the Church in Ireland. All holders of public office were required to take the Oath of Supremacy acknowledging Henry's position, and anyone who refused to take the oath was judged to be guilty of treason. The following year Henry ordered the closure of monasteries throughout the whole country. All of them in and around the city were confiscated and handed over or sold to laymen. In the case of the Priory of All Hallows (on the site of the present-day Trinity College), it was handed over to the mayor, corporation and citizens of Dublin and 'their successors for ever' in gratitude for resisting Silken Thomas. The following year a commission was appointed to destroy all relics, and remove images, ornaments and chalices from the churches, while many of the more valuable items were sent to England.

Up to this time Henry and his predecessors had the title of Lord of Ireland but in 1541 a parliament held in Dublin declared that Henry was King of Ireland. That parliament was the largest and most impressive held in Dublin for many centuries. In order to lend more importance to the decisions of the parliament a number of Irish chieftains were induced to attend. Various Anglo-Irish chiefs, who had seldom or never attended a parliament before, were also present. The king had given orders that the chieftains were to be treated with every respect, and since they were weary of continual strife, they were well disposed to accept Henry's offers of peace and reconciliation. The Irish chieftains and many of the Anglo-Irish lords did not understand a word of English so the Earl of Ormond translated the proceedings into Irish for their benefit.

———— ◎ ————

Among the few relics to survive the purge by Archbishop Browne were the heart of St Laurence O'Toole, which is still in Christchurch Cathedral, and the beautiful oak statue of Our Lady of Dublin. It is now on display in the Carmelite church in Whitefriars Street. According to tradition the statue escaped detection for many years by being sunk face down in the earth and the hollowed-out back being used as a pig trough.

Our Lady of Dublin, also known as the Black Madonna, is in the Carmelite church in Whitefrier Street. The statue has been in the church since 1822.

During penal times it reappeared in Mary's Lane Chapel but was later considered too shabby to be kept and was thrown out. A Carmelite priest, Father John Spratt, happened to see it in a junk shop in 1824 and brought it to Whitefriar Street Church where it has been venerated ever since.

———— ◎ ————

The latter years of Henry VIII's reign were relatively peaceful and even prosperous in Ireland. Apart from the religious question and the suppression of the monasteries, his treatment of Ireland was generally fair and conciliatory. By the time of his death the English power in Ireland was stronger than it had ever been before. He died in January 1547 and was succeeded by his son, Edward VI.

Edward, was only a boy at the time and was king in name only. The real power was in the hands of a council or regency. This council pursued a more active policy of spreading the Reformation in Ireland and met with a lot of opposition, including several insurrections. In 1551 the Lord Deputy, Sir Anthony St Leger, was ordered to introduce the new liturgy in Ireland, including the use of English in the churches. It proved impossible to enforce, however. In the greater part of the country there was no change and services were conducted as before, but in the Pale there was a patchwork of obedience. Sometimes the Mass was in English, sometimes parts were omitted, some priests acknowledged the king's supremacy, while others did not.

When Edward died in 1553, he was succeeded by Queen Mary, his half-sister. She was a fervent Catholic and immediately set out to restore the position of the Catholic Church in Britain and Ireland. But in Ireland there was no persecution of Protestants; they were quite free to practise their religion in their own way. However Mary was still a Tudor and so she retained the title 'Queen of Ireland'. Neither did she restore the confiscated lands to the monasteries.

In 1558 Mary died and was succeeded by Queen Elizabeth I, her half-sister. Immediately there was another reversal of policy. A parliament was assembled in Dublin in 1560 to restore the Protestant religion. The Act of Supremacy was revived and once more, office holders had to take the oath. The Act of Uniformity, which commanded all people to use the Book of Common Prayer and to attend Protestant services on Sundays under threat of punishment and fines, was reintroduced. The new regulations were mostly ignored throughout the country and even in Dublin and the Pale most people took no notice of them. Officially, however, Protestantism was the religion of the state in Ireland and was to remain so until the disestablishment of the church in 1869.

———— ◎ ————

The Dublin of Elizabethan times was surrounded for the most part by a great wall in which there were six main gates: St Nicholas Gate, New Gate, Bridge Gate, Gormund's Gate, Pole Gate and Dames Gate where the River Poddle flowed. Each gate had a cannon for protection. Outside the wall was a deep ditch running the whole length around.

The only part of the city not enclosed by the wall was along the Liffey but the height of the quays in this area provided good protection. There were also three defensive towers on the quays. These were, from east to west: Case's Tower, Fyan's Tower at Fishamble Street and Prickett's Tower on Merchant's Quay.

The citizens were constantly opening smaller gates for their own purposes and these had the effect of weakening defences in times of attack.

———— ◎ ————

There were no military barracks in the city at this time and so many soldiers wandered the streets that a 'cess' was introduced by the authorities to get money to provide for them. The cess meant that provisions could be seized by the authorities and their owners paid far less than the goods were worth. The old curse of 'Bad cess to you' owes its origin to this resented law.

———— ◎ ————

The first book to be printed in Ireland was *The Book of Common Prayer*. It was printed by Humphrey Powell in Dublin in 1551.

———— ◎ ————

7

◎

THE PRISONER
IN THE CASTLE
1556 – 1603

The accession of Elizabeth to the throne of England in 1558 coincided with the rise to power of the O'Neills of Tyrone and the O'Donnells of Donegal. In 1587 Sir John Perrott, the Lord Deputy in Dublin, concocted a plan for entrapping young Red Hugh O'Donnell, the son of Sir Hugh O'Donnell of Donegal. At the time the authorities feared an invasion from Spain where the Armada was even then in preparation. Perrott wished to secure hostages from the Irish chieftains to ensure their good behaviour and in particular from the O'Donnells whom he feared most of all.

In the autumn of 1587 Perrott sent a merchant ship laden with Spanish wine to Lough Swilly where it anchored near where young Hugh O'Donnell lived with his foster-father, Mac Sweeney. When Mac Sweeney offered to buy some wine he was told there was none left for sale but if he wished to come aboard there was plenty of wine to drink for free. The bait was taken. A party of Mac Sweeneys, along with the young Red Hugh, went on board. Then while the visitors were enjoying themselves the ship set sail and Hugh was brought to Dublin and imprisoned in the Bermingham Tower in the Castle.

Three years and three months slowly passed. Perrott was recalled to England and was replaced by Sir William Fitzwilliam, a man noted for his cruelty. One dark winter's evening in 1590 Red Hugh and a few companions managed to lower themselves by rope onto the footbridge over the water-filled ditch around the Castle. They were met by one of Hugh's people who gave them two swords, one for Hugh and one for Art Kavanagh, a young Leinster chief who escaped with him. Passing through one of the city's gates,

———— ◎ ————

In 1560 during the reign of Henry VIII the area now known as the Phoenix Park was confiscated from its owners the Knights Hospitallers. When the Earl of Chesterfield was viceroy during the reign of George II, in the 1730s, he stocked the park with deer and opened it to the people of Dublin as a public park. He was also responsible for the 'Phoenix' monument in the park in the mistaken belief that the park's name came from that mythical bird. In fact the name derives from a famous spring in the area of the present-day Zoological Gardens which was known as *Fionn Uisce* (pronounced feen ishke) meaning 'clear water'. Over the years further areas were absorbed into the park and it now comprises about 1760 acres.

———— ◎ ————

In 1560 three public clocks were ordered for the city by Elizabeth I. They were erected in St Patrick's Cathedral, Dublin Castle and the Tholsel which was in Christchurch Place at that time. Elizabeth also established a postal service two years later.

———— ◎ ————

The first ever book in the Irish language to be printed in Ireland was printed in Dublin in 1571. It was an Irish alphabet and catechism.

———— ◎ ————

In 1583 a dispute arose between two chieftains of the O'Connor clan, Teigh MacKilpatrick O'Connor and Connor McCormack O'Connor. It was decided that the matter should be settled by mortal combat in Dublin Castle in front of the Lords Justice and the council. The two combatants were stripped to the waist and armed only with a sword, a shield and a skullcap. At first they showed such lack of enthusiasm that they were told they were making a mockery of the Queen's justice. They therefore set to in earnest, resulting in Connor being wounded in the leg and eye, while Teigh was slashed in the ribs. The enraged Teigh then fiercely attacked his opponent, struck his head from his body and presented it to the Lords Justice on the point of his sword.

———— ◎ ————

which hadn't been closed for the night, they made their way to Three Rock Mountain in the Dublin hills. They continued until they reached Roundwood where they rested, being too tired to go further. Here they were joined by a local chief, named Phelim O'Toole.

Meanwhile soldiers from Dublin Castle had managed to track them to where they were hiding. Seeing that they were surrounded O'Toole made a pretence of arresting the fugitives and they were brought back in chains to Dublin Castle. There they were shackled in heavy iron fetters.

A year later Hugh and two companions, Henry and Art O'Neill, sons of the late Shane, escaped again on Christmas night by cutting their chains with a file which had been smuggled in. (It is suggested that the avaricious Deputy Fitzwilliam was bribed by Hugh O'Neill, Earl of Tyrone, to allow the escape.)

Outside the Castle they were met by a guide from Fiach Mac Hugh O'Byrne of Glenmalure. They managed to get outside the city walls but lost Henry O'Neill in the darkness. In harsh weather they pressed on, making their way further west by way of Killakee and along the route of the present military road over the Dublin mountains. They continued until at last they could go no further. While they sheltered as best they could behind a large rock, the servant ran on to O'Byrne's headquarters for help. Fiach immediately sent a small party with food and clothing but they were too late to save Art O'Neill, who died of exposure. (A wooden cross in the mountains near the Wicklow Gap marks the area where he died.) Hugh, who was stronger, managed to survive, even though his feet were badly frost-bitten. He was brought to safety in Glenmalure and rested in a secluded cottage recovering from his ordeal until a messenger from the Earl of Tyrone came for him.

Accompanied by Phelim O'Toole, Red Hugh managed to evade all the soldiers on the lookout for him. They crossed the Liffey at a ford just west of Dublin and eventually they made their way to O'Neill's Castle in Dungannon. From there Hugh eventually managed to reach his family castle in Donegal. His two big toes had to be amputated and it was a year before he was fully recovered. In May 1592 he was elected 'The O'Donnell', head of his clan.

Meanwhile Hugh O'Neill had been created Earl of Tyrone by the parliament held in Dublin in 1585 and eight years later was

——————— ◎ ———————

Crumlin to the west of Dublin was one of the four manors
in the county which were owned by the Crown. Due to the
'misbehaviour' of its tenants they were forced to pay a
higher rent than the others. In Hollinshed's Chronicle of
1577 we learn why:

'The Manor of Crumlin payeth a greater rent to the prince
than any of the other three, which proceedeth from this:
The Seneschal, being offended with the tenants for their
misdemeanour, took them up very sharply in the court, and
with rough and minatory speeches, began to menace them.
The lobbish and desperate clobberiousness, taking the
matter in dudgeon, made no words, but knocked their
Seneschal on the costard, and left him for dead. For which
detestable murder their rent was enhanced, and they pay at
this day ninepence per acre, which is double to any of the
other three manors.'

——————— ◎ ———————

In 1594 Walter Reagh Fitzgerald led a band of rebels into
Crumlin village and burned it to the ground. They
plundered the church and took the lead from its roof to
make bullets. Subsequently the parishioners were too poor
to repair the church.

——————— ◎ ———————

In 1591 Trinity College was established by charter on the
grounds confiscated from the Priory of All Hallows. The
space in front of the new college, which up till then was
called Hoggen Green, now became College Green.

——————— ◎ ———————

When Queen Elizabeth I died, Dublin's Catholics rejoiced
with cries of 'Jezebel is dead' and immediately wanted the
Mass restored. They were soon put in their place by James
I who told them that 'no tolerance will be given to the
Romish religion'.

——————— ◎ ———————

master of all Tyrone. He immediately set about drilling his men, small numbers at a time, until he eventually had a large army of trained soldiers.

The subsequent history of the Ulster chieftains does not concern us here. Suffice to say that the whole country outside the Pale became engulfed in war and disturbance during the reign of Elizabeth. Plantations were attempted and failed in Munster and Antrim. O'Neill and O'Donnell rebelled against the government, had some magnificent victories such as at the Yellow Ford in Armagh, but eventually suffered defeat at Kinsale in 1601 where a small Spanish expedition arrived too late and too far from the Ulster strongholds of the northern chieftains.

O'Neill held on for a time in the bogs and forests of Ulster but on the promise of life, liberty and title, agreed to submit to the Lord Deputy Charles Blount Mountjoy at Mellifont in County Louth in 1603. The death of Elizabeth had already taken place but this fact was concealed from O'Neill. A few days later he rode with Mountjoy to Dublin. Only then did he hear of the queen's death and he is said to have shed tears of rage when he discovered how he had been tricked.

When Hugh O'Neill's army besieged Dublin the inhabitants were fearful that he would cut off the city's water supply from the Dodder and the Poddle.

The Counter-Reformation saw a big change in the fortunes of many Dublin churches. A writer at the time declared, 'One church is used as the Deputy's stable. The vaults under Christchurch are let for tippling houses for beer, wine and tobacco, and these are frequented by the Papists.'

On Friday 11 March 1596 a tremendous explosion occurred on the quays between one and two o'clock in the afternoon. At the time a large number of barrels of gunpowder had been unloaded from a ship on the Liffey and were stacked on the quays at the end of Winetavern Street. Later reports said that the clerk in charge had gone off to have 'a pot of ale' in a nearby house leaving no one in charge and that children were seen playing with the barrels and actually rolling them in the street. (Perhaps the use of gunpowder was still so novel at the time that its dangers were not appreciated.) It is thought that a nail in one of the casks caused a spark, which set off the explosion. The count of the dead went on for days and at the end it was found that one-hundred-and-twenty-six men, women and children were killed, of whom seventy-six were Dubliners and the rest were strangers. There was widespread structural damage in the area of Winetavern Street, Merchant's Quay and Wood Quay. Inside the walls of the city nearly forty houses were flattened in Cook Street, Fishamble Street, Bridge Street, High Street, Castle Street and St Michael's Lane. The force of the explosion was such that the bell in the tower of Christchurch Cathedral over half a mile away cracked.

The first map of Dublin to be published was by John Speed in 1610. The map shows that the city walls were still intact and that most of the development of the city was south of the river with a single bridge connecting the two parts. On the south side it shows 'The Colledge' (Trinity) to be somewhat isolated from the hub of the city around the Castle. It also shows fourteen Protestant churches but no Catholic ones.

8

◎

THE SCOURGE OF
OLIVER CROMWELL
HITS IRELAND
1607 – 1654

After submitting to the Lord Deputy, Mountjoy, O'Neill retired to Tyrone but he was not allowed to live in peace. His enemies constantly spread false stories about him and he had to attend meetings of the Irish council in Dublin to answer various charges against him. A few weeks after one such meeting an anonymous letter was found outside the council chamber purporting to give details of a plot to seize Dublin Castle and murder the new Lord Deputy, Arthur Chichester. The writer turned out to be Christopher St Lawrence, Baron of Howth, who, when questioned about it, named several Ulster chieftains, but not O'Neill, as being implicated in the plot. Although the plot lacked credibility, many of those named feared for their safety and eventually fled to the continent, among them the newly appointed Earl of Tír Conaill (Donegal), Rory O'Donnell and the ageing Hugh O'Neill. This 'Flight of the Earls' took place in 1607. The Plantation of Ulster took place after they had left. The six counties of Tyrone, Armagh, Derry, Donegal, Fermanagh and Cavan were forfeited to the Crown. (It is interesting to note that when partition took place in the twentieth century that Cavan and Donegal were excluded but Antrim and Down were included.) With the departure of the Ulster chieftains and after four and a half centuries, the English conquest of Ireland was complete.

In 1613 a 'national' parliament was summoned, purporting to represent every province of Ireland, but, although the vast majority of the country were Catholics, when the parliament met in Dublin

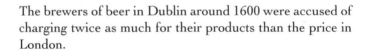

The brewers of beer in Dublin around 1600 were accused of charging twice as much for their products than the price in London.

In 1616 Dublin Corporation ordered that every fifth house should have 'lanterne and candlelight set forth' as a form of public lighting.

During the seventeenth century the Dublin town crier's job was to walk around the town every night in winter at 10.00 p.m., 12.00 p.m., 2.00 a.m. and 4.00 a.m., and in summer at 11.00 p.m., 1.00 a.m., and 3.00 a.m. giving news 'of the weather and the time of night'.

Another official was the town beadle whose job it was to 'turn beggars out of the town and keep the pigs out of the streets'.

During the seventeenth century the practice of deporting 'undesirables' to the West Indies began. Beggars and street traders were regularly rounded up and locked into a large cage in the Cornmarket before being examined for punishment or deportation.

During the seventeenth century some Dublin merchants issued their own coinage and notes and tokens.

it had 126 Protestants and 99 Catholics in the House of Commons, while the House of Lords had 20 Anglican Bishops and 20 Lords, of whom 14 were specially created. In spite of all this, it was probably the most representative parliament to sit in Ireland until independence was achieved in the twentieth century.

On 18 May 1613 the parliament was opened by a religious procession. Chichester led the state parade from Dublin Castle to St Patrick's Cathedral. There the Catholics stayed outside while the rest of the parade entered and attended the service. More discord occurred when the Houses assembled in their respective chambers in the Castle. The Catholics proposed one of their own, Sir John Everard, as Speaker of the House. This was opposed by their opponents, who withdrew temporarily to confer. In their absence the Catholics elected Everard and placed him in the chair. When the Protestants returned they elected Sir John Davys but Everard refused to move and he was forcibly ejected from the chair. The Catholics then withdrew from both the Commons and the Lords and the parliament was prorogued. When the parliament was recalled in 1614, among the bills passed was the attainder of O'Neill and O'Donnell and an act confirming the king's entitlement to their confiscated Ulster lands. A subsidy of £20,000 (a lot of money in those days) was granted to King James himself but in 1615 he dissolved the parliament. He had got all he wanted from it.

When James I died in 1625 he was succeeded by his son Charles I, who was perpetually short of money. That same year the Irish gentry, Catholic and Protestant, encouraged by the then Lord Deputy, Falkland, offered to pay the enormous sum of £120,000 in instalments to the king in return for certain concessions or 'Graces' as they were called. These Graces assured them that they would be secure in their estates and that the Catholics would not be discriminated against because of their religion. Once the king had the money, however, he broke his promises – the land titles were not confirmed and laws against the Catholics were enforced.

In 1633 the king sent over one of the most efficient deputies ever to hold power in Ireland – Thomas Wentworth, later Earl of Strafford. He had two objectives: to make the king absolute master in Ireland and to raise as much money as he could for him. He immediately got the gentry to give £20,000 to the king on the

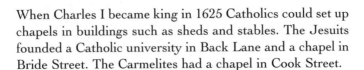

When Charles I became king in 1625 Catholics could set up chapels in buildings such as sheds and stables. The Jesuits founded a Catholic university in Back Lane and a chapel in Bride Street. The Carmelites had a chapel in Cook Street.

After Charles had got his money for the so-called 'Graces' he promptly forgot his promises. Catholics were once more persecuted. Fifteen religious houses and chapels were closed down, among them the Catholic University, whose buildings were handed over to Trinity College.

In the 1630s the population of Dublin numbered about 20,000 and this made the city second only to London in size.

In 1650 Dublin was stricken by a terrible plague in which up to sixteen thousand people died. Nine years later a census of the population of the city showed that the inhabitants numbered only 8,780, of whom 5,459 were 'English' and the rest were 'Irish'.

In 1657 the authorities in Dublin were complaining that that the Irish language was 'commonlie and usuallie spoken and the Irish Habit worne not onlie in the streetes and by such as live in the countrie and come to this cittie'. They said that this was so provoking to God that He might justly cause the plague and 'other judgements' to hit the city!

The first newspaper ever to be published in Dublin appeared in 1685. It was a single sheet of paper, printed on both sides. Each edition began with the word 'Sir' and was in the form of a letter to the readers. It soon began to include merchants' advertisements hoping to make their wares better known.

promise that penal statutes would not be enforced against them and that he (Wentworth) would summon a parliament in Dublin to have the Graces confirmed. In 1634 Wentworth duly assembled the parliament in Dublin Castle and got it to vote £240,000 to the king. But once again Charles avoided granting the Graces.

Thomas Wentworth not only constantly raised money for Charles I but also gathered an army of 10,000 Irishmen (mostly Catholics) and 1,000 horses to fight for the king in England. The army disbanded after Wentworth was recalled to England.

In 1639 Wentworth called another Dublin parliament and again got money for the king. He was now made Earl of Strafford and he raised a well-trained army of 10,000 men in Ireland to serve the king in England. But his career was drawing to a close. In 1640 he was recalled to England and in the following year was impeached by the House of Commons and later beheaded, the most damaging charges against him coming from Ireland.

When Wentworth was summoned to England the arrangements to transport his Irish troops to England went to pieces. There was no money to pay or feed them, so they readily took to the traditional practice of plundering the civilian population. Finally when they were disbanded, many joined continental armies and those who didn't proved to be a well-trained nucleus for the regiments of the Confederates in the civil wars which followed shortly.

The ruthless behaviour of Wentworth and the refusal of the king

———— ◎ ————

When Wentworth arrived in Dublin he set about putting an end to various abuses in the city. He closed the drinking houses under Christchurch, established open spaces at Stephen's Green, Oxmantown Green and College Green for the use of the citizens. He put an end to piracy on the Irish Sea, encouraged the linen trade, and was instrumental in providing the first professional theatre in the city. In 1637 the New Theatre opened in Werburgh Street under the charge of a Scotsman named John Ogilby. Wentworth appointed him 'Master of the Revels'.

———— ◎ ————

Wentworth was unquestionably the most efficient Lord Deputy ever to serve in Dublin. We have a description of him as 'clad in black armour, with a black horse and black plume and feathers'.

———— ◎ ————

It was during Wentworth's time that the vaults of St Michan's Church were repaired and used for the burial of some of Dublin's citizens, whose bodies are preserved to this day. Contrary to popular tradition the so-called 'crusader' among the bodies is in reality a citizen of Dublin from Wentworth's time.

———— ◎ ————

The Confederate threat to Dublin, which was held by the Parliamentarians, was to end with the Battle of Rathmines. After the battle a wounded horse wandered into a tavern near Portobello and the tavern owner later named his premises The Bleeding Horse – a name that has lasted to the present day.

———— ◎ ————

to grant the Graces eventually led to a determination by some Irish chiefs to obtain their rights by insurrection. The rising throughout the country was set to take place on 23 October 1641. Dublin Castle and other fortresses throughout the country were to be seized and their stores of arms taken. On the evening of 22 October, a man named Owen Connolly went to one of the Lords Justice, Sir William Parsons, and told him of the plans. Connolly had been drinking with two of the leaders in a tavern in Werburgh Street and had been told the secret. At first Parsons didn't believe the story, for Connolly was drunk. But when Parsons consulted the other Lord Justice, Sir John Borlase, they decided to arrest the two leaders, MacMahon and Maguire, on the morning of 23 October. (The two of them were subsequently hanged in London.) Another of the leaders, Rory O'More, escaped by rowing up the Liffey to Islandbridge to his daughter's house, where he was able to hide until it was safe to go further.

Although the authorities' actions succeeded in stifling most of the planned rebellion in the Dublin area, incidents did occur sometime later. A strong force of insurgents took over Carrickmines Castle and when a body of cavalry under the command of Sir Simon Harcourt set out from the city to take it back he found it too well defended and he had to send for reinforcements. Because these did not arrive until late that night he decided to wait for morning before making his attack. That night signal fires were lit on the battlements and others answering them lit up the surrounding hills. The great numbers of rebels thus revealed caused Harcourt to send for even more reinforcements. While he waited, sharpshooters on the castle inflicted many casualties among the besiegers, including Harcourt himself. He had stood out to give some commands and was shot in the chest by one of the marksmen. He was put into a vehicle and set out for the city under escort. The roughness of the journey caused him such pain that the party decided to stop at Merrion where he died the next day.

Further reinforcements, under the command of Lieutenant-Colonel Gibson, now arrived with artillery and proceeded to attack the castle mercilessly. After a fierce battle the besiegers managed to breach the walls and then set out to massacre the entire garrison, as well as a great number of women and children who had taken refuge there. Altogether about three hundred and fifty people were slaughtered.

The rising was much more successful in the north. At the end of a week nearly all of Ulster was in the hands of the rebels. Throughout the following months, terrible massacres were carried out by both sides throughout the country. Hundreds of settlers died as they vainly tried to make their way to Dublin in appalling conditions. Other refugees poured into the city from all over the Pale. Their pitiful condition was eagerly exploited as propaganda by the authorities. For many years afterwards pamphlets giving the gory details were used to inflame the Protestants.

One such pamphlet stated:

> Sir Patrick Dunstan's wife was ravished and the unfortunate gentleman slowly cut to pieces. They cut off his ears and nose, teared off both his cheeks, cut off his arms and legs, cut out his tongue, and after, ran a red-hot iron through him.

The two Lords Justice, Parsons and Borlase, sent out military parties from Dublin throughout the surrounding country. These massacred all they met, whether engaged in rebellion or not. Their general, Sir Charles Coote, committed terrible cruelties, particularly in Wicklow, killing and torturing men, women and children.

This period of Irish history is extremely confused and confusing. The following is an attempt to unravel it. There were four distinct parties in Ireland at the time, each with its own army.

First: The Old Irish whose leader was Rory O'More of Laois. They had suffered most from persecution and wanted complete independence from England. Their army under the command of Owen Roe O'Neill was mostly confined to Ulster.

Second: The Old Anglo-Irish Catholics were chiefly based in central and southern Ireland. These too had suffered because of their religion and from plantations. They wanted religious and civil liberty but not separation from England. Their army came under the command of Colonel Thomas Preston who had a distinguished career on the Continent.

Neither of these parties really trusted the other but together they formed the Confederate side.

Third: The Parliamentarians, who included the Presbyterians

Owen Roe O'Neill commanded the army of the Old Irish.

and the Scots of Ulster under General Robert Monroe. The English Parliament in its war with King Charles had sent a Scottish army to Ulster, where it had joined English troops already there.

Fourth: The Royalist party, which held Dublin. These were mostly Anglicans of the Established Church who opposed the Parliamentarians. They were the party of the king and they wished to make it appear that the Catholics were the king's enemies. Their leader was James Butler, the Lord Lieutenant and Duke of Ormond.

For some time the two Catholic parties worked together. O'Neill, with the Old Irish, carried on the war in Ulster against Monroe, while Colonel Preston, with the Anglo-Irish in Leinster, continued the war against the Royalists.

In June 1642 Owen Roe had a comprehensive victory over Monroe at Benburb in Co. Cavan. This had the effect of increasing the influence of the Old Irish party in the confederation. Then it became known that Ormond was in negotiations with the Parliamentarians to surrender Dublin to them. O'Neill and Preston were ordered to proceed to Dublin and take over the city.

The two armies arrived within a few miles of Dublin and O'Neill was so close that the city's anxious inhabitants could see hundreds of fires started by his army, raging from Castleknock to Howth. But there was a delay, mainly due to Preston wishing to make a deal with Ormond, instead of attacking the city at once. When Owen Roe heard of Preston's duplicity he withdrew his army. Ormond then surrendered the city to the Parliamentarians under Colonel Jones, and fled to France.

Soon afterwards Jones inflicted a heavy defeat on Preston and in the same year the Confederate army under Lord Taaffe was defeated in Munster. Now Ormond thought it a good time to return to Ireland and resumed command of the Royalist side. He concluded a peace deal with the Confederates but it was all too late – Charles I was beheaded that same year and Dublin was firmly in the hands of the Parliamentarians.

The execution of the king caused such a revulsion in Ireland that nearly all the Irish parties, including Ormond, the Confederates and the Scots and Presbyterians of Ulster declared for the Royalist cause against the Parliamentarians and proclaimed the Prince of Wales as King Charles II. The Parliamentarians under Jones still held Dublin and now Ormond marched with an army from Kilkenny and reached Castleknock on 21 June. The next day he moved on to Finglas, from where he made some half-hearted attacks on the north side of the city.

Jones had about 4,500 men to defend Dublin while Ormond had roughly the same amount. The city itself was in a very poor state to defend itself against attack. It had no proper fortifications and was low on provisions.

Ormond seems not to have known the poor state the city was in, for he delayed his attack for so long that the defenders managed to get new supplies from England and were able to strengthen the fortifications. He did very little until the end of July when he decided to march around the city to Rathmines. There was no village there at that time, only fields of pasture and tillage. Two roads, which correspond to the present-day Rathmines Road and Ranelagh Road, ran through the area. Ormond set up his camp on high ground between present day Palmerstown Park and Ranelagh. He then ordered that the River Dodder should be blocked, thus cutting off the water supply to the city. Next he attacked Rathfarnham Castle which was defended by a small garrison of Parliamentarians, and after a brief battle, gained possession. He ordered one of his officers, Major-General Purcell, to fortify the old castle of Baggotrath, not far from the mouth of the Liffey at that time but where the houses in Upper Baggot Street opposite Waterloo Road, now stand. Possession of the castle would mean that the city garrison would be unable to graze their horses on the pastures between the castle and the city. This action would have the effect of hampering the use of their cavalry.

On 1 August Purcell set out after dark with a force of 1,500 men to take and repair the castle. Not knowing the area, he had to employ local guides to show him the way but when Ormond rode over the next morning he found that little or no work had been carried out. By way of explanation, Purcell told him that the guides had deliberately led his army astray and that Jones had practically dismantled the castle beforehand, leaving it hardly worth the effort to fortify it.

Jones now decided to take immediate action rather than wait for Ormond's attack. He moved cavalry and infantry to the rear of the fortifications at Lowsy Hill (now Townsend Street), while Ormond drafted the bulk of his army over to Baggotrath, set up his artillery on Gallow's Hill (now Mount Street) and ordered his men to prepare for action. He then rode back to his camp to rest before the expected action the following day. Jones, however, sprang a surprise by attacking that same night, 2 August. He utterly routed Ormond's forces at Baggotrath, sending some of them fleeing to the mountains and the rest back to the main camp.

The sounds of gunfire had awakened Ormond and he rushed from his tent, only to be told of the collapse of his forces at Baggotrath. In spite of Ormond's efforts to rally his troops, the main body of his army now ran away and the Parliamentarians steadily advanced until they reached Ormond's artillery. Here he decided to make a last desperate stand against an infantry force advancing from the city. Unknown to him some of Jones' cavalry had circled around and now attacked him from the rear.

After a short skirmish Ormond's troops broke and ran. Ormond, himself, was struck by a musket ball but his armour saved him from injury. The destruction of his army left him with no alternative but to escape inland, leaving everything to the enemy. Meanwhile

Royalist forces under the command of Lord Inchiquin remained in possession of Rathgar Castle (where Rathgar Road meets Orwell Road) and Rathmines Castle (in Palmerstown Park). When Colonel Jones' troops advanced on the two castles the garrisons soon surrendered and most of them joined the Parliamentary side.

By this time the Parliamentarians in England under Oliver Cromwell were triumphant. He now turned his attention to Ireland with the intention of crushing the Royalists still active there. On 14 August 1649, accompanied by his son-in-law, Sir Henry Ireton, as second-in-command, Cromwell landed at Ringsend at the mouth of the Liffey. (According to reports he was violently seasick during the voyage.) He was accompanied by 9,000 foot-soldiers, 4,000 cavalry and a large supply of war materials and money. When his army arrived in the city he stabled his horses in St Patrick's Cathedral, which was in a bad state of repair at the time. His forces quickly captured the castles at Rathfarnham, Kimmage and Tallaght.

Later Cromwell addressed a large crowd in Dublin and told them that, by God's providence, he would 'restore them all to their just liberties and properties'. On 23 August he made an order forbidding the citizens from 'profaning, swearing, drinking and cursing, which were said to be the daily practice of the place'. Cromwell's supplies also included thousands of bibles, which were to be distributed among his soldiers and to the native Irish (who would not understand a word of their contents!).

Oliver Cromwell told the citizens of Dublin that he would 'restore them all to their just liberties and properties'.

On 31 August he left his lodgings at the corner of Werburgh Street and Castle Street (later demolished by the Wide Streets Commission in 1812) and proceeded against Drogheda where the taking of the town was followed by an appalling massacre. Over the next number of months he either took by force, or had surrendered to him, towns all over Ireland. By May 1650 the country was so much in the control of the Parliamentarians that Cromwell returned to England, leaving Ireton to finish the job. This he did so successfully that by 1652 the war was ended.

9

◎

KING JAMES II
AND THE BATTLE
OF THE BOYNE
1660 – 1690

The restoration of Charles II to the English throne in 1660 was greeted with great joy by Irish Catholics. They now expected some redress for their sufferings at the hands of the Cromwellians but they were to be bitterly disappointed.

In 1662 the Dublin parliament passed an Act of Settlement, giving the new settlers a title to their holdings. The Catholics strongly objected to this and after several years wrangling, the matter was finally settled by allowing the Protestants two-thirds of the lands and the Catholics one-third. This was a complete reversal of the situation before the Act of Settlement.

In 1675 a 'Popish Plot' to restore the Catholic monarchy in England was 'discovered'. While King Charles II was suspected of secretly being a Catholic, it was known that his brother James, Duke of York and later James II, was indeed one. An Englishman of low character called Titus Oates pretended to have discovered a plot to kill the king and install James on the throne with the help of a French invasion. While his evidence was extremely flimsy the Privy Council appeared to believe him. A veritable frenzy of persecution of Catholics ensued, leading to the execution of many leading (and innocent) Catholic gentlemen. The fury soon spread to Ireland and Archbishop Peter Talbot of Dublin was selected as the first victim. Although he was extremely ill in his bed at the time he was arrested and taken to Dublin Castle. He died there two years later. Two other 'conspirators' were also named: Lord Mountgarrett and a Colonel Peppard. Mountgarrett was in his eighties, confined to bed and senile, while no trace could ever be found of a 'Colonel Peppard' for the simple reason that he didn't exist.

James II succeeded his brother Charles II in 1685 and he set about restoring the Catholic religion in England and Ireland in such a heavy-handed, harsh and illegal fashion that the whole Protestant population rose against him. He sent Colonel Richard Talbot, Lord Tirconnell, to Dublin as commander of the armed forces. Talbot immediately set about disarming the Protestant militia and disbanded thousands of Protestant soldiers and officers and replaced them with Catholics. In 1687 he was appointed as Lord Lieutenant of Ireland and this panicked and enraged the Protestants even more.

When James II attended the parliament he had summoned in Dublin he wore a crown specially made for him in the city.

Mary, the eldest daughter of James by his first marriage, was a Protestant and heiress to the throne. She was married to William of Orange, also a Protestant. Then the queen, James' second wife, gave birth to a son who would be brought up as a Catholic and inherit the throne. With the prospect of a succession of Catholic monarchs before them the English people offered the throne to William of Orange.

─────── ◎ ───────

In 1666 Dublin contributed over 100,000 head of cattle to the citizens of London to feed them after the Great Fire there.

─────── ◎ ───────

In 1670 riots occurred when Dublin's second bridge across the Liffey was built on the site of present-day Watling Street Bridge. Some people, such as ferrymen and other merchants, who stood to lose money by the construction of the bridge, invited a group of apprentices to tear the wooden structure down. During their attack on the bridge twenty apprentices were arrested, and when their friends tried to rescue them, four apprentices were killed. The bridge got the name Bloody Bridge as a result.

In 1922 the corporation renamed the bridge Rory O'More Bridge to commemorate one of the leaders of the 1641 rebellion but the name is little used today.

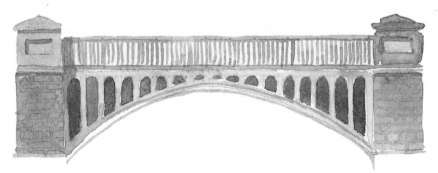

Queen Victoria (now Rory O'More) Bridge was completed in 1861. There were riots when the original wooden bridge was built in 1670.

─────── ◎ ───────

In November 1688 William, accompanied by his wife, Mary, the daughter of King James, landed in England. James fled to France in absolute terror. William then claimed the throne of England.

Lord Talbot, seeing these events unfold in England, immediately set about securing Ireland for King James. He raised a large, irregular, untrained and undisciplined army of Catholics and took possession of the most important places throughout the country. The take-over of garrisons in the south of the country met with little resistance but when the Jacobite army approached Derry on 7 December 1688 the older men and magistrates debated on what was the best course to follow. It was then that the Apprentice Boys closed the gates while the elders debated.

When James heard of Lord Talbot's actions on his behalf he plucked up courage and sailed for Ireland. (He was the first English king to come to Ireland since Richard II in 1399.) He landed in Kinsale in March 1689 and reached Dublin that same month. On Palm Sunday, 24 March he entered Dublin city through St James' Gate which then stood on the main road between Watling Street and Crane Lane. (St James' Gate was not a gate in the city wall but a barrier erected on the western approaches to the city.) He was given the freedom of the city by the Lord Mayor, a Protestant. He was also presented with the sword of state, which he handed to the Lord Deputy, to be carried before him in the royal cavalcade. The route to Dublin Castle was covered with gravel for the occasion and the streets were gaily decorated and lined with troops. At the Castle he attended a Catholic service in the chapel where a Te Deum was sung to celebrate his arrival. Later he was guest of honour at a magnificent banquet in a specially prepared house near the castle gate. The celebrations continued all night.

Just one day after his arrival in Dublin, James summoned a parliament in the city to meet on 7 May 1689. It met in the present-day King's Inns, which was formerly a Dominican Convent. James himself attended the opening ceremony, wearing his robes and a crown specially made for him in Dublin.

The parliament consisted mostly of Catholics and included both Irish and 'Old English' elements. The House of Commons had two members from each county and two from each city or borough. Patrick Sarsfield was one the members of the parliament.

———— ◎ ————

In 1676 another bridge was built at Capel Street with stones taken from the ruins of St Mary's Abbey. The bridge collapsed in 1687 due to a combination of an extremely high tide meeting the flood waters caused by a terrible storm. When the new bridge was built in 1755 the superstructure was allegedly based on that of London's Westminster Bridge. It has been altered a number of times since that date. Today it is known as Grattan Bridge.

Essex (now Grattan) Bridge was originally built in 1676 with stones taken from St Mary's Abbey. It was reconstructed several times during its history and the present bridge dates from 1875.

———— ◎ ————

The Thingmote, which had stood at College Green from the time of the Vikings, was levelled in 1681 by the City Recorder, Sir William Davis. Its massive size can be gauged by the fact that the earth from the site, when spread along what is now Nassau Street, raised the level of the road by over eight feet. The difference in levels of Nassau Street and College Park today show how much the road had been raised.

It was at this time that the 'long stone', the Steyne, was removed. It is not known what became of it later.

———— ◎ ————

Meanwhile the attempts to capture Derry were getting no further but when James was told that he only had to appear at the gates of that city and they would be thrown open to him, he set out for the North. After a miserable journey he eventually arrived at the south gate in the Derry walls but instead of being allowed in he was met with the cry 'No Surrender.'

Shortly afterwards he returned to Dublin, leaving others to direct the siege. He then summoned another parliament in Dublin, which passed several acts giving religious freedom to all, restoring some lands to their previous owners and declaring that other lands would be confiscated from those who sided with William. But all this legislation came to nothing. Before it could be implemented James and his government were gone.

To meet mounting expenses a tax was imposed on estates and base coinage was issued to the value of £1,000,000, the real value of which was only about £60,000. (A £5 coin was actually worth four pence!) Coins were minted from brass, copper, tin, old cannonballs, broken bells, pots and pans at the Royal Mint at 27 Capel Street. Many shopkeepers refused to accept such base coinage even when threatened with hanging for refusing. This 'brass money' ruined trade and caused such widespread poverty that Lord Talbot withdrew the coins sometime later.

The siege of Derry was only the beginning of the war. King William came to Ireland to conduct the campaign in person. James set out with his army from Dublin and met up with the Williamite army at the Boyne just west of Drogheda. The behaviour of James before the battle was very erratic, sometimes full of determination and at other times planning an immediate retreat. Finally he sent all his baggage and half of his field guns back to Dublin. When news of this spread throughout the army it didn't help the morale of the troops.

The battle started on 1 July 1690 with each of William's men wearing a sprig of green in his cap, while soldiers in James' army wore a little strip of white paper. James took no part in the battle, being content to watch proceedings from a safe distance on a small hill. William on the other hand played a very active part.

Towards the end of the day when James saw the way the battle was going he fled with 200 cavalry, leaving his men to look after themselves, and reached Dublin a little after nine o'clock in the

Although there are sixteen bridges across the Liffey in Dublin at present there used to be another major bridge which lasted from 1682 to 1802. It was called the Ormonde Bridge and was located between O'Donovan Rossa Bridge (connecting Winetavern Street and Chancery Place) and Grattan Bridge (connecting Capel Street and Parliament Street). The original structure was just a wooden platform but later railings were added 'to prevent people falling off the bridge into the river'.

In 1684 the bridge was replaced by a stone structure which had five arches, one of which was a wooden drawbridge which could be raised to allow the passage of ships. Later when Capel Street Bridge had its drawbridge removed the one in Ormonde Bridge served no purpose and was replaced with a stone arch. In 1752 the bridge was in a very poor state and an examination revealed that the piers of the bridge had been built on 'the naked bed of the river'. Some repairs were made but in 1802 the whole structure collapsed during a flood in the river and was never rebuilt.

Yet another bridge was built in 1683 connecting Queen Street and Bridgefoot Street. It, too, collapsed in 1763 due to a raft of timber lodging in the central arch during a flood and causing the whole bridge to be swept away. The bridge was rebuilt in 1768. It was renamed 'Mellowes Bridge' in 1942 to honour Liam Mellowes, the IRA leader executed in 1922.

Arran (now Liam Mellowes) Bridge was built in 1768 to replace one swept away in a flood in 1763. It is the oldest bridge on the river.

evening. He is reputed to have complained to Lord Talbot's wife, 'The cowardly Irish have run away,' only to get the reply, 'It seems your majesty has won the race.'

During the Battle of the Boyne the gates of Dublin were closed and the citizens were not allowed out of the city, while Protestants were ordered to stay indoors for the day. After the battle many of the defeated soldiers made their way back to Dublin and by nightfall the city was filled with weary, exhausted soldiers.

The next morning King James left Dublin for Wexford and eventually, France. He had carefully provided for his own safety by placing two troops of horses at Bray to make sure the road to Wexford was kept open. With the departure of James, Lord Talbot was put in charge and he immediately gave orders to march to Limerick.

William of Orange

The victorious Williamite army made its way to Dublin after the battle and camped on the Common in Crumlin. (They brought with them the body of the great old soldier, Duke Schomberg, who had been killed in the battle. His body was later interred in St Patrick's Cathedral.) On 16 July William rode into the city to a rapturous reception from the Protestant population, who showered the soldiers with flowers and gifts and even hugged their horses. One account describes how 'they ran about shouting and

———— ◎ ————

During his stay in Dublin King William presented a new mayoral chain to the Lord Mayor to replace the original one which had been lost in 1688. The new chain is still in use to the present day.

———— ◎ ————

Dublin Corporation set out St Stephen's Green in the middle of the seventeenth century. Up till then it had been a common and had one gallows at Merrion Street corner and another at Harcourt Street corner.

———— ◎ ————

In the seventeenth century large numbers of Huguenots (Protestants who were fleeing persecution in France) came to settle in Ireland. At the beginning they were resented by the citizens of Dublin and in fact there was a riot in the city when 300 people gathered to attack the refugees. The Huguenots supported King William against James and a Huguenot regiment fought for William at the Battle of the Boyne. Many of these Huguenots remained in Dublin after the Treaty of Limerick and were joined by their wives and children.

By the early eighteenth century the Huguenot community was well established in the city, particularly in the Coombe area where they established a strong weaving industry. Many of the Huguenot community came to prominence in Dublin life, including the La Touche and D'Olier families. In 1693 a plot in Merrion Row was purchased to serve as a Huguenot cemetery and up to 600 persons were buried there up to 1901 when the cemetery was closed

———— ◎ ————

embracing one another and blessing God for His wonderful deliverance. The poor Roman Catholics [were] now lying in the same terror as we had done some days before.'

In August 1690 William and his army set out from Dublin and besieged Limerick. He finally abandoned the action in September and returned to Dublin and then to England. The Williamite army eventually had a victory over the Jacobite army at Aughrim and a second siege of Limerick followed which ended with a negotiated settlement. The Treaty of Limerick was signed on 15 October, 1690.

Patrick Sarsfied. When challenged for the password at Ballyneety during the siege of Limerick the answer was 'Sarsfield is the word and Sarsfield is the man.'

———— ◎ ————

Before the arrival of King James a businessman named Giles Mee was paid £7 17s 6d to repair St James' Gate for the royal visit. The following year, in 1690, the corporation gave permission to Mee to start a brewery nearby. In 1759 that same brewery became the property of one Arthur Guinness and is known worldwide as St James' Gate Brewery. The lease granted to Arthur Guinness was for 9,000 years, so it has some time to go yet!

———— ◎ ————

In July 1701 an equestrian statue of King William by Grinling Gibbons was erected in College Green. From the beginning it was subject to continuous abuse, mostly from students of Trinity College who objected to William having his back to the College and facing towards the Castle. In 1710 two of the students were fined £100 and sentenced to six months in jail for defacing the statue. In 1805 it was painted black on the eve of King William's birthday by a daring individual who informed the watchman that he had been sent by the corporation and who even got the watchman to guard his paints!

In 1836 it was blown apart by a bomb but the pieces were collected, pieced together again and the statue erected once more. However, when it was again blown up in 1929 it was never replaced. The monument to Thomas Davis occupies the site today.

———— ◎ ————

10

◎

FROM PENAL LAWS
TO UNITED IRISHMEN
1690 – 1782

The terms of the Treaty of Limerick were quite fair and King William was well disposed towards the Irish; he restored many of them to their estates and granted numerous pardons. He often declared that he 'had come to deliver Protestants but not to persecute Catholics'.

In October 1692 Lord Sidney, the Lord Lieutenant, summoned a parliament in Dublin, exactly a year after the Treaty of Limerick. The parliament was exclusively Protestant, for the very good reason that every member had to take an oath that the Chief Doctrines of the Catholic Church were false. Of course, no Catholic could take such an oath. Sidney, representing the king, opposed the measure but was outvoted. All the Catholics immediately walked out.

One of the first things this parliament did was to declare that it was independent of the English Parliament. A money bill sent from England was rejected on the grounds that it had not originated in the Irish House of Commons. The Lord Lieutenant was so angry at this snub to the English Parliament that he twice suspended the Dublin parliament and in November 1693 he finally dissolved it.

By 1695 Lord Capel was appointed Lord Lieutenant and he at once summoned a new parliament in Dublin which sat for several sessions, during which some of the 'Penal Laws' were passed. There had been many penal laws against Catholics in the years before this but they were passed only at long intervals and, often enough, not carried out. But now they came in quick succession, growing more and more severe as time went on. These laws were for the most part enacted by the Irish Parliament, which as already stated was entirely Protestant. The first action of the 1695

In 1700 the arrival in Dublin port of the sailing ship the *Ouzel* caused consternation in the city. The galley had set sail for Turkey in 1695 and no word of her had been heard for five years. It had been presumed that she had sunk and in fact an insurance claim had been paid to the owners.

Now, not only had it the same captain and crew but it was laden with a rich cargo of pirated goods. The captain's story was that they had been captured by Algerian pirates who then used the *Ouzel* as a pirate ship while the captain and crew were held captive in Algeria. They said that five years later the Irishmen had succeeded in recapturing the *Ouzel* and its cargo.

The *Ouzel* Galley

Five more years were to pass after their arrival in Dublin before an agreement was reached about the disposal of the cargo. Eventually it was decided that it should be sold and the proceeds used as a benevolent fund for merchants who fell on hard times. It later emerged that the Algerian pirates of the time kept accurate records of all their captures but there was no trace of any capture of the *Ouzel*. It is suspected that the Captain and crew had indulged in some piracy of their own.

parliament was to confirm all the minor provisions of the Treaty of Limerick and to omit all the important ones. The bill passed easily through the Commons but some peers, seven Protestant bishops and seven laymen, vigorously condemned this breach of faith. Once this bill was passed the parliament passed a whole series of penal laws in 1695 and 1697. The number of these laws is too large for them all to be listed here but some of the more important were as follows:

(i)   Catholic schoolteachers were forbidden to teach
(ii) Catholic parents were forbidden to send their children abroad for education
(iii) The lands of Catholic landowners were taken from them and given to others
(iv) If a Catholic had a valuable horse any Protestant could take it from him for £5
(v)   No Catholic could have a vote
(vi) Catholics were forbidden to travel more than five miles from home, to keep arms, to take cases to court or to be guardians or executors
(vii) Any Catholic priest who came into the country could be hanged.

This was only the first instalment; worse was to follow. When the Duke of Ormonde (grandson of Ormond of Cromwell's time – from 1662 onwards he spelled his name with an 'e') became Lord Lieutenant he passed further penal regulations. Two of these were as follows:

(i)   If the eldest son of a Catholic declared himself a Protestant he became owner of all his father's land.
(ii) No Catholic could vote or hold any public office.

These and many more such laws reduced the Catholic population to abject misery. It must be remembered that elsewhere in Europe similar penal laws were passed by Catholics against Protestants and by Protestants against Catholics but only in Ireland was there an attempt by a small minority to suppress the religion of a whole nation among whom they lived. Not all the penal laws were enforced, however, and by the middle of the eighteenth century they were gradually relaxed.

———— ◎ ————

During the eighteenth century capital punishment by hanging was an extremely common occurrence. Pirates on the Irish Sea were especially savagely treated as a warning to others. Four pirates were executed in St Stephen's Green in 1766. Two of the bodies were left hanging by chains on the rocks near Poolbeg. The other two bodies were hung on the South Wall but they stank so much that the locals objected and the bodies were removed to Dalkey Island.

———— ◎ ————

Where offenders escaped hanging they very often got whipped instead. A frequent route was from High Street down along Dame Street to College Green where the poor unfortunates were whipped from one end of the course to the other. Public whipping was meted out until 1815.

———— ◎ ————

In 1734 the students of Trinity College disliked their Junior Dean, Edward Ford, so much that they murdered him!

———— ◎ ————

Anatomy lessons at Trinity were primitive affairs in the eighteenth century. An observer described how 'the professor of anatomy had his subject on a board before him, part of the human body, and as he dissected, frequently put the knife in his mouth'.

———— ◎ ————

Dublin's citizens of the period certainly did not lack for drinking opportunities. There were about two thousand ale-houses, three hundred taverns and twelve hundred shops selling brandy in the city.

———— ◎ ————

In the days of sailing ships it used to take anything from eighteen to thirty hours to cross from Holyhead to Ringsend. In fact it was not uncommon, due to stormy weather or adverse winds, for the journey to take a week or ten days.

———— ◎ ————

However, there was one important avenue for progress open to Catholics. While ownership of land and participation in the professions was denied to them, they were able to prosper in trade. Many of them indeed became rich, especially in the larger towns such as Dublin.

When exports of goods of various kinds such as livestock, meat and dairy products to or from England or the colonies were banned in the seventeenth century (to protect British producers' markets), Catholics began to apply themselves to other industries, especially that of wool, brewing and tanning. But when this trade began to flourish it too was destroyed by statute.

Public life in Ireland in the eighteenth century, especially that of the Protestant minority, centred on the Parliament. It was always held in Dublin and, from 1731 onwards, in the building in College Green now occupied by the Bank of Ireland. From 1715 to 1783 the parliament met for only one session of six months every second year. In the House of Commons there were 200 members and all had to be members of the Established Church. The higher government officials were nearly all Englishmen and formed the 'Court' Party, always willing to carry out the wishes of the king and English council. By fair means or foul they were always able to command a majority in their favour. But among a certain section of Irish Protestants the power of these English officials, and the unjust laws that had wreaked such havoc on Irish trade, provoked feelings of resentment towards the English Parliament and rekindled a growing sense of patriotism.

They were only a small group and they became known as the 'Patriot' Party. They had two main objectives: to remove restrictions on trade, and to make the Irish Parliament independent of that of England. Among their leaders were Jonathan Swift, Charles Lucas, Henry Flood, Edmund Burke and Henry Grattan.

Gradually as the years went by, the small party grew in strength and ultimately they succeeded in their main objectives but it was to be a long drawn-out process. The struggle between the Patriot Party and the Court Party was to be the main feature of the political history of Ireland for most of the eighteenth century.

In 1698 the Member of Parliament for Dublin University, William Molyneux, published an essay called *The Case of Ireland's being Bound by Acts of Parliament in England Stated.*

———— ◎ ————

In 1706 Tailors' Hall in Back Lane was built on the site of the Jesuit College which had been built in 1627. It is the oldest guildhall in the city.

———— ◎ ————

The first lighthouse in the world to use candlepower instead of burning coals was erected on Dublin Bay in 1761.

———— ◎ ————

On 17 September 1773 the Drogheda mail coach was held up at Santry 'by two young men of good address'. They robbed the passengers of their cash and watches, except for the purse of a priest, which they returned. One of the robbers was caught a week later and informed on the other.

———— ◎ ————

An improved system of public lighting was introduced in 1785. Oil lamps replaced the candles and burning torches.

———— ◎ ————

An old print of Dublin Bay from the eighteenth century gives a clear indication of the origins of the name 'Beggarsbush'. The view was sketched from a point on Haddington Road and clearly to be seen is the bush under which beggars of the day used to shelter. Three beggars, two standing and one sitting, are shown waiting by the roadside.

———— ◎ ————

Towards the end of the eighteenth century the Dublin port authorities built a massive wooden house at the port entrance to serve as a watch house, store house and a place of shelter for travellers forced to stay there because of the weather. A man named Pidgeon was given the job of caretaker and he found the place was frequented by so many people that he started supplying meals and refreshments to visitors. He also had a boat for hire to his guests and his hostelry became quite famous as 'Pidgeon's House'. Later it became known by its present name, the Pigeonhouse.

———— ◎ ————

Henry Grattan lived for a time at 56 St Stephen's Green East. After the Act of Union ended the life of the parliament he had declared independent, he said 'I sat by its cradle and I followed its hearse.'

In his essay Molyneux denounced the many injustices inflicted on Ireland and claimed Ireland had a right to make her own laws, independent of the English Parliament. The essay caused great anger in England and Parliament ordered that it be burned publicly by the hangman.

A strange court case, which occurred early in the eighteenth century, greatly added to the friction between the parliaments. A dispute over some property arose between two Irishmen called Sherlock and Annesley. When the case was brought to the Dublin court it decided in favour of Annesley. On appeal to the Irish House of Lords the judgement was reversed in Sherlock's favour. Next Annesley appealed to the English House of Lords, which reversed the decision once more for him. They also fined the sheriff of Kildare for not obeying their ruling. Then the Irish House of Lords cancelled the fine, declared the appeal to the English House of Lords illegal, praised the sheriff for his action and arrested the members of the Dublin court who had given the first judgement in favour of Annesley!

The English Parliament at last put an end to the farce by passing

———— ◎ ————

On one occasion when Dean Jonathan Swift's printer, George Faulkner, returned from London he went to visit Swift dressed in a laced waistcoat, 'a bag-wig and other fopperies'. He was asked, 'Pray, sir, who are you?' 'Why, I'm George Faulkner, the printer,' was the reply. 'You, George Faulkner, the printer! Why thou art the most impudent, bare-faced impostor I ever heard of. George Faulkner is a sober, sedate citizen and would never trick himself out in lace and other fopperies. Get about your business and thank your stars that I do not send you to the House of Correction!' Poor George went home and having changed out of his finery, went once more to visit the Dean. This time Swift received him warmly and welcomed him 'on his return from London', saying: 'There was an impudent fellow here in a laced waistcoat who would fain have passed for you; but I soon sent him packing with a flea in his ear.'

———— ◎ ————

Before his death Dean Swift had gradually sunk into increasing dementia and when he died in 1745 he left a legacy for the founding of St Patrick's Hospital for psychiatric patients in Steeven's Lane near Kingsbridge. He also wrote of the bequest:

> He left the little wealth he had
> To build a house for fools and mad
> And showed by one satiric touch
> No nation wanted it so much

———— ◎ ————

Jonathan Swift is buried under the floor of St Patrick's Cathedral at the west end of the nave. The Latin inscription on the wall nearby was written by Swift himself. It has been freely translated by Yeats as follows:

> Swift has sailed into his rest
> Savage indignation there
> Cannot lacerate his breast
> Imitate him if you dare—
> World besotted traveller, he
> Served human liberty.

———— ◎ ————

in 1720 an important act known as 'The Sixth of George I' (so called because it was passed during the sixth year of his reign). This act declared that the English Parliament had the right to make laws for Ireland and that the Irish House of Lords had no right to hear appeals.

Perhaps the greatest opponent of the Court Party was not a member of parliament at all but a clergyman named Jonathan Swift, dean of St Patrick's Cathedral. He was angered by the destruction of Irish industry for the benefit of English traders. In an essay encouraging Irish people to retaliate he coined the famous phrase 'Burn everything English except their coal.'

Towards the end of the reign of King George I another event occurred which strengthened the opposition of the Irish Parliament to control from England. The event is known as the 'Affair of Wood's Halfpence'.

Since the reign of Edward VI (1546–1553) there had been no money minted in Ireland – all the coins circulating in Ireland were made in England. During King George's reign there was a great shortage of small coins in Ireland and this affected the poor in particular. In July 1722 the English treasury granted a patent for minting small coins to the king's favourite, the Duchess of Kendal. She sold the patent to a Wolverhampton Iron Master named William Wood, allowing him to mint 60 tons of copper into halfpennies and farthings to the face value of £108,000. The duchess and Wood hoped to make a very large profit as only £15,000 in small coins was needed.

The Irish Parliament strongly objected to all this. The minting of coins was a State prerogative and the granting of the patent to an individual was regarded as deeply insulting. The Parliament protested to the king but a committee appointed by the English Privy Council to look into the matter dismissed their protests and added that the king was not bound to consult the Irish Parliament on anything at all. Then early in 1724 a letter was published, under the name of MB Drapier, which vigorously attacked 'Wood's Halfpence'. The author was supposed to be a Dublin shopkeeper but in reality was Jonathan Swift.

The First Drapier letter played on the prejudices of the ignorant multitude. It claimed that 'Wood's Halfpence' would soon become the sole currency of the whole Kingdom.

———— ◎ ————

Lord Charlemont's Casino in Marino was built around 1772. The Palladian building has four state rooms on the ground floor, four bedrooms on the first floor and eight other rooms in the basement with numerous statues of Roman gods and various other sculptures. The casino came under state guardianship in 1932 and full ownership in 1972.

———— ◎ ————

The building known as Marino Crescent near the junction of the Malahide Road with Fairview was built in 1792 by a builder, Mr Ffolliot of Aungier Street. He was accused by Lord Charlemont of blocking the view of Dublin Bay from his Marino Casino. In an attempt to stop the building Charlemont imposed very heavy dues on building materials passing through his tollgates. Ffolliot responded by conveying his materials across the bay by barge and built his houses of a height to completely block Charlemont's view! (One resident of the houses was Bram Stoker, the author of *Dracula*, who was born in number 15 on 8 October 1847.)

———— ◎ ————

In the eighteenth and the first half of the nineteenth centuries the port of Dublin was largely under the control of the Ballast Board. In 1793 the board established offices at 6 Lower Sackville Street and later in 1801 moved to the corner of Westmoreland Street and Aston Quay. The building had a rather unusual timing device on its roof, a 'time ball'. It consisted of a four-foot diameter copper ball with a wooden pole through the centre. A clock in the Ballast Office was connected by telegraph to Dunsink Observatory. An impulse from the observatory was sent every second to this clock which in turn controlled the copper ball. At precisely 1·00 p.m. every day the ball was released to slide down the wooden pole. Ships' captains on the Liffey could thus get the exact time each day. The ball is now in Dunsink Observatory. (Incidentally, ballast was necessary for the safety of ships to ensure their stability when they had no cargo. The usual ballast was sand, gravel or stone. The Ballast Board had the task of regulating where ballast could be excavated and also where unwanted ballast could be dumped.)

———— ◎ ————

When Jonathan Swift was three years old his devoted nurse kidnapped him from Dublin and brought him to England. His two great loves were Vanessa (Esther Vanhomrigh) and Stella (Hester Johnson).

The Second letter was not much different but Swift began to show his real purpose in the Third letter. He railed against the insults offered to the Irish Parliament and asked were not Irish people as free as those in England. (Swift's 'Irish people' were of course the colonists – he had little or no concern for the ordinary Irish Catholics.)

The Fourth Drapier letter was the most famous. It appeared in October 1724 and was addressed to the 'whole people of Ireland' (but once more the Catholic population was not included). Again it attacked 'Wood's Halfpence', criticised the assumed power of the English Parliament to legislate for Ireland and pointed out that force alone would make Ireland accept this.

The authorities were outraged and offered the then huge reward of £300 for information on the author. Although many people knew it was Swift, no one came forward to claim the reward. The authorities then prosecuted the printer of the letters but the Dublin Grand Jury refused to accept the charge. The Grand Jury was dissolved and a new one appointed. The new jury not only threw out the charge again but said that anyone who accepted Wood's coins was an enemy of the king.

———— ◎ ————

The bridge which is now named after Daniel O'Connell started out as the Carlisle Bridge in 1791. It was designed by James Gandon and named after the Lord Lieutenant at the time. It was opened to pedestrians in 1792 and to carriages in 1795. It originally had an obelisk at each corner but these were removed in 1804 because they interfered with the vista from Westmoreland Street to Sackville Street. Frequent criticisms of the bridge over the years for its narrowness and the fact that it was 'hump-backed' led to it being completely redesigned and reconstructed. The work began in 1877 and the wide level bridge we know today was fully opened to traffic in 1880. The Port and Docks Board had the name 'Carlisle Bridge' carved on the parapets but the corporation placed bronze plaques over that name when they renamed the bridge O'Connell Bridge in 1880.

Carlisle (now O'Connell) Bridge used to be hump-backed and had an obelisk at each corner. The present bridge was opened in 1880.

———— ◎ ————

The authorities gave in – the patent for the coins was withdrawn, Wood was compensated and the king announced in 1725 that the whole affair was at an end.

In the meantime the struggle between the two parties in the parliament went on. The Patriot Party opposed government policy and harassed the Court Party at every turn. These early 'patriots' were concerned with the wellbeing of the Protestant people only and cared little about the disadvantages suffered by their Catholic fellow-countrymen. Indeed some of them were selfish and corrupt and were later bought off with high positions or pensions.

One of the greatest causes of dissension was the Pension List. Large pensions were given to persons who had done little to deserve them and all had to be paid by the Irish Exchequer. The leader of the Patriots, Henry Flood, attacked this scandalous system and he was aided by an extremely able and eloquent young man called Henry Grattan. Grattan was not yet at that time a Member of Parliament but he strongly supported Flood in his criticisms. Another great bone of contention was the duration of parliament. In England it could only last seven years at most but in Ireland the parliament could last as long as the king wished. The preceding parliament had lasted for the entire reign of George II, some thirty-three years!

In 1767 the Patriots under Charles Lucas petitioned the English council to bring in the Seven Year Bill to limit the length of any Irish parliament to seven years. The council accepted the request but changed the limit to eight years. The passing of the bill was greeted with great approval in Ireland.

All this time the Catholics were silent, taking no part in the political proceedings. All they wished for at the time was a quiet life and to be allowed to get on with their trading interests. More and more Catholics were entering trade as it was one of the few outlets where Catholic activity was permitted.

The American War of Independence was the catalyst for the relaxation of the penal code in the 1770s. Both Protestants and Catholics in Ireland were strongly pro-American. The events in America also provided the excuse for Protestant patriots to form the Irish Volunteers. They were formed ostensibly to protect Ireland against invasion but they were seen to be a useful lever in wringing concessions from England. The Irish Volunteers were

———— ◎ ————

A strange fact about 'Grattan's Parliament' is that Grattan was always a member of the opposition.

———— ◎ ————

St Stephen's Green was commonly used as a place of execution at the time.

In 1691 a certain Mark Baggot was arrested as 'a spy in women's clothing' and hanged. In 1695 a Mary Bacon was burned at the stake for killing her child and in 1722 a Mary Allen was found guilty of a similar offence and also burned at the stake.

———— ◎ ————

In 1738 Lord Santry, who owned Santry village, was convicted of the murder of one of his servants and was sentenced to death for his crime. When efforts to have the sentence quashed were unsuccessful his uncle, Sir Compton Domville, came up with a novel scheme to aid his nephew. At that time all of Dublin's water was supplied from Templeogue and Sir Compton happened to own Templeogue. He threatened to cut off the city's water supply unless Lord Santry was released. The threat worked and Santry was allowed to 'escape' and eventually made his way to Italy.

———— ◎ ————

The principal post office was located in Fishamble Street for thirty years from 1680. The Music Hall was opened in the same street in 1741 and it was there that Handel conducted the premiere of *Messiah* on 13 April 1742 in front of an audience of over seven hundred. (He had already composed *Messiah* before coming to Dublin.) So many people wished to attend that the ladies were asked not to wear their hooped skirts, and because they agreed, many hundreds more saw each performance. During his nine-month stay in Dublin Handel lived in Abbey Street and performed on many occasions in the Music Hall during that time. (Incidentally the S–bend in Fishamble Street is thought by some to follow a line of defence for the early Norse settlement in Dublin.)

———— ◎ ————

almost completely Protestant but Catholics were generally favourable towards them.

In Dublin various professions and classes began to raise their own corps; noblemen and lawyers were two examples. Each corps selected its own uniform which the men bought for themselves. Where they were too poor to do so, they were provided from a general fund. They bought their own weapons too, although in some cases the Castle authorities very reluctantly handed out a few thousand rifles.

Gradually the threat from external forces receded and the Volunteers began to focus more on domestic issues but they were still loyal to the British connection and were Protestant led.

In October 1779 parliament met again and the Volunteers made demands for redress of their grievances. Their usual assembly point in Dublin was around the statue of William of Orange in College Green. By this time Henry Grattan had become their spokesman in parliament. He demanded free trade and a motion to that effect was passed unanimously by the house. Dublin was in a state of great excitement and the Houses of Parliament in College Green were besieged by huge crowds demanding the quick implementation of the free trade motion. A solemn procession from the Parliament House, led by the Speaker carrying the demand and followed by the members of the House of Commons, made its way up Dame Street to Dublin Castle. The streets were lined on both sides with Volunteers in uniform who presented arms as the procession passed. At the Castle the petition was presented to the Lord Lieutenant, Lord Buckinghamshire.

The British Parliament subsequently acceded to the petition and in November 1779 passed three Free Trade Acts: the first permitted free export of wool and woollen goods; the second allowed free export of glass products; the third allowed free trade with British colonies. The news was greeted with great rejoicing in Dublin and the standing of the Volunteers was greatly enhanced.

Having flexed their muscles and tasted victory they now demanded more, in particular, the repeal of Poyning's Law (which stated that the Irish Parliament could not pass any law without the permission of the authorities in England), and 'The Sixth of George I' (which stated that the English Parliament could pass laws governing Ireland).

Dublin has two canals connecting the city to the river Shannon – the Grand Canal and the Royal Canal. The Grand Canal was commenced in 1755 and by the end of the century it had reached a terminal basin near James' Street. The canal was opened to traffic on 2 February 1779 and a passenger-boat service operated between Dublin and Sallins, Co. Kildare, the following year. It was then decided to continue the canal to Dublin port and the project was completed by 1796. The grand opening was performed by the Earl of Camden who sailed his yacht into the newly constructed Grand Canal docks at the mouth of the river.

For some years the scheme was successful and five hotels were constructed along its length, including the best known one at Portobello Bridge. The rise of the railways brought about a decline in canal traffic however and although a good trade continued between Dublin and Limerick until the 1930s the last boats ceased business in 1959–60. In more recent years there has been something of a revival for the canal, with increasing tourist traffic.

The Royal Canal was also started at the end of the eighteenth century and it too was between Dublin and the Shannon. By 1806 the first passenger-boat service connected the Liffey at North Wall Quay to Mullingar in Co. Westmeath. Eleven years later the canal finally reached the Shannon but like the Grand Canal it also had to compete with the railways and was not a great success. It was finally closed by CIÉ in 1961.

A storm which occurred on 28 January 1792, breached the South Wall of Dublin Harbour and in the words of the *Dublin Chronicle* 'His grace the Duke of Leinster went on a sea party, and after shooting the breach, sailed over the Low Ground and the South Lotts and landed safely at Merrion Square.'

On 16 April the parliament again met in Dublin where Grattan, although quite ill at the time, made an impassioned speech in favour of the repeal of the two acts. The motion was passed unanimously and when the action moved to the English Parliament, the Commons and the Lords both agreed to end the right granted by 'The Sixth of George I'. The Act of Repeal, as it was called, was communicated to the Irish Parliament in Dublin on 27 May 1782. The news was received with great acclaim by the people of Dublin and in gratitude the parliament voted 20,000 men and £100,000 to the British Navy.

The former Houses of Parliament in College Green are now occupied by the Bank of Ireland. The original buildings on the site were at various times, a hospital (1603), a mansion (1612), House of Commons (1730), House of Lords (1787) and finally a bank (1808).

Acknowledging the great efforts of Henry Grattan, the parliament voted £100,000 to him but he would only accept £50,000, (and then very reluctantly). He later purchased and took up permanent residence in Tinnahinch House beside the Powerscourt Estate in Enniskerry

In January 1783 the English Parliament passed the Act of Renunciation declaring that Ireland's right to be bound only by the laws made by the king and the Irish Parliament was established forever. From now on, the only connection between the two parliaments was to be that the king was head of both.

———— ◎ ————

John Philpott Curran was born in 1790 in 4 Ely Place. When he was young he had such a bad stammer that he was given the nickname 'Stuttering Jack'. By practising the speeches of Shakespeare in front of a mirror he completely overcame his disability and became 'the wittiest and dreamiest, the most classical and ambitious' member of the Bar. The writer, Jonah Barrington, describes Curran thus:

> His person was mean and decrepit, very slight, very shapeless – with nothing of the gentleman about it; on the contrary, displaying spindle limbs, a shambling gait, one hand imperfect, and a face yellow and furrowed, rather fat and thoroughly ordinary. But his rapid movements, his fire, his sparkling eye, the fine and varied intonations of his voice – these conspired to give life and energy to every company he mixed with.

———— ◎ ————

In 1791 work began on a bridge over the Liffey at Islandbridge. This was to replace a previous bridge which had been damaged by a flood in the river in 1787. That stone bridge had been built in 1577 at the site of one of the earliest fording points on the river. The new bridge was completed in 1793 and was first named Sarah Bridge after the wife of the Lord Lieutenant, Westmoreland. Many regard the bridge, which has a single elliptical arch, as the most graceful bridge of all the Liffey bridges. In 1922 the corporation renamed the bridge Island Bridge.

Sarah (now Island) Bridge

———— ◎ ————

The Irish parliament of the time was rotten to the core. Of the 300 members of parliament over 100 were government hacks who would vote as directed. Any man could become a member by paying money to a borough owner. The borough owner would then direct the people to elect the donor. (Borough owners could earn up to £10,000 a seat in this way.) Less than eighty members were elected in a free democratic way. Some boroughs had only about a dozen electors, so it was relatively easy to bribe them. Although Catholics constituted four-fifths of the population they were totally excluded – they could neither vote nor be elected.

Parliamentary reform was, therefore, obviously needed and the Volunteers took up the question. They wanted to end bribery and corruption and ensure that all members were elected by free votes. A general convention of the Volunteers was held on 10 November 1783 in the Rotunda at the corner of present-day Parnell Square. After much debate certain reforms were listed and were introduced by Flood in the parliament in College Green shortly after. Despite a powerful speech by Flood, supported by Grattan and John Philpott Curran (in his maiden speech), the government side voted down the proposals. The result caused great bitterness and for a time there was danger of a clash between the government and the Volunteers. But eventually on 2 December the Volunteer Convention adjourned, with no fixed date for reassembling. This in effect was the end of the influence of the old Volunteer movement. From this time on they became more revolutionary in their ideas under the influence of events in France. They now formed themselves into clubs and groups, which held their meetings in secret.

In Dublin, as elsewhere, they began to drill and arm both Catholics and Protestants. The government increased the army to 15,000 men and also revived the militia – a much-hated force. The country saw outbreaks of violence everywhere. Mobs of Volunteers roamed the streets of Dublin, attacking and injuring soldiers, ransacking shops and upbraiding any shopkeepers who sold English goods.

Some efforts by the then Chancellor of the English Exchequer, William Pitt, to remedy the imbalance of trade between the two countries were defeated by the English Parliament. Other proposals, much less favourable to Ireland, were passed in London

———— ◎ ————

The present-day Kilmainham Jail opened in 1796 on a site known as Gallows Hill on the South Circular Road. There had been a jail in the area since1210 but by the eighteenth century it was in a deplorable condition and had to be replaced. The new jail had fifty-two individual cells and these were soon filled to overflowing at the time of the rebellion of 1798. Again in 1857 it was felt that the prison needed alteration and by 1863 the redesigned building was ready for occupation. Kilmainham has played 'host' to a long list of famous Irish leaders including Robert Emmett, Charles Stewart Parnell, the 1916 leaders, Eamon de Valera and many others. The jail was closed in 1924 and is now open to the public as a national monument.

Kilmainham Jail

———— ◎ ————

but when they were presented to the Dublin parliament there was uproar. Flood and Grattan made eloquent and fiery speeches against the bill. After an angry all-night debate the government had a slender majority of nineteen. So small was the margin that the government thought it prudent to withdraw the bill. So things remained as they were until the Act of Union.

From 1785 onwards great agitation spread throughout the country. Secret societies sprang up, such as the 'Right Boys' and the 'Defenders' on the Catholic side and the 'Peep-o-Day Boys' on the Protestant side. Atrocities were committed by both parties – they fought, maimed and killed each other and caused havoc throughout the country.

Dublin was as much disturbed as the rest of the country and in an effort to quell disturbances in the city a special body of constables was set up to aid the existing watchmen. (This force of constables was in time to become the Dublin Metropolitan Police which was eventually incorporated into the Garda Síochána in 1925.)

The French Revolution of 1789 greatly affected political thought in Ireland at the time. The ruling classes in general supported the Royalist side and the Catholic clergy constantly warned their flocks against the new ideas being promoted on the continent. At the same time there were many in the country who eagerly embraced the new ideas. Political clubs were formed to promote the cause of political reform. Whig Clubs were established in Dublin, Belfast and elsewhere and included among their members such people as Theobald Wolfe Tone, Napper Tandy, John Philpott Curran, Henry Grattan and others.

In October 1791 Tone, who was born at 44 Stafford Street (now Wolfe Tone Street), founded the Society of the United Irishmen in Belfast and later another branch was formed in Dublin with Napper Tandy as its secretary. The stated aims of the United Irishmen were to unite Irishmen of all religions and classes, to reform government and to repeal the Penal Laws.

On 2 December the more progressive members of the Catholic Committee, which had been founded in 1757 with similar aims to the United Irishmen, now called a meeting of Catholic delegates from all over Ireland. They met in the Tailors' Hall in Back Lane, joining Nicholas Street and High Street. (The assembly was often

Theobald Wolfe Tone, who was born at what is now 44 Wolfe Tone Street, founded the Society of the United Irishmen.

subsequently called the 'Back-Lane Parliament'.) A petition to the king was drafted and five delegates were appointed to bring the petition directly to London.

They were introduced to King George III by Edmund Burke and as a result the king sent a request to the Irish parliament to remove some of the inequalities suffered by Catholics. The parliament, however, rejected the request with contempt, but was later forced in 1793 to grant Catholics substantial concessions. The 'Forty-Shilling Freeholders', i.e. men who owned land worth at least forty shillings more than the rent they had to pay, were given the vote, were allowed to attend Trinity College and get degrees; they could serve on juries and be justices of the peace. But one thing was denied them – they could not be elected to parliament.

The same parliament which reluctantly passed these relief laws also passed two coercion acts: the Convention Act forbidding any gathering of delegates like the Back-Lane Parliament, and the Gunpowder Act forbidding the importation or sale of gunpowder or arms.

In spite of the Convention Act, the United Irishmen continued to meet and at a gathering held in Cope Street near the Parliament buildings in February 1793, Archibald Hamilton Rowan (who had been a member of the Volunteers and was now a United Irishman) distributed a pamphlet calling on the Volunteers to take up arms in the defence of Ireland and calling for complete Catholic emancipation. Secret government agents were at the meeting and brought the pamphlet to the notice of the authorities. Sometime later Rowan was arrested for distributing the pamphlet to the Volunteers. His trial began on 29 January 1794.

Large crowds gathered outside the Four Courts in the snow and his defence counsel, Philpott Curran, was chaired home· by torchlight procession each evening. Soldiers were on guard right inside the building and detachments of cavalry patrolled the surrounding streets. Although eloquently defended by Curran, Hamilton Rowan was found guilty by the jury after only ten minutes deliberation. He was sentenced to two years' imprisonment and a fine of £500. He was smuggled out the back door to avoid a riot and brought to the 'second' Newgate Prison in Green Street.

While Rowan was in prison a Protestant clergyman named William Jackson arrived in Ireland from France to sound out the leading United Irishmen about an invasion by the French. Accompanying Jackson was a London attorney called Cockayne in

The 'Back-Lane Parliament' met in Tailors' Hall in 1791. Over the years the building deteriorated and was in danger of collapse. It was beautifully restored in 1966.

———— ◎ ————

When 'Black Jack' Fitzgibbon became Lord Chancellor he had a magnificent golden coach built in 1790 at the then enormous cost of £7,000. On occasions when he used it in the city the coach and its highly unpopular occupant were pelted with stones and once a dead rat was thrown into it. On the death of Queen Victoria the beautiful golden coach was painted black as a sign of mourning. It has now been restored to its former glory and is on view in Newbridge House Open Farm in Donabate in Co. Dublin.

———— ◎ ————

During the 'reign' of Fitzgibbon an Englishman, Dr Richard Twiss, visited Dublin and later wrote a scathing criticism of Black Jack and his cronies. In retaliation a manufacturer friend of Fitzgibbon printed a portrait of Twiss on the bottom of his earthenware chamberpots. Black Jack's wife, Lady Clare who was a sister of Buck Whaley, then composed the following:

> Here you may behold a liar
> Well deserving of hell-fire
> Everyone who likes may p—
> Upon the learned Doctor T—

———— ◎ ————

The United Irishman, Archibald Hamilton Rowan, lived to the age of eighty-three and died in 1834. He was described as a 'majestic figure, a model for the sculptor, with a native oaken sapling in his hand, and two gigantic Danish wolfhounds at his heels'. He was 'an early riser, temperate in his habits, and when not provoked to choler, bland, courteous, amiable, and capable of winning and retaining the most devoted friendship'. A companion who went on a walking tour of England with him describes 'his practice at starting from our inn, of a wet morning, of rolling himself into the first pool he met in order that he might be beforehand with the rain!'

———— ◎ ————

whom he confided his plans. Cockayne was in reality an English
government spy but he acted his part well. The two men had
meetings with Tone, Hamilton Rowan and others, including
Leonard McNally, a Dublin lawyer. (McNally, who was born at
22 Harcourt Street, was a trusted friend of the United Irishmen, he
knew their secrets and retained their friendship and confidence till
he died. It was only after his death, when his heir claimed the
continuation of the secret service income of £300 a year which his
father had received since 1798, that it was discovered that he also
had been a government informer. He is buried in the vaults of the
Church of Adam and Eve on Merchant's Quay.)

John Philpot Curran had his favourite daughter buried in the
lawn of the Priory, his country home in Rathfarnham. Houses
have since been built over the area, so her grave may be
under somebody's house today.

During the meetings a statement was issued by Tone at Rowan's
insistence to say that the people of Ireland were near to open
rebellion, that Ireland was 'a conquered, oppressed and insulted
country' and that the Catholics and Defenders 'would throw off the
yoke, if they saw any force in the country sufficiently strong to
resort to for defence'. Tone later withdrew his statement but
allowed Rowan to make a copy of it. Rowan did so and added some
embellishments of his own. Jackson later posted copies of the

statement to France. The letters were intercepted and Jackson was arrested. When Rowan heard of Jackson's arrest he decided to escape from prison. He bribed a jailer to allow him to visit his house in Sackville Street where he escaped through a back window and eventually made his way to France. The following year Jackson was brought to trial and convicted of treason. He cheated the hangman, however, as he managed to take a dose of arsenic and dropped dead in the courtroom.

The striking success of republican French forces on the Continent at this time now had an effect in Ireland. Prime Minister Pitt decided on a policy of conciliation, to drop coercion and remove all remaining disabilities suffered by the Catholics in Ireland. He sent over a new Lord Lieutenant, the Earl of Fitzwilliam, to carry out his orders.

Fitzwilliam was a just and liberal man and was received with great enthusiasm by the Catholics of Dublin who knew what his mission was. He immediately set about reforms by removing from office various officials who opposed any improvements. A month later Grattan introduced a bill to give permission to Catholics to sit in Parliament. Just when it seemed that the bill was on the point of being passed a small clique led by 'Black Jack' Fitzgibbon, Lord Chancellor of Ireland, managed to convince Prime Minister Pitt and King George that the Protestant religion would be endangered in Ireland if it was passed. The bill was defeated, Fitzwilliam was recalled, the deposed officials reinstated and the old policy towards Catholics resumed. Fitzwilliam left Ireland on 25 March 1795 amid scenes of great mourning throughout the city. To rub salt into the wounds Fitzgibbon was promoted to the title 'Earl of Clare'.

11

◎

FROM REBELLION TO UNION
1798 – 1801

At first the United Irishmen was an open organisation and exclusively Protestant. Then, when it was banned by the government in 1794, it changed to being a secret society. Large numbers of Catholics were admitted as members and by 1795 the policy of the United Irishmen was to become more and more republican, influenced greatly by the events in France.

On 9 April 1795 a massive meeting of Catholics was held at the Franciscan church in Francis Street. Over 4,000 people attended amid a welter of excitement. They were told by the leaders that they could not hope for any concessions from England by peaceful means. Rumours that a union of the two countries was planned by Pitt as the price to pay for Catholic emancipation invoked passionate speeches. The speakers declared that they would never trade the independence of their country for their own religious liberty and that they would never abandon their Protestant brethren.

When Fitzwilliam was recalled from Dublin, and hopes of reform began to fade, the leaders began to think more and more of rebellion. Lord Camden, Fitzwilliam's successor, arrived in Dublin in 1795 and a furious riot occurred in the streets. The military were called out to quell the disturbance and two citizens were killed.

All of this added to the unrest which was spreading throughout the country. The United Irishmen's leaders began negotiations with the French government in 1796. Tone, who had thought it prudent to leave Ireland in 1795, first went to America but in the following year he made his way to France. He joined several prominent members of the United Irishmen in Paris who were in negotiations with the French authorities for military aid for an Irish

———— ◎ ————

Leinster House was built by the first Duke of Leinster in 1745–7. On being told that he was foolish building in what was then an unfashionable part of Dublin he is said to have replied, 'They will follow me wherever I go.'

When Lord Edward Fitzgerald got into trouble with the authorities, Leinster House was ransacked for incriminating documents. One time he wrote in a letter, 'I confess Leinster House does not inspire the brightest of ideas.'

———— ◎ ————

Frescati House was occupied by the Fitzgeralds from 1766 until 1802 and later became a school for boys. In 1983 the house was demolished to make way for the enlargement of a supermarket on the site in spite of vigorous protests.

———— ◎ ————

In the eighteenth century many beggars in Dublin were sent to Newgate Prison close to where Green Street Courthouse is today. Thieves were not so lucky; they were taken straight from court to the gallows. The entrance gate to Newgate Prison is now preserved in Kilmainham Jail.

———— ◎ ————

A curious event took place in the late eighteenth century when a Turkish gentleman, Dr Achmet Borumborad, arrived in the city and set up hot and cold seawater baths which became very popular. Some years later, when the 'Turk' wanted to marry a local lady he shaved off his beard and revealed himself as Patrick Joyce from Kilkenny!

———— ◎ ————

In the early part of the nineteenth century Thomas Whaley, better known as Buck Whaley, lived on the southside of St Stephen's Green. He won a bet that he would travel to Jerusalem and back on foot, except where a sea crossing was unavoidable, play ball against that city's walls and return within one year. Another bet he undertook almost cost him his life. He bet that he could jump over a mail coach and did so by having the coach drawn up beneath an upstairs window. The jump crippled him for life, however.

———— ◎ ————

insurrection. Among them was Lord Edward Fitzgerald.

Lord Edward Fitzgerald, the son of the first Duke of Leinster, was born at the family home at Carton in County Kildare. His family became Protestants at the time of the Reformation and had supported William of Orange against King James. Edward was a delicate child at first but later developed into an active healthy boy. When the Kildares bought a villa at Blackrock in south County Dublin in the 1760s they enlarged it and gave it the name Frescati. The countess took her family there because of its healthy aspect and proximity to the sea.

Lord Edward Fitzgerald fought for the British side in the American War of Independence.

At the age of sixteen Edward joined the British army and by 1781 found himself fighting against American forces in the War of Independence in South Carolina. An escaped slave called Tony Small found Edward wounded and unconscious on the battlefield at Eutaw Springs. He carried him to safety, bound his wounds and undoubtedly saved his life. When Edward sailed for home some time later he took Tony with him and the former Black slave became his devoted servant for the rest of his life.

Subsequently Lord Edward followed a varied career of travel

During the eighteenth century, stagecoaches ran from Dublin to the principal towns in the country. They carried five passengers, one on top and four inside. Gates were put across the roads at many points and a toll had to be paid for the coach to be allowed through. The usual toll for a stagecoach was five and a half pence. In 1841 the mail coach from Sligo to Dublin took 15 hours and 15 minutes to complete the journey. In 1866 the train did the same journey in 7 hours 40 minutes for thirty-seven and a half pence.

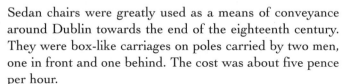

On 24 March 1798 the mail coach from Dublin to Belfast was stopped at Santry by an armed gang of rebels. They told the coach driver and guard that they were friends and that they had stopped the coach to prevent it falling into the hands of a large group of insurgents who were waiting for the coach in Swords. They invited the driver and guard into a house to wait and when they were inside the rebels set fire to the coach. They did not rob the passengers, however, nor did they harm them in any way. The driver later said that there was up to 1,000 other rebels in the fields nearby.

Sedan chairs were greatly used as a means of conveyance around Dublin towards the end of the eighteenth century. They were box-like carriages on poles carried by two men, one in front and one behind. The cost was about five pence per hour.

Every well-to-do family had its own chair and more than four hundred others were for hire in the city. The story is told of one Connacht man who, on hiring a chair, stepped into it only to discover that the bottom had fallen out of it. Instead of complaining however, he cheerfully walked all the way. When he got out at the end of his journey he remarked, 'Only for the honour of the thing I might as well have walked!'

and politics, including election to the Irish Parliament in College Green where he caused uproar for supporting the Volunteers when the house condemned them for celebrating French military victories. Gradually Lord Edward grew more and more republican in outlook and became so involved with the United Irishmen that by 1798 he was one of the leaders of the movement.

On 15 December 1796 over forty warships and 15,000 men left France bound for Ireland with Wolfe Tone on board one of the ships. The fleet was under the command of General Hoche. From the start the expedition was dogged by ill fortune. In a perfectly calm sea one ship hit a rock and sank with over 500 men; four other ships collided; several more, including that of Hoche, went astray. Less that half of the ships reached Bantry Bay and four days of ferocious storms prevented any landing. Finally the dispirited remnants sailed back to France.

Meanwhile the government embarked on a policy of repression, first in Ulster and later in the rest of Ireland. Anarchy, atrocities, burnings and pillaging by soldiers were widespread throughout the country. In May 1797 Grattan made another attempt in parliament to get some concessions on Catholic Emancipation but was voted down by the government side by four to one. Grattan and his supporters then withdrew from parliament in disgust.

The United Irishmen's leaders now decided that only force would gain the concessions they needed from the government. They settled on 23 May 1798 as the day the rebellion would start with the taking of Dublin Castle but unknown to them every move they made was betrayed to the authorities by informers. One of these was a man called Thomas Reynolds whom Lord Edward had recruited into the United Irishmen in Kildare. On Lord Edward's insistence he became a colonel in the United Irish army, a fatal move on Lord Edward's part, because Reynolds was more interested in his own advancement than anything else. When Fitzgerald revealed to him the plans for the coming rebellion Reynolds negotiated with the Castle authorities for a sum of £5,000 and £1,000 a year for life in return for betraying his friend.

Reynolds also let the Castle know of an early morning meeting of some of the leaders in the house of Oliver Bond, 9 Lower Bridge Street, opposite the Brazen Head tavern in Dublin on 12 March. Shortly after ten o'clock a magistrate called Major Swan arrived at

———— ◎ ————

When General Humbert, the leader of a French expedition to Ireland in 1798, surrendered after the battle of Ballinamuck, Co. Longford, he and his fellow officers were put on parole and lodged in an hotel in Dawson Street. Before they eventually departed for France they presented the hotel owner with their swords.

———— ◎ ————

Many of the bodies of those who were executed or killed in the fighting in 1798 were buried in mass graves in Croppies' Acre in front of the Royal Barracks (now Collins' Museum) at Wolfe Tone Quay. It is thought that part of the original Croppies' Acre now lies under the quay itself. In 1985 a large block of granite marked with a cross and the date '1798' was erected at the site to commemorate the dead buried there.

———— ◎ ————

Among the 'rebels' executed in Dublin were some lamplighters for neglect of duty and a Doctor Esmonde whose yeoman coat was turned inside out to show that he was a traitor.

———— ◎ ————

the house with a detachment of constables in uniform. When Swan gave the password 'Is Ivers of Carlow come?' he was admitted to the house. Swan flung open the door of the meeting room and found all the leaders present but the most incriminating documents were burned before he could prevent it. Thirteen members of the committee were arrested and only Lord Edward of the five-man executive remained at liberty.

Various other houses were raided by the military the same day and more of the leaders taken into custody. They failed to capture Lord Edward Fitzgerald, however, and a reward of £1,000 was offered for his capture. The Castle sent out two search parties with warrants to arrest him but though they searched Frescati and his home, Leinster House, they failed in their task. In fact Lord Edward was at home when the search party arrived but his faithful servant Tony smuggled him out to safety in Merrion Street. In the days and weeks that followed Lord Edward assumed almost mythical proportions in the eyes of his followers, appearing among them in various disguises, in spite of intense efforts by the authorities to find him.

In March 1798 the government declared the whole country to be in a state of rebellion and gave the newly appointed army commander, General Lake, a free hand to impose martial law. His soldiery spread terror and savagery throughout the country. Burnings, floggings, mutilations and rapes were the order of the day. 'Croppies', that is those who favoured the United Irishmen and adopted the fashion of cutting their hair short, were especially targeted. Pitch-capping, where the head of the victim was covered with a paper or cloth cap filled with tar and set alight, became commonplace.

Lord Edward stayed at various locations in the city during this time, including the home of a Mrs Dillon in Portobello and that of a feather merchant called Nicholas Murphy, in Thomas Street. Plans for the rising were completed by early May and it was agreed that it would start in the city on 23 May by stopping the mail coaches from departing for the provinces. The non-arrival of the coaches in the surrounding towns was to be the signal for the waiting rebels to rise up and in this way the rebellion would spread throughout the country.

Lord Edward had his magnificent uniform of green jacket and

———— ◎ ————

Lord Edward Fitzgerald was described as 'of a cheerful, intelligent countenance, an artless gaiety of manner, without reserve but without intrusion, and a careless, yet uneffusive intrepidity both in conversation and in action'.

———— ◎ ————

After Lord Edward Fitzgerald was arrested in Thomas Street the house owner, Nicholas Murphy, was also arrested and spent a year in jail, during which time his house was used as a barracks by the soldiers. He later complained that some fine examples of silverware were stolen by the men and that they destroyed 'six dozen as fine wine as could be found – claret, port and sherry – I purchased it in the wood' and that when the soldiers got tired of drinking his wine 'they were selling it in the morning for sixpence a bottle and buying whiskey with the money'.

———— ◎ ————

Lord Edward Fitzgerald is buried in the crypt of St Werburgh's Church. Major Sirr is buried in the graveyard of the same church.

———— ◎ ————

Francis Higgins, the 'Sham Squire', was born in a cellar in Lord Edward Street. He became in turn, a messenger boy, a shoe-black, a waiter in a pub, a clerk in a law office and finally a lawyer himself. He became exceedingly rich and the owner of the *Freeman's Journal*. He was an unmitigated rogue and gained all his wealth and position by underhand means. He got the nickname 'Sham Squire' because he pretended to be a landed gentleman in order to get a lady to marry him. (She is said to have died of grief as a result.) Later it was proved beyond doubt that he betrayed Lord Edward Fitzgerald to the Castle authorities for £1,000. He was 'to be seen daily with Buck Whaley on Beaux Walk in Stephen's Green, wearing a three-cocked hat fringed with swan's down, a canary-coloured waistcoat with breeches to match, a bright green body coat and violet gloves'. He died in 1806 aged fifty-six years of age.

———— ◎ ————

matching trousers trimmed with scarlet braid brought to his hiding place in Thomas Street in preparation for leading the troops into battle. The weather at the time was unusually fine and warm and everything seemed set for successful action but the army of spies and informers at last came up with hard information.

The paid informer, Francis 'Sham Squire' Higgins, discovered that Fitzgerald was hiding in 152 Thomas Street and told the authorities. On 19 May 1798, at seven o'clock in the evening, Major Swan and a soldier entered the house and burst into the room where Lord Edward Fitzgerald, who had a slight fever, was lying in bed. Swan was confronted by the owner, Nicholas Murphy, who asked him what his business was but when Swan saw Lord Edward in the bed he rushed past, yelling 'You are my prisoner'. Lord Edward sprang up and attacked Swan with a dagger which he had concealed. A Captain Ryan then rushed into the room and grappled with Lord Edward who repeatedly stabbed at him with his dagger. The fatally wounded Ryan still grimly held on and Major Swan then joined in the struggle. At that moment Major Sirr rushed into the room and shot Fitzgerald twice in the shoulder, causing him to drop the dagger, after which he was overpowered.

Later it was claimed by the authorities that Fitzgerald had a pistol with which he shot the soldier in the stomach before attacking the major with the dagger. Murphy categorically denied this and said that the soldier was also wounded by the knife, as Lord Edward was unable to reach his pistols. After his arrest he was taken to Newgate Jail and an armed guard was placed inside his cell in case an effort was made to rescue him. In fact a number of butchers from Patrick Street and some others from the Liberties did set out to do just that but gave up the attempt when told that a squadron of horses was already on its way up Castle Street to attack them.

On 21 May two lawyer brothers, Henry and John Sheares, who were members of the United Irishmen, were arrested. They were convicted of treason on 12 July and publicly beheaded outside Newgate Prison two days later. Henry was actually reprieved but the order arrived five minutes too late to stop the execution. (Their remains lie today in the vaults of St Michan's Church.)

On the evening of the 23 May Samuel Neilson, one of the United Irishmen leaders, called a meeting of fifteen officers from

Dublin city and assigned to each a position to occupy. The chief assembly points were Smithfield, north of the Liffey and Newmarket, beside the Coombe on the southside. After his meeting with the officers, Samuel Neilson made his way to Newgate Prison to plan an attack on it to release the wounded Lord Edward Fitzgerald, Oliver Bond, Henry Jackson and others, who were prisoners there but he was recognised by the jailer and arrested.

The Castle authorities, through one of their many spies, were soon aware of the plans for the rising made at the meeting of 23 May and troops were immediately despatched to occupy Smithfield.

> The cavalry and infantry were, in some places, so compactly interwoven, that a dragoon could not wield a sword without cutting down a foot soldier, nor a foot soldier discharge his musket without knocking down a trooper. The cavalry being elevated, could breathe freely in the crowd; but the infantry could scarcely avoid suffocation. A few hundred insurgents, with long pikes, coming on rapidly in the dark, might, without difficulty, have assailed the yeomen from five different points.
>
> *Sir Jonah Barrington*

Newmarket was similarly occupied and all main roads and Liffey and canal bridges were blockaded. Large numbers of rebels who converged on the city that same day were stopped by the waiting troops or turned back when they found there were no officers to lead them. An account of the time tells of how:

> The columns of the rebels which surrounded the town waited one for the other to begin, and had any daring officer been found to lead his men under fire, the others from Ringsend, Eccles Street, Clontarf and Harold's Cross, in all of which places were large bodies of them, would have probably followed the example, which might have been of the worst consequences as the garrison was so weak, and the troops from Loughlinstown camp did not arrive till two in the morning.

The next day the lanes and alleys around Smithfield were found to contain large amounts of pikes and muskets which had been abandoned by contingents of rebels on finding the area occupied by the king's troops.

With the capture of Neilson there was no leader left to take command. Some minor skirmishes did occur at Rathfarnham, Crumlin, Tallaght, Rathcoole, Clondalkin and other areas. The new Lord Lieutenant, Charles Cornwallis, ordered that 'any man in a brown coat who was found within several miles of the field of action was to be butchered without discrimination'. Many innocent people were killed and their remains were piled up in carts to be paraded through the streets of Dublin. The bodies of several of the victims were displayed in the Castle yard, while others were hung outside barracks throughout the city. Many more prisoners were hanged from lampposts.

Wholesale arrests reduced the United Irishmen organisation within the city to a helpless condition and on-the-spot hanging of prisoners at various points in the city, including Carlisle Bridge, acted as a powerful deterrent to others. Within a week the threat to the capital was over and the main focus of attention shifted to Wexford.

The rising began in Wexford on 24 May 1798 and the rebels were mostly Catholics although many of the leaders were Protestant. They met with considerable success at first but were eventually defeated at Vinegar Hill. Meanwhile Lord Edward's wounds had festered and he gradually lapsed into a fever and died on 4 June 1798. He was thirty-two years old.

In the North of Ireland some success attended the risings in Antrim and Down but eventually that too ended in failure. Whereas the rebellion in Wexford was Catholic led, in the North it was predominantly Protestant. At the end of both uprisings the yeomanry and militia committed dreadful atrocities. Their many outrages were matched on the rebel side by roving bands throughout the country, free of all restraint.

In August 1798 a small French expedition under the command of Admiral Bompart, who was accompanied by Theobald Wolfe Tone, arrived in Lough Swilly. After a fierce battle once more the French surrendered. Tone was recognised and sent in chains to Dublin. There he was court-martialled and sentenced to be hanged. On Sunday 11 November he was told that he was to be hanged the next day at Newgate Prison. The part of his sentence requiring that 'his head be struck off, fixed on a pike and placed in the most conspicuous part of the city' was cancelled by the Lord Lieutenant. That night Tone tried to commit suicide by cutting his throat with his penknife, although controversy continues to surround this, some believing it was the authorities who tried to kill him. He was found at 4.00 a.m. in a pool of blood with his windpipe severed. Four surgeons were called in and his wound was sewn up. Frantic efforts were now made by the lawyer, Philpott Curran, to overthrow the guilty verdict but on the morning of Monday 19 November 1798, Wolfe Tone died.

His body was taken to 52 High Street where his parents were living. He was laid out on the floor and a plaster cast was taken of his face. His hair was cut and divided among the family. For two days large numbers of mourners filed past the coffin. He was later buried quietly in Bodenstown, Co. Kildare.

12

◎

IRELAND AND GREAT BRITAIN BECOME THE UNITED KINGDOM 1800

As early as 1703 and 1707 the Irish Houses of Parliament had actually petitioned the British government for a union of the two countries but the request was refused outright. With the passing of time the desire for union waned greatly and by 1784 the Lord Lieutenant, Lord Rutland, declared that anyone who suggested union would be tarred and feathered. By the end of the century, however, the English Prime Minister, William Pitt, was convinced that a union of the two countries would indeed be of benefit to both countries. He thought that the Catholics might see in the union a means of achieving emancipation but he knew that opposition from the Protestant side would be extremely strong. The opposition from the Dublin ruling classes was certain. The corporation, the bankers, the merchants and members of the Bar would be implacably opposed to the loss of their Houses of Parliament.

Knowing the difficulties he faced, Pitt set about overcoming them. He began a campaign in the press to woo people to the idea. Merchants were told that trade would increase and English capital would flow into the country. The Catholics were told that Catholic emancipation could be granted to them since they could never hope to attain a majority in the new union parliament.

In February 1799 the matter was brought before the English Parliament by Pitt and was approved. He then set about preparing for a successful vote in the Irish Parliament during the next session. Office holders who were known to be against the measure were

———— ◎ ————

Dublin Bay was described by a traveller in 1800 as follows: 'The numerous wrecks which take place every winter, apparent from the masts, which are seen here and there peeping above the surface of the water, as it were, to warn others of their fate, are convincing proof of the assertion that the locality is a most dangerous one to shipping.'

———— ◎ ————

The word 'quiz' is also reputedly to have been introduced into the English language around this time as the result of a bet. The story goes that a theatre manager named Daly made a bet that he could coin a new word and he won his bet by having the letters Q-U-I-Z written on walls around the city. The citizens 'quizzed' each other as to what the word meant.

———— ◎ ————

In 1815 a public flogging at the Royal Exchange building (now the City Hall) attracted such crowds that nine people were killed in the crush.

———— ◎ ————

Leinster House was rented to the Royal Dublin Society by the third Duke of Leinster in 1815 for £10,000 and a yearly rent of £600. In 1922 the Irish Government obtained part of the building for parliamentary purposes and took over the whole building in 1924.

———— ◎ ————

dismissed or threatened with dismissal. Those borough owners who had the disposal of seats in the Irish Parliament were bought off by direct payments – about £15,000 (a very large sum in those days) was paid for each seat. The entire cost of buying out the 'rotten' or 'pocket' boroughs was £1,260,000.

To buy individual votes, twenty-eight new peers were created, thirty-two existing peers were promoted, and bribes in the form of pensions, judgeships, government positions and direct cash were offered to others. Pitt's chief agents in this were the Lord Lieutenant (Lord Cornwallis), Lord Castlereagh and Lord Clare (John Fitzgibbon). To give him his due, Lord Cornwallis was disgusted with the methods he was forced to use. He was convinced that half of those who voted for the Union would have been delighted if the bill were defeated.

However, even though the majority vote in favour was obtained by bribery, corruption and coercion, there were some who thought it was the correct thing to do.

In January 1799 the Irish parliament met in College Green. The king's speech, which was read to the assembly, asked for a discussion on the question of union. The House of Commons debated for a long time but in the end there was a majority of only two in favour of the idea. This was tantamount to a defeat, as the motion was only for a discussion. Pitt, however, would not accept that the cause was lost and said that he would keep bringing the matter before the House until it was passed. In the same month the two Houses of Parliament in England discussed the proposal and very few opposed.

Seven months passed before the matter was brought before parliament again. Bribery and corruption continued unabated and achieved some success in changing the minds of several more opponents of the measure.

On 15 January 1800 the Irish Parliament in College Green opened for the last session. This time the king's speech made no reference to the Union but the subject was raised by those opposing the idea. During the debate that followed, Henry Grattan, who had been absent from the House for a long time due to illness, made a dramatic appearance.

He was dressed in the blue Volunteer uniform, with red cuffs and collar. He wore his cocked hat, square to the front, and kept it

After the ailing Grattan made his famous speech against the Union, Isaac Corry, the member for Newry, stood up and attacked him, accusing him in so many words of encouraging the United Irishmen in their rebellion. Corry had at one time been an enthusiastic supporter of Grattan but when he saw an opportunity for advancement on the Government side had switched allegiances. Accepting the challenge, Grattan replied with a devastating speech in which he called Corry 'a political pedlar, an unprincipled trimmer, who prostituted both his principles and his talents, such as they were, first for bread, and then for station'. Corry in turn replied with more charges against Grattan: that he had aided and abetted traitors, had encouraged the rebellion and had then run away until it was over. Grattan then accused Corry of being a greater traitor than a rebel. 'I agree that the rebel who rises against the Government should be punished but I missed on the scaffold the right honourable gentleman', and much more in the same vein.

A duel followed, as was intended. It took place in a field in Ballsbridge. Corry had first sent a message asking for a reconciliation but Grattan refused. When the order to fire was given, Grattan hit Corry in the arm with his shot, while Corry missed. On being told to fire a second time, Grattan deliberately fired above his opponent's head but it is not known if Corry fired. Afterwards Grattan visited Corry while he was recovering from his wound and while he was there Corry's brother Edward came in; Corry said, 'Here is my brother Edward; Edward, here is Mr Grattan, and he will shoot you whenever you deserve it!' Later when Grattan was living in Brighton in England, Corry visited Grattan and was warmly received by him.

After the Union fashionable Dublin went into decline when the Lords and Ladies turned their attention to London society rather than Dublin. Many fine buildings of Mountjoy Square, Gardiner Street, Henrietta Street and Summerhill became tenements over the following century and in time became some of the worst slums in Europe.

on until halfway up the floor of the house. He then stopped, took off his hat and 'looked round the House with a steady and fearless eye, as if he wished to let them know that, though exhausted, he was yet prepared to give battle'.

Getting permission to make his speech while remaining seated, Grattan spoke eloquently for two hours against the proposed union. Other speakers joined in and the debate lasted for eighteen hours altogether. When the vote was taken, the side opposing the Union lost by forty-two votes. This caused the Lord Lieutenant some uneasiness as forty-two votes was not regarded as a safe enough majority, especially as Grattan's speech was bound to have an effect by the time the actual vote on the Union was taken.

In March the proposal was put in front of the two Houses of Parliament in England. It was approved by both. The bill was then drawn up in its final form and put before the Irish Houses of Parliament in College Green. The first reading on 21 May 1800 showed a Government majority of sixty. At the second reading on 26 May the majority fell to forty. The final step took place on 7 June, when the Parliament of Ireland voted for its own extinction, most of those opposing the bill having withdrawn in a body. So, at the final session there were many empty seats in the chamber in College Green although the galleries were crowded. When the final moment came, the Speaker of the House, John Foster, who had vehemently opposed the bill:

> . . . rose slowly from the chair . . . he looked steadily around him on the last agony of the expiring Parliament. He at length repeated in an emphatic tone, 'As many as are of the opinion that this Bill do pass, say aye.' The affirmative was languid but indisputable; another momentary pause ensued; again his lips seemed to decline their office; at length, with an eye averted from the object he hated, he proclaimed with a subdued voice, 'The Ayes have it.' The fatal sentence was now pronounced; for an instant he stood statue-like; then indignantly, and with disgust, flung the Bill upon the table, and sunk into his chair with an exhausted spirit.

An independent country was thus degraded into a province – Ireland, as a nation, was extinguished.

Sir Jonah Barrington

———— ◎ ————

Three years after the Union the Parliament Buildings in College Green were taken over by the Bank of Ireland. The House of Commons was converted into boardrooms and offices but the House of Lords was left untouched and can still be viewed today.

———— ◎ ————

O'Donovan Rossa Bridge between Winetavern Street and Chancery Place was originally called Richmond Bridge. It was built in 1813 and opened to the public in 1816. It has three arches and is constructed in granite. During excavations for the bridge various artefacts were found, including Tudor combs and two long wooden boats, in one of which was a human skeleton. The bridge was given its present name in 1922.

Richmond (now O'Donovan Rossa) Bridge

———— ◎ ————

On 1 August 1800 the Act of Union became law and on 1 January 1801 it came into operation. The occasion was celebrated with a gunfire salute and a new standard, the 'Union Jack', showing the cross of St Patrick, red on a white ground, together with the crosses of St George of England, and St Andrew of Scotland, floated for the first time over the Castles of Dublin, London and Edinburgh.

The main provisions of the Act of Union were as follows:

> The two kingdoms to be henceforth one – The United Kingdom of Great Britain and Ireland; Ireland to have one hundred members in the House of Commons and thirty-two peers in the House of Lords; the Irish Established Church to be continued forever and united with that of England; Ireland to contribute two-seventeenths of the expenditure of the United Kingdom for twenty years.

13

◎

ROBERT EMMET, 'THE DARLING OF IRELAND' 1778 – 1803

Robert Emmet, born in 1778, was the younger brother of Thomas Addis Emmet, one of the United Irishmen. (His family lived at 124 St Stephen's Green, since demolished). In 1798 Robert was a student at Trinity College and he was so outspoken in favour of French revolutionary ideas that he was expelled from the college and came under the notice of Dublin Castle authorities as a dangerous person. In 1800 he went to France as an agent of the United Irishmen and managed to get an interview with Napoleon. He was given some assurances of assistance for an Irish rising but it seems no firm promises were

Robert Emmet

made. When he returned to Ireland he immediately set about planning the insurrection by gathering around him like-minded individuals but no prominent names took up his cause – at least, none became known to the authorities.

His father died in 1802 and Robert used a legacy of £2,000 to rent two houses to be used for storing arms and to purchase materials for their manufacture. He soon had gathered a stockpile of hand grenades, pikes and gunpowder. He used the newly built debtors' prison (the Marshalsea) at the rear of Bridgefoot Street as an arsenal. He also stored munitions in Butterfield House in Rathfarnham where he lived with Anne Devlin as his housekeeper. (Anne was a cousin of the famous Wicklow rebels Michael Dwyer and Hugh O'Byrne and was intensely loyal to Emmet.)

Emmet's main plan was to attack three separate targets, the Pigeon House, Dublin Castle and the Artillery Barracks at Islandbridge. The Pigeon House was to be attacked by a force of 200 men at low tide. The Artillery Barracks were to be taken by 400 men, while Emmet himself was to lead the attack on the Castle.

It seems that Emmet learned the lesson from the '98 Rebellion that the less that knew the plans the better. His tactics appear to have been so successful that even after an accidental explosion in one of his depots in Patrick Street the authorities did not seem to have been much the wiser.

After the Patrick Street explosion Emmet felt that he had to act quickly, even though he wasn't completely ready. On the evening of Saturday 23 July 1803, at nine o'clock, with some of his lieutenants and about a hundred men, Emmet sallied out into Thomas Street. His followers had no firearms but a good amount of pikes. Waving his sword and calling on the passers-by to join him, Emmet set off towards the Castle. Most of the people in the street merely watched but hangers-on and vagabonds joined the group in the prospect of plunder and loot. Emmet soon realised that to attack the Castle was hopeless, so he proposed to his followers that he would lead them out to the Wicklow Mountains where they would wait until reinforcements arrived. The local toughs were in no mood to take this course of action. They murdered an unfortunate soldier who was riding by and dragged Lord Kilwarden, the Chief Justice, from his carriage, murdering him and his nephew who was with him.

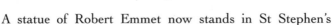

Nine Martello towers were built around Dublin Bay in 1804 as a defence against a possible Napoleonic attack. (Ironically enough, the name Martello comes from Cape Mortello in Corsica where a similar type of tower successfully resisted a British attack in 1794.) The towers were built from Sutton along the shore to Bullock Harbour. There was also one on Dalkey Island whose garrison was the first permanent residents of the island for hundreds of years. (When all other garrisons were disbanded at the end of the Napoleonic threat the Dalkey garrison was forgotten by the British War Office and continued to be paid until late in the century when most had either died of old age or had left the island.)

The towers were not all of the same size or design – the tower at Sutton could house a garrison of 16 men, while that at Sandycove may only have served as a watchtower. An interesting feature in the towers was a shot furnace in which cannon balls were made red-hot so they would set fire to the sails or timbers of attacking ships. It appears that none of the towers was ever called into action.

Seven of the towers are still there today and the tower at Sandycove features in James Joyce's *Ulysses*.

A statue of Robert Emmet now stands in St Stephen's Green opposite the house where he was born.

Michael William Balfe, the composer and violinist, who wrote *The Bohemian Girl* and other operas, was born in 10 Pitt Street (now Balfe Street) in 1817. He made his first appearance as a violinist at the tender age of nine, but he had already produced compositions at the age of seven.

A story is told of his hotly disputing the merits of a new German opera with a friend who praised it as quite original. 'Original!' exclaimed Balfe. 'What do you mean by that?' 'Why, I mean that it has never been heard before,' said his friend. 'Well, I say it is music which will never be heard again!' was Balfe's reply.

Emmet was filled with despair and sorrow and made his way to Ballinascorney and later from there to his house in Rathfarnham. He probably could have escaped from the country except that his love for Sarah, the daughter of Philpott Curran, caused him to delay until he could say goodbye to her. He was eventually arrested by Major Sirr in a house in Mount Drummond Avenue in Harold's Cross on 25 August.

Many other arrests were made and large numbers of prisoners were held in prison ships in Dublin Bay. (One of the ships bore the name *The Lovely Peggy!*) Anne Devlin was one of those arrested. She was interrogated and tortured and finally suspended at the end of a rope from the shafts of an upturned cart but she steadfastly refused to give any information about Emmet. She was then charged with high treason and was imprisoned for three years in Kilmainham Jail. At one period she was held in a basement cell directly beneath the cell holding Emmet. (She later became a servant with another family and finally died in poverty and obscurity in 1851.)

A special commission was set up to try Emmet in Green Street Courthouse and he unfortunately chose as his counsel none other than Leonard McNally. (McNally was the informer who was in the pay of the Castle authorities and who had 'defended' the United Irishmen.) Not that Emmet had much of a defence, as his guilt was all too obvious. In his eloquent speech from the dock he set out his motives and the principles which guided his actions. He then spoke the immortal words that have been quoted so frequently ever since: 'When my country takes her place among the nations of the earth, then, and not till then, let my epitaph be written.'

He was inevitably sentenced to death and at noon the following day, 20 September 1803, he was hanged on a scaffold in front of St Catherine's Church, Thomas Street. His body was then beheaded and his head given to George Petrie for a death mask to be made; his head was never recovered. The rest of his body was buried near Kilmainham Jail but later removed and reburied in a place unknown to this day. Of the nineteen others tried for taking part in his rebellion, seventeen were hanged.

What is now commonly called the Halfpenny Bridge was
built in 1816. Building began at the time of the Battle of
Waterloo and for a time it was called the Wellington Bridge
after the duke. Its official name at present is Liffey Bridge.
When it was opened to the public a toll of one halfpenny
was payable to cross the bridge and a toll remained until it
was ended about 100 years later in 1916. Although
advertising hoardings were forbidden on the bridge, for
years it carried signs for 'Holloway's Pills and Ointments'
and 'Spratts Patent Chicken Meal and Dog Cakes'.

At one time it was proposed that the bridge should be
pulled down and a stone bridge, incorporating a gallery to
house the Hugh Lane paintings, should be built in its place.
The proposal was never acted upon and the 'Haypenny'
Bridge remains intact to the present day.

The Halfpenny Bridge was so called because a toll of one
halfpenny was payable by pedestrians.

---◎---

In 1817 the foundation stone of the Wellington monument in the Phoenix Park was laid. When the huge pillar was completed there was no money left to cast the bronze panels commemorating the duke's victories. The panels were cast from cannons captured in the Peninsular War. Forty years later the panels were completed and the sloping steps around the monument put in place. The steps replaced plinths at each corner that were intended to hold statues of the duke with lions.

The Wellington monument

---◎---

———— ◎ ————

When King George IV visited Dublin in 1821 it was
decided to honour the occasion by building a bridge to
provide a direct route from the Royal Hospital in
Kilmainham to the Royal (Collins) Barracks on the other
side of the Liffey. The cornerstone of Kingsbridge was laid
in 1827 and the cast-iron bridge opened to traffic in 1828.
In January 1922 the corporation renamed the bridge
Sarsfield Bridge and finally in 1941 it became Heuston
Bridge after Seán Heuston, the 1916 leader.

Kingsbridge (now Heuston Bridge) was the earliest cast-iron
bridge made in Ireland. There used to be depictions of royal
crowns on the parapets but they have been removed.

———— ◎ ————

14

◎

DANIEL O'CONNELL,
THE GREAT LIBERATOR
1775 – 1848

Most Catholics were persuaded that the Act of Union would see an improvement in their lot. Catholic emancipation was promised and anyway the Irish Parliament hardly represented their opinions to any great extent. Be that as it may, there was great indignation and anger when emancipation was refused after the Union was passed. The reason given was that King George III regarded himself as bound by his oath of coronation to refuse the measure. Pitt made no effort to change the king's mind, although it is probable that he could have done so if he had really tried.

For twenty-nine years Catholics in every part of the United Kingdom were denied the concession and it was only by the efforts of Daniel O'Connell that the British government were forced at last to concede.

Daniel O'Connell was born near Cahirciveen, Co. Kerry in 1775. His family were relatively well off and he was given a good education both in Ireland and the continent. While a student in France he saw some of the excesses of the French Revolution and he was twenty-five years of age when the Rebellion of 1798 occurred. Both events are said to have had a lasting impression on him, so that all his life he abhorred the use of violence to attain political ends. He became a highly successful barrister and for most of his life he pursued the twin careers of lawyer and politician. He studied law in London at Lincoln's Inn and Gray's Inn, and in Dublin at King's Inn.

He read wisely and widely, spending many hours in the library at Eustace Street. At one time he was so enthusiastic about the

———— ◎ ————

In 1815 O'Connell referred to the 'beggarly' corporation of Dublin in one of his speeches. By his standards it was a very mild 'insult' indeed, and was greatly surprised to be asked by John D'Esterre, a Protestant and member of the corporation, if he had indeed used the expression 'beggarly'. O'Connell replied that he had, but that 'no terms attributed to me, however reproachful, can exceed the contemptuous feelings I entertain for that body'. The expected response to this would have been a challenge to a duel. D'Esterre was an ex-navy officer and a noted duellist but his response was calculated to be really insulting. He went to the Four Courts with a whip, supposedly to chastise O'Connell. But when O'Connell made his way there, D'Esterre had moved to the Liffey quay to parade up and down. The next day the challenge did arrive. Arrangements were made to meet at 3.30 p.m. the following day at Bishop's Court, Co. Kildare.

A priest hid in a nearby cottage in case O'Connell was shot. His second, a Major MacNamara, changed O'Connell's white tie for a black one to make a less conspicuous target. He also removed various large medallions from O'Connell's watch chain for he knew they would make a terrible wound if driven into his body.

The two duellists took positions ten yards apart. Hundreds of spectators had gathered to watch. At the drop of a white handkerchief, D'Esterre took aim and fired. His shot was extremely bad for such a skilled marksman and hit the ground in front of O'Connell, who fired at the same time, aiming low to wound and not to kill. D'Esterre was hit in the thigh and fell to the ground.

O'Connell then drove back to Dublin where he was given a rapturous reception. That night bonfires blazed all over the city, while bailiffs rushed to D'Esterre's house in Bachelor's Walk where he lay seriously ill. Two days later he died and was buried at night by the light of lanterns. O'Connell conveyed his 'deep and lasting sorrow' at his death to D'Esterre's widow and vowed that he would never fight another duel – a promise he kept for the rest of his life. For many years after the duel O'Connell would raise his hat as he passed D'Esterre's house on his way to the Four Courts.

———— ◎ ————

When Daniel O'Connell apologised to the then Archbishop of Dublin, Dr Murray, for taking part in the duel with D'Esterre, (duelling was banned by the Church), the reply he got was 'Heaven be praised. Ireland is safe'.

United Irishmen that 'Sham Squire' Higgins reported him to the Castle authorities as 'a blood-thirsty republican'. Later he became a member of the Lawyers' Yeomanry Corps. As such, he was on duty on one of the bridges over the canals to enforce the curfew and engaged in the search of the Grand Canal Hotel in James' Street for 'croppies' after Emmet's abortive rebellion – in fact all his life he was a man of contradictions.

In May 1798 he was called to the Bar – the day after they arrested Lord Edward Fitzgerald. He took up residence in 30 Merrion Square South (now 58) and he was in Dublin when the Act of Union ended the Irish Parliament. He heard the bells of St Patrick's Cathedral ring out in celebration and saw the first flying of the new flag over Dublin Castle, with the Irish harp relegated to a little corner. He is reported to have said about that day, 'My blood boiled and I vowed that morning that the foul dishonour should not last if I could put an end to it.'

Soon afterwards he spoke against the Union at a public meeting which he had helped to organise. When the meeting was in progress it was raided by the notorious Major Sirr. The assembly waited in trepidation while the major read the resolutions passed by the meeting and breathed a sigh of relief when he then threw them down on the table with contempt.

———— ◎ ————

There are numerous stories told of O'Connell's extraordinary knowledge of the law and expertise in court. On one occasion a client was acquitted of stealing a dead cow because O'Connell argued that the man should have been charged with stealing meat.

———— ◎ ————

In a case about a contested will a witness kept saying the testator was alive when he signed the will. O'Connell noticed that he repeatedly used the Irish phrase '*Bhí beatha ann.*' (There was life in him.) Suddenly Dan had a brainwave. 'When you say, "There was life in him", do you deny that there was a live fly in the dead man's mouth when his hand was put to the will.' The shocked witness admitted the deception.

———— ◎ ————

In a murder case the strongest evidence against the defendant was his hat which was found at the scene of the crime and positively identified by the prosecution witness. O'Connell lifted the hat and started to examine the inside, spelling out the accused's name 'J-A-M-E-S . . . Were these words inside the hat when you found it?' he asked. 'They were,' replied the witness. 'Did you see them in the hat?' he was asked. 'I did.' 'This is the same hat?' 'It is.' 'Now, my Lord,' said O'Connell to the judge.'That's the end to the case – there is no name whatsoever inscribed in the hat.'

———— ◎ ————

When O'Connell approached King George III at a function immediately after the granting of emancipation, he saw the king's lips move in what he took to be some words of congratulation. Greatly pleased he took the pudgy hand held out to him and kissed it with reverence. Later when he asked the Duke of Norfolk (who had been standing close to the king) what the king had said, he was told the words were, 'There's O'Connell, God damn the scoundrel!'

———— ◎ ————

O'Connell soon came to realise that opposition to repeal of the Act of Union was immense both in England and Ireland. He decided that he had a much better chance of gaining Catholic emancipation, which after all, had been promised prior to the Act. Along with his friend Richard Lalor Sheil, he started the Catholic Association which was to be financed by voluntary contributions. Each Catholic was asked to contribute one penny per month, the clergy in each parish to oversee its collection and safe keeping.

The plan was a great success. Even though, at best, only one Catholic in twelve contributed regularly, the first eight months saw £7,573 collected, the next three months, £9,263, and £5,680 in the second half of 1826. The money was used to provide free legal aid to Catholics in trouble with the law and to finance the various political campaigns fought by the association.

The campaigns were successful: pro-emancipation candidates (all Protestants of course) were elected in nine counties. Then in 1828 the MP for County Clare, William Vesey Fitzgerald, accepted an appointment in the Duke of Wellington's government and this meant, by the rules of the day, that he had to stand for re-election. After much persuasion O'Connell agreed that he himself should stand for election. An extraordinary campaign followed and O'Connell was elected with a majority of two to one.

The British government was greatly alarmed but they saw that public opinion, both in England and Ireland, favoured emancipation of Catholics. And so, after stormy debates in the English Houses of Parliament, the bill to that effect received the royal assent on 13 April 1829.

When O'Connell went to Westminster to take his seat, he was told that the Act of Emancipation only applied to those elected after the passing of the act. He was offered the old oath repudiating the Catholic faith and refused to take it. This meant that he had to be re-elected before he could take his seat. He stood for election again in Clare and was returned with an even bigger majority. At the opening of the new session of parliament he duly appeared and took his seat.

O'Connell now devoted nearly all his energies to political work. He had left agitation for the repeal of the Act of Union 'on the back burner' while working for emancipation. Although the campaign for the repeal of the Act of Union started in 1810, it wasn't until

———— ◎ ————

When King George IV visited Dublin in 1821 he was warmly welcomed by the citizens of Dublin. He landed at Howth so drunk that he could hardly stand. Later in the viceregal Lodge in the Phoenix Park the king drank the health of the Irish gentry. O'Connell, who wore a blue sash and rosettes for the occasion was so overcome with enthusiasm that he proposed the building of a palace to commemorate the visit. Later, as the king boarded the boat in Dun Laoghaire Harbour, O'Connell presented him with a laurel wreath. After the king's visit Dun Laoghaire was renamed Kingstown. The name became Dun Laoghaire again in 1922. The Dublin Society was also allowed to use the word 'Royal' in their name because of their address of loyalty to the king at the time.

———— ◎ ————

A memorial obelisk standing on four large stone balls erected near the harbour to mark the occasion of the king's visit is still there today.

———— ◎ ————

One of the most notorious judges in O'Connell's time was John Toler, Lord Norbury, known as the 'Hanging Judge'. When he died, the gravediggers buried him at twice the normal depth 'so that he should have rope enough'. He was something of a buffoon. As he warmed to a case he would become more and more agitated. He would stand up, throw off his robes, even his wig, pour out the most outlandish gibberish – anecdotes of his youth, snatches of poetry or Shakespeare – rising to a crescendo of roars and bellowing until he often fell over, only to rise, blowing and laughing.

———— ◎ ————

During the 1820s, fashionable men in Dublin wore a buff vest, a swallow-tailed coat with bright buttons, a frilled shirt with ruffled cuffs and 'a large gold seal hanging from a fob'. In the 1840s, countrymen wore blue coats, corduroy breeches, and blue stockings.

———— ◎ ————

1840 that O'Connell started a vigorous campaign, when he founded the Repeal Association.

In November 1841 he was elected unopposed as Lord Mayor of Dublin. He was the first Catholic mayor for the city for one hundred and fifty years. On his election he promised to abstain from partisan politics, and on the whole, he kept his promise. Always the showman, dressed magnificently in crimson robes with sable collar and white satin bows all crowned with an enormous cocked hat, he addressed cheering crowds outside his house in Merrion Square. He attended various functions dressed in his ceremonial robes but refused to wear them when he attended Mass 'for the Lord Mayor can be a Catholic but his robes must be Protestant'. He would never wear the Lord Mayor's chain of office to Mass either, because it contained the medallion of King William which still adorns it to this day.

But by the end of 1842 he was becoming bored with his life as Lord Mayor and in February 1843 he took up his Repeal work again. He began holding huge public meetings throughout the country, the so-called 'monster' meetings. Thirty such meetings were held in that first year alone.

Crowds of over 100,000 attended each of these meetings. In August a million people heard him speak at Tara in Co. Meath. Although these meetings were eminently peaceful, the Lord Lieutenant, Lord de Grey, was getting very nervous about them as he suspected that things were in danger of getting out of hand. When O'Connell announced in August that he intended holding the greatest monster meeting ever in Clontarf and reference was made to 'Repeal cavalry' in a public notice about the meeting, the authorities decided that something had to be done.

Peel was convinced O'Connell would back down at the threat of an open confrontation and decided to call his bluff. On 7 October 1843, a day before the meeting, a proclamation was issued declaring the Clontarf meeting to be an unlawful assembly. O'Connell was in a dilemma; he could call off the meeting and suffer the tremendous loss of face or he could go ahead with it and risk a disaster. But true to his non-violence principles he called it off. Clontarf was a watershed in O'Connell's career – after this his course ran downhill all the way.

In October he and seven others were arrested and charged with

———— ◎ ————

Lord Norbury once ordered a poor wretch to be flogged from College Green to the quays. When the victim said 'Thank you, my lord, you have done your worst', Norbury said viciously, '. . . and back again'. Another who had stolen a watch was sentenced to death with the words, 'Ha-Ha! You made a grab at time, but you caught eternity.'

———— ◎ ————

On one occasion at a Bar dinner Norbury asked Philpott Curran if the meat was fresh, to which Curran replied, 'You try it and it is bound to be well hung!'

———— ◎ ————

Curran was noted for his wit and, even on his deathbed it didn't desert him. 'I fear you cough with more difficulty,' his doctor said to him. 'That is strange,' replied Curran, 'for I have been practising all night.'

———— ◎ ————

During the nineteenth century it was quite the 'done thing' for men to bathe completely nude on beaches such as Ringsend and Sandymount. The modern-day practice of nude bathing at the Forty Foot at Sandycove is thought to be a survivor of the practice.

———— ◎ ————

In 1807 two troopships the *Prince of Wales* and the *Rochdale* which had set out from the Pigeon House harbour were forced to turn back because of a violent storm in the Irish Sea. The *Prince of Wales* ran aground at Blackrock and the *Rochdale* was wrecked at Sandycove. Altogether three hundred and eighty people lost their lives. Some of the dead were buried in Booterstown graveyard where their memorial stone can be seen today against the wall of the old graveyard near the Tara Hotel.

———— ◎ ————

conspiring to change government policy by intimidation and demonstrations of great physical force. It was confidently thought that no Irish jury would convict them. But the Castle made its own rules. When the trial started in Dublin on 15 January 1844 the prosecution challenged eleven Catholic jurymen on the grounds that they were 'Repealers'. The end result was that the jury was composed of twelve Protestants, mostly Orangemen. Despite a vigorous defence, all but one of the accused were found guilty and remanded on bail for sentence.

Eventually O'Connell was sentenced to a year's imprisonment and a fine of £2,000. The others were given nine months each and a £50 fine. They were allowed to choose their place of detention, so they all presented themselves, accompanied by a procession of their supporters, to the Richmond Bridewell in Grangegorman. There they were treated with every possible consideration until they were released three months' later on 6 September. O'Connell was having dinner with the prison governor and assistant governor when a messenger rushed in, shouting 'You're free, Liberator, you're free!' It is reported that the governor fainted on the spot, while the assistant governor wept with relief. O'Connell went home that same evening but returned to the jail the next morning for a public release and a triumphal procession. The Lord Mayor and members of the corporation were there in person to greet him as he left the prison once more.

All along the route from the prison to Merrion Square thousands of people gathered to line the streets in perfect order to welcome O'Connell back to his house. His supporters had taken out of retirement the carriage which had been used in previous triumphs. To the roars of the crowd the ten kilometre procession wound its way down the quays, past the Four Courts, over the bridge towards the Castle which they jeered in passing, and down to College Green. Here O'Connell stopped the carriage and pointed to the old Houses of Parliament in a symbolic gesture to the delirious applause of the crowds. When he reached Merrion Square he addressed his followers but the old spirit was gone. His speech lacked fire and no longer roused the audience as his speeches had done in the past.

Things rapidly deteriorated after that. The old spark and drive never returned and anyway the country was soon to be gripped by

———— ◎ ————

One of the greatest natural disasters ever to hit Ireland occurred on the Feast of the Epiphany, 6 January 1839. On that night the country was devastated by a storm of such ferocity that the date is forever known as 'The Night of the Big Wind'. The day started out calm, with snow from previous days still lying on the ground. Gradually, however, it began to warm up, unnaturally so, one woman feeling it was 'like the air in a hothouse'.

By ten o'clock a light breeze had turned into a gale. Inexorably, it grew steadily worse, until by midnight it had become the most destructive storm ever to hit the country. Trees went down like ninepins, whole roofs sailed through the air, walls and houses collapsed, factory chimneys folded and streets became impassable.

The storm reached its peak between 2.00 and 5.00 a.m. Torrential rain fell amid crashing thunder and lightning flashes. One curious phenomenon noted in various parts of the country was the fact that many of the rain showers fell as salt water – whipped up, no doubt, by the hurricane as it swept in from the ocean.

Many citizens sought refuge under the portico of the Bank of Ireland building in College Green and in churches throughout the city.

The next morning when daylight broke, the full extent of the destruction could be seen. Hardly a town had escaped. Rivers were swollen and choked with debris. Nearly 300 people lost their lives and thousands more were injured.

In Dublin every part of the city suffered damage. Trees were uprooted throughout the city. The roads everywhere were practically impassable. The ball on top of the spire of St Patrick's Cathedral was blown down, as were the steeples of Simmon's Court Church and the church in Irishtown. The belfry of Phibsborough Church was almost destroyed. Houses in every part of the city were devastated. Six people lost their lives in a fire in Mary Street. Other casualties were the malt kiln at Jameson's distillery and the stables of Arthur Guinness, where nine horses were killed.

———— ◎ ————

the deadliest of all foes – famine! In the winter of 1846 O'Connell made a passionate plea in the Westminster parliament for Ireland's starving poor but his voice fell on deaf ears.

He retired to Kerry for a while and then came back to Dublin in January 1847. The next month he made his final appearance in the London parliament where he declared: 'Ireland is in your hands . . . She is in your power . . . I predict that one quarter of her population will perish unless you come to her relief.' The House rose and cheered him to the echo as he sat down but his speech had little effect on those in power.

Shortly afterwards he began to decline in health, greatly affected by the devastation the famine was causing to the people of Ireland. In 1847 he set out on a journey to Rome, partly on pilgrimage and partly for health reasons but he never reached there. He died in Genoa on 15 May 1847 at the age of seventy-one. In accordance with his wishes, his heart was enshrined in the wall of the Irish College in Rome while the rest of his remains were brought back to Dublin.

As the steamer *Duchess of Kent* sailed up the Liffey with his body on board, it was passed by the *Birmingham*, an emigrant ship carrying emigrants to a new life in England. As the ships passed each other there came from the *Birmingham* the traditional Irish 'keen' for a dead leader. Tremendous crowds attended his funeral through the streets of Dublin to Glasnevin cemetery. The *Freeman's Journal* reported that even though the crowd was immense 'not a sound was heard – all was unutterable sorrow'. Later a monument in the likeness of an ancient Irish round tower was erected over his grave.

———— ◎ ————

Before the granting of Catholic emancipation in 1829 the composition of Dublin Corporation was one hundred per cent Protestant even though Catholics were in the majority in the population.

———— ◎ ————

At one time a statue to O'Connell stood outside the City Hall in Dame Street but it was later removed to inside the building to protect it from weather erosion. The plinth on which it stood remains outside.

The statue of O'Connell, which today stands in O'Connell Street, is by John Henry Foley. The 'angels' around the base are by Thomas Brock who completed the work eight years after Foley died. Some of the angels bear bullet holes suffered during gun battles in the street in the twentieth century.

The O'Connell monument

———— ◎ ————

Sir William Crampton (1777–1858) was Surgeon General during the reign of Queen Victoria. He was a founder member of the Royal Zoological Society and was responsible for obtaining the present site for the zoo in the Phoenix Park. One night a messenger roused him from his bed and told him that a great personage had fallen from his horse in College Green. Crampton rushed immediately to the scene to find that the statue of King William had been blown from his horse by an explosion.

A memorial to Crampton once stood at the corner of Hawkin's Street and College Street. It was damaged in 1959 and for the sake of better traffic flow was never replaced.

When Father Theobald Mathew held his temperance meeting behind the Customs House in Dublin in 1840 he drew an enormous crowd. Nearly 5,000 people 'took the pledge' that day and nearly 100,000 people had taken it by the end of the year. Good intentions did not last however, and most pledges were broken, much to the relief of the brewers who feared a serious threat to their business. (A statue to the memory of Father Mathew was later erected in O'Connell Street.)

Father Mathew gave a medal to all who took the pledge. Unable to pay for all these thousands of medals he was arrested and lost the chance to be Bishop of Cork as a result.

————— ◎ —————

A remarkable mode of transport was inaugurated between Kingstown and Dalkey in 1843. This was known as the Atmospheric Railway. It was championed by the great engineer, Brunel, but denounced by the famous locomotive expert, Stephenson. The system relied on the pressure of the atmosphere to pull the railway carriages uphill to Dalkey and to allow the force of gravity to carry them back down again. This is how the system worked: a continuous metal pipe, about 30 cms in diameter, was laid in the middle of the track across the sleepers. The air was extracted from the pipe by a steam-driven air pump placed about 100 metres from the end of the line at Dalkey. The resulting vacuum caused a plug, or piston, to move up along the pipe propelled by the atmospheric pressure behind it. This moving piston had a metal framework six metres long attached to it. At the end of the framework was a metal rod, which was attached to the train. The metal connecting rod travelled along the pipe in a slit covered by soft leather flaps which opened and closed as the rod passed along. The leather flaps were covered with a mixture of wax and tallow and after the slit was opened by the connecting rod, a wheel attached to the rod pressed down on the flaps and sealed them again.

A copper heater, filled with burning charcoal was supposed to melt the grease mixture and so improve the seal. This device failed to work, however, as the train moved too rapidly for it to work. As a result a man had to follow each train to grease and press down the flaps manually. When the train reached the end of the pipe its momentum carried it the rest of the way into the station and a lookout man at the pumping station would stop the pump. The piston was removed from the tube in Dalkey and hooked under the train to be carried back down on the return journey and re-inserted once more in Kingstown.

Strange as it may seem, the system worked very well and continued in use for nearly eleven years. The main reason for the abandonment of the system was the difficulty in keeping the leather flaps airtight. The greased leather also proved a great attraction for rats which caused constant damage.

————— ◎ —————

In 1847 the Richmond Gate which spanned the quay at Watling Street Bridge was removed and rebuilt as the western gate to the Royal Hospital in Kilmainham. Its removal was financed by the Great Southern and Western Railway because it restricted traffic to Kingsbridge Station.

The Richmond Gate

William Rowan Hamilton, one of Dublin's greatest sons, was born in 1805 at 36 Lower Dominick Street. He could read Hebrew at the age of seven and could speak thirteen languages by the time he was fourteen, but it is as a mathematician that he is best remembered. On 16 October 1843 he was walking with his wife across the bridge over the Royal Canal at Broombridge in Cabra when suddenly, in a flash of inspiration, 'he discovered the fundamental formula for quaternion multiplication' and in his elation he carved the formula on the stone of the bridge. (The formula reads $i^2 = j^2 = ijk = -1$.) The event was commemorated in a memorial on the bridge unveiled by Eamon de Valera one hundred years later.

One of the most famous contemporaries of Daniel O'Connell was the blind Bard of the Liberties, Michael Moran, otherwise known as Zozimus. He was born in Dublin's Liberties in 1794 in a street called Faddle Alley off Blackpitts, and seems to have been blind from birth. At the age of twenty-two he began his career as bard and busker. Dressed in corduroy trousers, a long coat with a cape around the shoulders, a misshapen tall hat and what he called his 'Francis Street brogues' he wandered the streets reciting his poems and telling his stories to all who would listen. One of his favourite spots was on Carlisle Bridge where he would stand and after asking, 'Is there a crowd about me now?' would launch into his repertoire of ballads, stories and biblical tales.

His great fear was that his body would be used for anatomical studies in the Royal College of Surgeons when he died but his friends had him buried in Glasnevin cemetery. A limestone memorial was erected over the grave in 1988 by a group of his admirers.

Michael Moran (1794 – 1846), known as 'Zozimus, the Bard of the Liberties' may have got his name from a hermit of the same name in Palestine.

15

◎

THE GREAT HUNGER
STALKS THE LAND
1845 – 1848

Although there had been other famines in Ireland in previous times, particularly in the thirteenth, fourteenth and eighteenth centuries, that which devastated the country in the middle of the nineteenth century was the most terrible. The 'Great Famine' began in 1845 when the potato crop failed for the first time. The crop promised to be a plentiful one early that summer but later on the tubers were reduced to a rotten, stinking mass within a few days. Potatoes dug early that year seem to have escaped the disease so that in many cases the peasants managed to survive the winter.

When the blight hit in 1845 all sorts of reasons were advanced as the cause of the trouble: the influence of the moon, lightning and thunder storms, the wind, the type of manure. The real cause was a fungus that grew on the underside of the leaves of the potato plants. This fungus produced spores that were rapidly spread by wind, rain and insect. The disease passed quickly down to the tubers, which developed small black spots and then quickly rotted.

In November 1845 the Archbishop of Dublin, Dr Murray, gave orders for prayers to be said in all the churches that God would spare the people in the coming year. The prayers were in vain. The blight was even worse in 1846 – over three-quarters of the crop was destroyed countrywide.

The British Prime Minister, Sir Robert Peel, introduced three measures: he ordered a large supply of 'Indian corn' (maize) from America for sale in Ireland; he appointed a Relief Commission in Dublin to oversee its sale and to introduce work schemes by which the people could earn money to buy the corn; and he removed

With the growth of knowledge in human anatomy in the eighteenth and nineteenth centuries was a parallel growth in the need for human bodies to study. This led to the activities of the 'body snatchers', who stole the bodies of recently buried people to sell to hospitals for the medical students to practise on.

In 1825 one such body snatcher, Thomas Tuite, was captured in Bully's Acre at Kilmainham in possession of five bodies and a pocketful of full of teeth! The bodies were worth ten shillings each and a full set of teeth was priced at £1. Tuite was sentenced to six months in jail but no doubt he considered it worth the risk as he was a regular supplier to four surgeons in the Dublin hospitals.

Because body snatching became so commonplace five watchtowers were built in Glasnevin Cemetery and guards with bloodhounds patrolled the grounds. The *News Letter* gives an account of a gun battle which took place on 27 January 1830 between the sentries and the body snatchers. The 'sack-em-ups' weren't easily defeated, however, and returned the following night. The alert sentries drove them off once more, wounding several of them in the process.

The *News Letter* reported a strange tale the next month.

A few nights ago a corpulent midwife named Maginnis, rather aged, died on the north side of the city and on the night of her burial it was discovered that the leader of those who attempted to disinter the poor woman and deliver her body up for dissection was one of her own sons. On the fellow being accused of the crime he said, 'Sure even if I did so, a tenderer hand couldn't go over her.'

Dan Donnelly, the renowned bare-knuckle pugilist from Townsend Street, was buried in Bully's Acre in 1820 but his body was dug up shortly afterwards. He was 'rescued' and reburied but not before his arm was cut off. It is now on display in The Hideout tavern in Kilcullen, Co. Kildare.

The passing of the Anatomy Act in the British Parliament in 1832 put an end to the body snatchers. The act allowed dissection of legally acquired bodies in medical schools. Bully's Acre graveyard, was officially closed that same year.

protectionist duties on the import of corn into Britain and Ireland to reduce the price of bread. (This latter measure was of little use to the Irish poor who couldn't afford bread at any price.)

The man appointed to oversee the relief measures was a British civil servant, Charles Trevelyan, a man in his late thirties who firmly believed that no action should be taken which would interfere with market forces.

Although the Indian corn from America was stored in government depots from January 1846 it was not generally released to the poor until May. Another example of the government's strict application of the trade laws was the fact that food was leaving the country in vast quantities all this time. Food was also coming in. Nearly four times as much wheat was imported as was exported but it was not for the starving population.

Then Trevelyan ordered the closure of the grain depots because too many people were calling on them for food!

Naturally enough, rural Ireland was the first to suffer the effects of the famine. Dublin workhouses were not full in 1845 but by 1846 so many thousands of destitute people were streaming into the city that guards were placed on the approach roads in an effort to turn back as many as they could. (The huge increase in the numbers flocking into Dublin marked the beginning of a problem that was to bedevil the city for many generations – that of overcrowding in the tenements housing the poor.)

Many of those going into the city were heading for ships to take them to England or America but vast numbers had no such plans – all they wanted was food and they thought their chances were better in the city. The workhouses were filling up rapidly and were being stretched to the limit to provide food for them all. The main food staple, potatoes, was obviously not available, so substitute foods had to be found. Two pints of porridge and half a pint of milk was provided for breakfast and rice and milk or bread and soup for dinner.

Soon the workhouses were unable to take in any more, so that whole families were turned away. So many thousands were starving on the streets that the 'Soup Kitchen Act' was passed by which soup kitchens were set up to feed the local communities. Each adult was to get a bowl of soup and a pound of bread per day.

One famous soup kitchen was set up in Croppies Acre in front

◎

In 1848 the Dublin Sanitary Association opposed the introduction of pipes to carry sewage from houses because they feared that germs and diseases would pass through the air from the pipes to the people in the houses.

◎

In 1849 while the ravages of the famine were still fresh, Queen Victoria paid a royal visit to Dublin. In spite of everything she was given a great welcome. There were parades, tours of various places of interest, and Nelson's Pillar was illuminated by the new-fangled electric lighting for the occasion. During her visit she viewed the *Book of Kells* in Trinity College and was shown the autograph of Elizabeth I who founded the college. Victoria then signed her name on a sheet of parchment which was later incorporated into one of the volumes. This was to give rise to the false charge that she autographed the *Book of Kells*.

Queen Victoria

◎

of the Royal Barracks on the quays near Kingsbridge (Heuston Bridge). A French chef, Alexis Soyer, who worked in the Reform Club in London, was invited to Dublin by the Lord Lieutenant to prove his theory that a bowl of his special soup and a piece of bread were sufficient for a grown man for a day. His 'magic' recipe for the soup was: oxheads, corn, carrots, turnips, onions, cabbage, peas, leeks and water. His 'New Model Soup Kitchen' in Croppies Acre which was constructed on the site had a boiler holding three hundred gallons of soup and a wooden hut about 40 feet long and 30 feet wide with a door at each end. One hundred clients could be served at a time.

Each client was given a bowl to which a spoon was attached by a short chain. They then entered by one door of the hut, drank their soup and ate their bread and exited by the other door. The bowls were taken from them, rinsed, and given to the next batch. The demand was so overwhelming that the crowds fought each other for their share and at the height of the famine, up to eight thousand, seven hundred and fifty portions were served in one day.

The Soup Kitchen Act gradually began to have an effect. By the middle of 1847 over three million people (nearly half of the total population) were receiving relief. This 'extravagance' raised alarm in the Treasury. Trevelyan's secretary wrote to each Poor Law Union (workhouse) telling them that he suspected that the act was being 'applied solely as a means of adding to the comforts of the lower classes' instead of for 'the utterly destitute'. Later he complained about the demand for rations 'continuously increasing'. The remedy was brutal – all government relief under the Soup Kitchen Act was to cease by October 1847.

By the end of September, while a million people were still getting free rations, more than two million others were cut off and had to depend on the workhouses. The workhouses were meant to be just that, the able-bodied would be fed if they worked.

Trevelyan now wrote, 'It is my opinion that too much has been done for the people. Under such treatment the people have grown worse instead of better, and we must now try what independent exertion can do.' He complained that the work of the previous two years was 'the hardest in his whole life'. So he took time off for a fortnight's holiday in France.

The winter of 1847–8 was as bad as anything that went before.

Thousands died from starvation and disease. (In fact more people died of cholera than starvation.) The hopes of millions rested on the crops of autumn 1848 but these hopes were dashed when the blight was as bad as ever that year.

It is hard to believe that all this time the high life continued among the upper classes in Dublin. In 1848 the Lady Mayoress held a ball at which dancing continued until late into the night and food and refreshments were in endless supply. Social activities at Dublin Castle continued unabated. Fancy Dress Balls, 'drawing rooms' and other social events were held as if life in the city was completely normal.

At the end of the famine the Dublin *Freeman's Journal* was asking, 'Do we live under a regular or responsible government? Is there justice or humanity in the world that such things could be, in the middle of the nineteenth century and within twelve hours' reach of the opulence, grandeur and power of a court and capital the first upon earth.'

16
◎
THE FENIAN CHIEF
1824 – 1901

As O'Connell's career was beginning to wane, a group of young men, 'Young Ireland', inspired by the writings of Thomas Davis was gathering. This group became more and more disenchanted with the non-violent attitudes of O'Connell and grew increasingly outspoken and extreme in their writings and speeches. One of their number, John Mitchel, the son of an Ulster Presbyterian minister, soon began to openly advocate rebellion. As the Young Irelanders, led by Mitchel, grew increasingly militant

Thomas Davis lived at 67 Lower Baggot Street. A walk in the Phoenix Park with John Blake Dillon and Charles Gavan Duffy led to the start of the *Nation* newspaper.

In the early nineteenth century St Stephen's Green was an open area consisting of about sixty acres of rough and wild land. It was so wet and marshy that the gentry used to shoot snipe over it and the corncrake made its home there in summer. Then when the corporation was in need of cash it sold off all but twenty-seven acres for building purposes. The remaining land was levelled and a wall was built all around it. The area was drained by means of a continuous ditch, which was dug inside the wall. Two gravelled walks were laid out, one ten metres wide, between the wall and the ditch, the other, more narrow one, on the other side of the ditch. Trees and shrubs were planted along the walks, while the central area was left as grazing land. With the passing of time, however the park once more became neglected, until in 1814 it was cleaned up again. The ditch was filled in, iron railings replaced the wall and an extensive tree-planting scheme was carried out. The park now became private property; gates were installed at various points and a fee of one guinea was charged for a key.

Needless to say the citizens of Dublin strongly objected to the new state of affairs but nothing was done until 1877, when Sir Arthur Guinness took a hand and had the park reopened once more to the public. He was also responsible for the transformation of the central area of the park from rough grazing land into the delightful park we have today. On the west side there is a statue erected to the memory of Lord Ardilaun, Sir Arthur Guinness.

A more gory history attached to St Stephen's Green is the burning alive there of a Mrs Herring on 24 October 1773. Another woman, a bishop's cook, found guilty of poisoning a number of people is supposed to have been boiled alive there on a different occasion.

the authorities decided to act. Mitchel, William Smith O'Brien and Thomas Francis Meagher were arrested and Mitchel was tried two months later under the Treason Felony Act. He was found guilty, taken in chains to Dublin's North Wall and transported to Tasmania. Smith O'Brien and Meagher were released because the jury could not agree. When Mitchel was deported, the leadership was assumed by Smith O'Brien – as unlikely a revolutionary as ever there was!

He was an upper-class Protestant, an MP at Westminster, educated at Harrow and had a pronounced English accent. This was the man who found himself leading a small troop of about a hundred men, largely unarmed, when the 'rising' took place in the south of Ireland in August 1848. The tiny force reached Ballingarry in Co. Tipperary and attacked a small group of police who had occupied a house belonging to a widow named McCormack. After a skirmish which later became known derisively as 'the battle of the Widow McCormack's cabbage garden' O'Brien and his followers made off into the countryside as best they could.

One of O'Brien's lieutenants at the battle was James Stephens, a young Protestant from Blackmill Street in Kilkenny. He had charge of forty or fifty men during the skirmish with only a few guns between them. Police reinforcements arrived and Stephens gave the order to fire. Several constables were killed. When the police returned fire some men dropped dead at Stephen's side. He himself was struck by two bullets, one of them in the thigh. As he fled from the scene, he was struck again and rolled into a ditch, half-conscious. When the police had left, he climbed out of his ditch and eventually made his way to Urlingford.

The authorities made a determined effort to arrest all of the leaders of the abortive rebellion but the 'funeral' of Stephens halted the search for that particular leader. A sympathetic obituary appeared in the *Kilkenny People* on 19 August 1848 lamenting the death of 'poor James Stephens . . . A most inoffensive man . . . a most excellent son and brother'. A coffin filled with stones was buried in the graveyard near St Canice's Cathedral in Kilkenny. A headstone over the grave bore the inscription:

> Here lies James Stephens. Born in Kilkenny AD 1824.
> Died from the effects of a wound at Ballingarry, 1848.
> Aged 24 years. R.I.P.

———— ◎ ————

In 1840 an omnibus service was introduced to the city. The 'bus consisted of an enclosed horse-drawn vehicle which could accommodate ten passengers on the roof and a further twenty inside on a straw-covered floor. In 1872 horse-drawn trams were introduced which could carry more passengers more cheaply. By 1881 there were 186 trams and over a thousand horses. The horse-drawn trams continued in use until 1901. The first electrically-powered trams were introduced in 1896 and continued in use until 1949, although the Howth tram continued for another ten years and made its last journey on 31 May 1959.

———— ◎ ————

In 1851 a census held in Ireland revealed that while the population of Ireland had fallen by twenty per cent, the population in the Dublin area had risen by nine per cent to a figure of over a quarter of a million. The increase in numbers led to appalling poverty. The grand houses were now tenements, with over one hundred people living in houses that used to serve one family. In 1914 it was found that nearly a quarter of Dublin's citizens lived in one-room tenements with an average of six persons to each room.

———— ◎ ————

The Rotunda Hospital did not get water closets until 1855; the first three baths were installed in 1868.

———— ◎ ————

On 14 February 1853 the steamship *Victoria* from Liverpool went aground at the Bailey lighthouse on Howth Head during a snowstorm. Fifty-five people lost their lives.

———— ◎ ————

The following year 'the largest sailing merchantman ever built', the *John Tayleur*, en route from Liverpool to Melbourne was wrecked off Lambay Island on 21 January 1854. A rope was connected from ship to shore but when large numbers of passengers were making their way along the rope the ship lurched and most were drowned. Over 200 people lost their lives, including 177 women.

———— ◎ ————

Shortly afterwards Stephens was smuggled on board a ship en route to England, disguised as a lady's manservant. He landed in Bristol and the following day reached France, where he spent the eight years. On returning to Dublin he was depressed by the lack of enthusiasm in the revolutionary movement. His health wasn't the best at this time, so much so that one old friend thought that he was 'not long for this world'.

After a tour of the country to assess the state of the organisation he began a successful career as a French language tutor in Killiney in Co. Dublin. All the time, however, he was actively engaged in his organising work and on St Patrick's Day 1858 in Peter Langan's timber yard in Lombard Street near Westland Row in Dublin the Irish Republican Brotherhood was formally established.

James Stephens was 'buried' in a Kilkenny cemetery forty-three years before he died!

Each aspiring member was required to swear an oath saying:
> I . . . , in the presence of Almighty God, do solemnly swear allegiance to the Irish Republic, now virtually established; and that I will do my very utmost, at every risk, while life lasts, to defend its independence and integrity; and, finally, that I will yield implicit obedience in all things, not contrary to the laws of God [or 'the laws of morality'] to the commands of my superior officers. So help me God. Amen.

William Dargan, who was born in 1799, was one of the greatest engineers Ireland has ever produced. He was responsible for the first Irish railway, that from Westland Row to Kingstown. The work commenced in 1832 and the first horse-drawn train made the journey in July 1834. The first steam-driven train left Westland Row in December 1834 and completed the journey in nineteen minutes.

Dargan was subsequently involved in the construction of nearly every other railway in the country. He became extremely rich but also earned a well-deserved reputation for generosity so that his employees called him 'The man with his hand in his pocket'. He built a magnificent house for himself and family in the south Dublin area of Goatstown. (His house, Mount Anville, has since become a famous school for girls.) He owned a second house at 2 Fitzwilliam Square.

William Dargan, who lived in Mount Anville, was one of the greatest engineers Ireland ever produced.

That same year Stephens organised a great public funeral for Terence Bellew MacManus, a Young Irelander who had died in America. Stephens had witnessed the tremendous funeral of Daniel O'Connell and realised the propaganda value of such events. When MacManus' body was brought home, Stephens set about arranging something similar, with thousands of marchers wearning black badges, carrying torches and accompanied by brass bands in the procession to Glasnevin cemetery.

In October 1858 Stephens went to America to contact leaders of the Fenian Brotherhood and to organise and assess the movement there. Before he left for Ireland a year later, he appointed John O'Mahony as director of the IRB in America. After Stephen's departure O'Mahony changed the name of the organisation to the 'Fenian Brotherhood'. From then on the term 'Fenian' was applied to all members of the movement.

On his return to Dublin in August 1864 Stephens went around the country on an organising tour. Drilling, making of pikes, gathering of arms and subversion of army personnel proceeded with new intensity. Stephens repeated on every occasion, 'Next year will be the year of action'.

The following year (1865) was indeed the 'year of action' but for the Castle authorities, not the Fenians. On the night of 14 September raids took place all over the country. The offices of the *Irish People*, the Fenian newspaper, which were rather daringly situated almost at the gates of Dublin Castle, at 12 Parliament Street, were raided and many compromising documents were discovered. The Castle had an informer, by the name of Pierce Nagle, in the *Irish People* offices, who had been supplying information to the police all along. A letter urging rebellion 'this year', written on 8 September by Stephens, and stolen by Nagle, had alarmed the authorities.

The raids, however, failed to deliver Stephens to the police and he remained free for the next two months. Despite Nagle's best efforts to discover his hiding place, Stephens was living quietly as 'Mr Herbert' in Fairfield House, Sandymount. And then, as a result of a tip-off, police swooped on the house on Saturday 11 November between six and seven o'clock in the morning. Because of the large force surrounding the house, Stephens knew there was no sense in resisting arrest. He and three companions were

The great exhibitions of Paris (1849) and London's Crystal Palace (1851) inspired William Dargan to become involved in the Great Dublin Industrial Exhibition of 1853 in which he invested £100,000, a colossal sum of money at the time.

The exhibition took place in massive halls on Leinster Lawn and on 12 May 1853 a state procession from Dublin Castle to Merrion Square was led by the Lord Lieutenant, the Earl of St Germans. Thousands of Dublin's citizens lined the streets for the opening parade which included the Lord Mayor and hundreds of other dignitaries, while inside the exhibition hall a thousand singers greeted the arrivals with the English national anthem and a selection of hymns. Dargan was offered a knighthood by the Lord Lieutenant on behalf of the queen but he refused the honour. Even though the exhibition was successful in many ways Dargan is reported to have lost about £20,000 on the venture.

On 30 August Queen Victoria, accompanied by Prince Albert, the Prince of Wales and Prince Alfred, visited the exhibition and later visited Dargan in Mount Anville.

Dargan continued his railway building and by the time of his death was responsible for over 1,000 miles of track. However a fall from his horse in 1866 left him severely injured and both his health and his business declined. A broken man and almost bankrupt, he died in 1867. His funeral with over 700 railway workers accompanying the hearse to Glasnevin cemetery was the largest seen in Dublin for many years. The *Irish Times* of the day commented, 'Wherever there is an Irish railway there is his monument, more noble than the pyramids.'

A statue bearing the single word 'DARGAN' stands today in front of the National Gallery in Merrion Square.

During Queen Victoria's visit to Dublin she endeared herself to the onlookers as she and the princes were being driven through the city streets. Something Prince Alfred did annoyed her so much that she snatched the cap off his head and delivered a slap across his face!

immediately brought to the Lower Castle Yard and there remanded by the Chief Magistrate to Richmond Jail until 14 November.

Brought once more before the Chief Magistrate Stephens was committed for trial on 27 November and sent back to Richmond Jail. But ten days later he escaped. Nine men, led by John Devoy, armed with revolvers and carrying a rope ladder, turned up outside the prison walls on 24 November. At one o'clock a Fenian member of the prison staff unlocked Stephen's cell with a key which had been made from a wax impression taken by the prison's night watchman.

Stephens and his helper then went into the prison yard to a high wall separating the yard from the prison governor's garden. They had planned to use a ladder in the yard to cross the wall but now found it was too short. They had to bring out tables, on which they placed the ladder, and thus got over safely. The outer wall was easily scaled by use of the rope ladder and Stephens was quickly brought to a safe house. Later he moved to a house in Kildare Street where he remained until he left the country. The police offered a reward of £1,000 for his capture and £300 for information on his whereabouts. A strangely worded description of Stephens was given as follows:

> James Stephens is about 42 years of age, 5 feet, 7 inches high, stout make, broad high shoulders, very tight, active appearance, fair hair, bald all round the top of his head; wore all his beard which is sandy, slightly tinged with grey, rather long under chin, but slightly round jaw approaching the ears, tender eyes which defect seems to be constitutional, and has a peculiar habit of closing the left eye when speaking; high cheek bones and rather good-looking; hands and feet remarkably small and well-formed, and he is generally dressed in black clothes.

The following March 1866 Stephens was smuggled aboard a ship on the Liffey and was brought to safety in Scotland. He then travelled to France and later in May he once more landed in America. In January 1867 he returned to France and was still there when the long-threatened Fenian rising took place in Ireland.

There was no fighting in Dublin City itself but a contingent of Fenians assembled at Terenure and marched out through Templeogue to the Dublin Mountains on 5 March 1867. They attacked a police barracks at Tallaght at midnight but suffered two deaths and twelve wounded when the police opened fire with sixty rifles. The attackers had few guns and were taken totally by surprise by the volley. The night was pitch dark and all that the few rebel riflemen could do was to aim at the flashes. A second volley from the police caused more casualties and completed the rout. The rest of the rebels retreated back to the city where most were arrested as they crossed the heavily guarded canal bridges. They were brought to the Upper Castle Yard where they sank exhausted to the ground after their long marches.

The Fenians were more successful in other parts of the county. Police barracks were attacked in Stepaside, Glencullen and Dundrum. The barracks in the first two locations were captured by the rebels and large quantities of rifles fell into their hands. They suffered no fatalities during the operations.

The leader of the attack in Glencullen was a man called Lennon. When he had finished inspecting the captured barracks he emerged to find a priest berating his Fenians and ordering them to go home. Lennon went up to the priest and pointing a revolver at his head, declared 'If you don't get out of here, I'll give you the contents of this!' The priest promptly departed. The same Lennon rescued a fellow officer, John Kirwan, who had been wounded in the Dundrum attack and was under police guard in a Dublin hospital. Lennon himself was later arrested and sentenced to fifteen years' penal servitude. By the end of March, the rising was over.

While all these events were happening in Ireland, Stephens was in Paris, living in very poor circumstances and watching in silence as the rising fizzled out. All through the 1870s he remained in poor health and at times on the edge of starvation. His plight was so desperate that the *Freeman's Journal* started a fund to assist him. Such was the affection in which the old leader was held that the fund was generously supported.

Then in September 1891 Stephens and his wife came back to Dublin. They took a small cottage in Sutton. Jane Stephens died there in 1895 and six years later on 29 March 1901, James

Stephens, the Fenian chief, died in his brother-in-law's house at 82, George's Avenue, Blackrock, Co. Dublin. His funeral was a massive affair, taking over five hours for the journey from Blackrock to Glasnevin. The coffin was draped in the Fenian flag of green, white and orange. Michael Davitt led the mourners and also present were the Lord Mayor of Dublin and John Redmond, leader of the Irish Parliamentary Party. When the cortege reached Glasnevin Cemetery Stephens was buried in the Martyrs' Plot. His grave has the inscription 'A day, an hour, of virtuous liberty is worth a whole eternity in bondage.'

17

◎

'THE BLACKBIRD OF AVONDALE' 1846 – 1891

On 27 June 1846 one of Ireland's most famous leaders was born in Avondale, Co. Wicklow, the seventh child and third son of a rich Protestant Irish landlord and an American mother. His name was Charles Stewart Parnell. (The Stewart part of his name came from his mother, Delia Stewart.)

At the age of six the young Charles was sent away to boarding school in England. Apart from the fact that it was customary at the time for children of the gentry to be educated abroad, it was also hoped that the boy would be cured of a stammer that he was acquiring from imitating his brother John. In 1855 his eldest brother, Hayes, was killed in a hunting accident and Charles was brought home for a time. He was sent back to England to a boarding school in Kirk Langley, Derbyshire. Four years later his father died suddenly in the Shelbourne Hotel in Dublin. In his will he had made Charles 'heir-in-law to all intents and purposes', John, Charles' older brother, having inherited a fortune from an uncle. Thus did Charles inherit the house and estate of Avondale at Rathdrum in Co. Wicklow.

Mrs Parnell did not wish to live at Avondale and would have preferred to live in Paris or America but could not take the children out of the country because they had been made wards of court. She therefore rented Khyber Pass, a house in Dalkey in south County Dublin. Later the Parnell household moved to Kingstown and for some further years lived at 14 Upper Temple Street in Dublin in the then fashionable north city.

Avondale House itself was rented out to an engineer working on the Dublin–Wicklow–Wexford Railway line, which was nearing

Charles Stewart Parnell lived at 14 Temple Street which at one time was a hiding place for Fenians wanted by the police.

completion at the time. Only the dower house, 'Casino', in the grounds of the estate was kept for the use of the family.

Charles was sent to England once more to a clergyman at Chipping Norton in Oxfordshire to prepare for entrance to Cambridge University. During his summer holidays he went back to 'Casino' and played a lot of cricket, a game at which he was quite talented. His companions at the time were all members of the same upper class as himself and Parnell was very typical of young landed gentry society. In March 1865 he was commissioned as Lieutenant in the Wicklow Militia at the age of eighteen years.

During these early years Parnell showed little interest in politics. He was aware of the Fenian activities of the 1860s but they didn't seem to occupy too much of his attention. While the Castle authorities were holding trials of Fenian prisoners in January 1866 he attended the first reception of the year held by the viceroy in Dublin Castle.

Searches for arms and arrests of Fenians continued unabated. Many Irish-American ex-soldiers who had returned to Ireland to aid the Fenian cause were arrested and held without trial. Three of these Americans had been befriended by Mrs Parnell as a fellow-countrywoman before they were arrested. They had even visited the Parnell house in Temple Street and the news of these visits

—————— ◎ ——————

Parnell was described as being 'tall, slim and handsome', with the 'figure and grace of a Greek statue'; he had a slight frame, brown eyes 'with strange inscrutability of expression; a long nose, straight and well-chiselled; a small mouth, easily mobile with pride, passion or scorn. He had a fine lofty white forehead'. He spoke English with an upper class Irish accent.

—————— ◎ ——————

A dreadful accident occurred on Portobello Bridge in 1861. A horse-drawn 'omnibus' returning from Rathgar to Nelson's Pillar stopped on the bridge to allow a passenger to get off. When the driver tried to re-start the horses, instead of going forward they started to back down towards the Rathmines end of the bridge. In spite of the best efforts of the driver, the horses continued to go backwards until they demolished the fence protecting the canal lock on the south-western side of the bridge and the vehicle tumbled end-first into the lock. When the horses were dragged in they pulled the vehicle down until it was once more resting on its wheels. There was only a metre depth of water in the lock at the time and the passengers would have been able to escape had not the lock keeper opened the sluice gates in the hope of floating the vehicle free. In the darkness and confusion, all the passengers, six in number, were drowned. Only the driver escaped. Among the victims was Mr Michael Gunn of the well-known theatre family.

—————— ◎ ——————

reached the ears of the police. A few doors away in a chemist's shop, at 3 Upper Temple Street, Fenian activity was indeed going on. The police raided the shop and found a letter from a Mr Parnell in the owner's pocket. When the chemist's assistant was questioned he told them that they had a 'patient' at Number 14. Although the patient in question was Mrs Parnell herself, the police thought that they were on the verge of apprehending some important Fenian.

They raided the Parnell house on the morning of 6 December 1886. Although the search was conducted with some civility and Mrs Parnell had not expressed outrage at the time, nevertheless some weeks later she complained bitterly to the Chief Secretary, Lord Naas, about the 'outrage' and 'insult to her family'. Since nothing incriminating was discovered, she received an apology and all the letters that the police had removed for examination were returned. The incident was evidently regarded as closed, for Mrs Parnell was a welcome guest at a great ball given by the viceroy at Dublin Castle on 7 March 1867, two days after the Fenian skirmishes in Tallaght. (The change in attitude of Mrs Parnell from the time of the raid to her later indignant complaint to the Chief Secretary has been attributed by some commentators to the reaction of her son, Charles, when he returned from Cambridge for his Christmas holidays and he learned what had happened.)

In May 1870 an important event took place in Dublin. A semi-private conference heard a proposal from a Donegal man, the son of a Protestant pastor, to the effect that 'the true remedy for the evils of Ireland' was 'the establishment of an Irish Parliament with full control over all domestic affairs'. The proposer was Isaac Butt and the adoption of the resolution marked the establishment of the Home Rule League.

Parnell showed not the slightest interest in Irish politics at the time and he spent a lot of his time in France and America when the fledgling Home Rule League was finding its feet. But the two issues, the Land Question and Home Rule, were to become the greatest concerns of Parnell's later political life.

For two years, 1872 and 1873, he stayed at Avondale, engaging in the usual pursuits of a country gentleman. In 1873 his brother John suggested that he should continue the old family tradition and take an active interest in public affairs. To John's surprise Charles replied that he had been thinking about it and that he favoured the

——————— ◎ ———————

A bridge, little known to most Dubliners, was built across the Liffey in 1877. More properly known as the Liffey Viaduct, it was built specifically to allow the passage of trains from Kingsbridge Station past Cabra, Glasnevin and Drumcondra to the North Wall. The viaduct traverses the bridge and leads to a tunnel, (about a kilometre in length) which goes under Conyngham Road and the Phoenix Park. The start of the tunnel under the park can be identified by the closed archway in the park wall on Conyngham Road.

The Liffey Viaduct

——————— ◎ ———————

Land League and Home Rule.

In early March 1874 he applied for membership of the Home Rule League at a meeting in Dublin and was gladly accepted. Isaac Butt said at the time, 'We have got a splendid new recruit, an historic name, young Parnell of Wicklow; and unless I'm mistaken the Saxon will find him an ugly customer.'

Parnell was immediately put to the test – a by-election had been called in Co. Dublin and he was put forward as a Home Rule candidate. Against all expectations he proved to be a nervous, hesitant speaker. It is said that he clenched his hands so tightly behind his back that his nails made his hands bleed. Many observers were of the opinion that if he got elected he would either stay silent or be known as 'single-speech Parnell'. However, he applied himself to canvassing, attending meetings and forcing himself to speak no matter how painful it was for himself – and for his listeners!

He addressed a two-hundred-strong meeting in Kingstown Temperance Hall and was well received, even if his speech was dull. Three days later a meeting he called in Terenure had to be cancelled when no one turned up to listen. Another meeting in Rathmines two days before polling day was more successful and a pre-arranged question on the release from jail of Fenian prisoners allowed him to give his view that they should all be released. This reply gained for him the support of Fenian sympathisers. The election ended in defeat, however. Parnell only got half the votes of the other candidate, a result that was in line with the expectations of his party – the exercise was something of a trial run.

Another chance presented itself in 1875 when a by-election was held in Co. Meath. The Home Rule party again put Parnell forward. This time he hit all the right buttons – he spoke in favour of Home Rule, the rights of parents to have their children educated in the religion of their choice and the 'Three Fs' for tenants – Fair Rent, Free Sale and Fixity of Tenure. With the endorsement of so many different groups, it was no great surprise when he had a comfortable victory – gaining nearly twice as many votes as his nearest rival. Parnell was on his way at last. On Thursday 22 April 1875, he entered the English House of Commons for the first time. He was twenty-eight years old. He made his maiden speech four days later and spoke thirteen times in the three and a half months

In 1879 a metal 'swivel' bridge was opened to traffic across the Liffey and was named in honour of Isaac Butt. The bridge could swivel horizontally on its central pillar to allow shipping to berth at the quays. When the railway bridge, known as the Loopline Bridge, was built just east of Butt Bridge in 1890 shipping could no longer pass through.

In 1932 the present concrete Butt Bridge, with a central span of thirty-three metres to allow barges to pass through, replaced the swivel bridge.

Butt Bridge

In 1885 the Prince and Princess of Wales visited Dublin. The prince, later to become King Edward VII, was interested in housing for the working classes. His entourage finally agreed that they would probably be safe if the couple went incognito. So, along with the Duke of Clarence, they went from Dublin Castle in an unmarked carriage along Werburgh Street to Golden Lane. As the duke stepped from the carriage a woman in one of the tenement's emptied a large pot of water in which cabbage had been boiled into the street. He lost his footing in the cabbage water and fell to the ground, much to the amusement of the prince and princess.

The people of the tenements soon learned who their visitors were and a huge crowd gathered within minutes. They gave three cheers for the prince and princess and many of them shook the prince's hand. The royal party then went inside the tenements and saw for themselves the desperate conditions in which their inhabitants lived. (The prince later returned to Dublin in 1903 and 1904 as King Edward VII.)

of that first parliamentary session.

Prior to his election the Home Rule party had already begun to adopt the policy of obstruction in the parliament. Because of the overwhelming odds facing any Irish group in the English parliament they decided that the only effective opposition they could mount against any obnoxious legislation was to obstruct the proceedings at every turn by interminable speeches and the raising of constant 'points of order'. Isaac Butt supported the tactic but it was a Belfast pork butcher, by the name of Joseph Biggar, MP for Cavan, who used it to the limit.

The very first day that Parnell attended parliament Biggar gave a typical display. He spoke for nearly four hours against a Coercion Act. Parnell was a quick learner and no doubt found the performance quite instructive.

In the summer of the same year he was taking an active part in events in Dublin too. It was the centenary year of the birth of Daniel O'Connell and a grand parade was organised to celebrate the event. The organising committee was under the control of the Lord Mayor of Dublin, Peter Paul MacSwiney, who was not a Home Ruler. He formed an anti-Home Rule alliance to prevent the take-over of the celebrations by the Fenian-dominated Amnesty Association, which was agitating for the release of the forty Fenian prisoners still in jail.

On the day of the parade, 6 August 1875, a tremendous crowd gathered to pay homage to the Liberator's memory. As the procession made its way through the streets of the city the Amnesty group, with black banners and a huge black flag on their carriage, attempted to join in. Fighting broke out and in the melee someone cut the traces of the carriage, allowing the horses to walk on through the crowd, leaving the carriage behind. The Amnesty men were not deterred, however. Tying themselves with ropes to the carriage they hauled it along to Carlisle Bridge (now O'Connell Bridge) to where the speakers' platform was located.

When the Lord Mayor's gilt coach eventually reached the platform he found it surrounded by the Amnesty supporters. The great black flag was displayed and black banners draped with real chains bearing the inscription 'Still in Chains', were everywhere. The Lord Mayor attempted to speak but his voice was drowned out by the rattling of chains and chants of 'Butt! Butt!' He eventually

———— ◎ ————

A committee, formed in 1902 to erect a fitting memorial to Parnell's memory, originally wished to buy Avondale but when they were unsuccessful they had a monument erected at the top of O'Connell Street. The foundation stone was laid in 1899 but it took twelve years before the monument was completed. It consists of an eight-foot statue of Parnell standing at the base of a large column bearing his words on the 'march of a nation'. One day after the completed monument was unveiled by John Redmond the nearby Great Britain Street was renamed Parnell Street.

The Parnell Monument took twelve years to complete.

———— ◎ ————

gave up the struggle and Butt and other Home Rulers, including Parnell, took over the platform.

Back in the British parliament Parnell continued the obstructionist policy and all through 1877, 1878 and 1879 the conflict raged. Butt never fully approved of the tactics adopted by the newer members of the Home Rule Party and in 1877 he was pushed aside and Parnell was elected leader.

The final push against Butt occurred shortly after a huge rally of supporters in the Rotunda Rooms in Dublin on 21 August 1877. The venue was packed with over four thousand people and many more were locked outside. Parnell and Biggar were given a rousing welcome but when Parnell rose to speak the reception was so tremendous that it was ten minutes before the cheering died down. Referring to criticism of the obstructionist tactics he declared, 'I care nothing for the English parliament and its outcries. I care nothing for its existence, if that existence is to continue as a source of tyranny and destruction to my country.'

After the meeting, cheering crowds escorted the two men down Sackville Street to the Imperial Hotel (which stood on the site now occupied by Clery's Department Store). Parnell eventually responded to the pleas of the crowd and addressed them from the balcony, 'The work begun here tonight will be heard throughout the world and will strike terror to the Saxon heart.'

As president of the Home Rule Party Parnell gave many rousing speeches both in Ireland and England. One particular speech in Castlebar, Co. Mayo included the famous words, 'Let no man lightly define the measure of Irish independence. Let no man assign a *ne plus ultra* to the march of a nation.' And later he added the words 'Let no man say; "Thus far shalt thou go and no further."'

In April 1879 a meeting was held in Irishtown, Co. Mayo, to protest against the excesses of a landlord who refused to reduce his rents. The Mayo Land League was formed as a result. The driving force behind the league was Michael Davitt. His family had been evicted from their home in Mayo and had emigrated to Lancashire in England. While working in a cotton mill there, he had an accident which resulted in the loss of his right arm. He became a Fenian and was imprisoned in 1870. In December 1877 he was released on parole, two years early. A few days later he met Parnell in London to thank him for making representations on his behalf.

At a meeting in the Imperial Hotel in Dublin on 21 October 1879 the Irish National Land League was formed. The aim was to organise the tenants of the whole country in an effort to eliminate rack-rents and to gain ownership of the land for the tenants. The early days of the Land League were filled with optimism but the mood was soon to change as the extremely wet summer that same year led to great hunger and shortages during the winter. Famine once more faced the peasants. Parnell and John Dillon went to America to raise funds for the Land League and the starving peasantry and succeeded in raising over £50,000 for their cause.

In the general election held in 1880 Parnell stood in three constituencies, in Cork, Mayo and Meath. He won all three seats but chose to sit for Cork City. During that same election a minor Clare landlord, by the name of Captain William O'Shea, was also elected as a member for Clare for the Home Rule Party. The event was to have a profound effect on the subsequent career of Parnell.

Catherine, the Captain's wife, was then thirty-five years old. She was described as being 'a beautiful woman, tall and dark with a mouth expressive of tenderness and sweetness and wistful eyes and a head crowned with a wealth of soft, glossy black hair.' She had married Willie O'Shea when she was twenty-one and by this time had three children; a boy aged ten and two daughters aged seven and five years.

Some time later when she visited the London Parliament she met Parnell for the first time. When he came out she saw 'a tall gaunt figure, thin and deadly pale. He looked straight at me smiling and his curiously burning eyes looked into mine with a wondering intentness that threw into my brain the sudden thought, "This man is wonderful – and different."'

That summer Parnell went to the Ladies' Gallery in the House to meet Katie O'Shea several times. He also took her in a hansom cab on drives out in the country and seems to have met her on many occasions before the summer recess of parliament. He returned to Avondale but wrote frequently to Katie saying he was missing a 'certain kind and fair face'. Later he wrote:

> My own love, you cannot imagine how much you have occupied my thoughts all day and how very greatly the prospect of seeing you again very soon comforts me. Yours always, C.

Willie O'Shea challenged Parnell to a duel over his friendship with his wife, Catherine O'Shea.

The activities of the Land League, as branches and numbers increased, seemed to be leading to a clash with the English authorities. Land League meetings became increasingly militant. They were accompanied on many occasions by groups of horsemen dressed in green and carrying long staves tipped with metal so that they resembled lances. The British government under Gladstone were increasingly determined to act.

On Wednesday 3 November while Parnell was at lunch in the Imperial Hotel in Dublin he was approached by a plain-clothes police officer and handed an indictment for conspiracy on nineteen counts. Among other things he was charged with conspiracy to stop tenants paying their rent, to stop legal evictions and to prevent others taking over farms from which tenants had been evicted. He was also charged with advocating boycotts. Thirteen other men were also served with indictments. The charges came to nothing however, when the jury declared that 'they were unanimous about disagreeing'.

All this time he was deeply involved with Katie O'Shea. It seems that Captain O'Shea was unaware of the affair at the time, at least he gave no sign in his dealings with Parnell that he was aware of anything. However, Katie told a friend that her husband knew well what was going on and that he knew Parnell stayed with her during her husband's absences. Be that as it may, on 12 July 1881, Captain

O'Shea wrote to Parnell challenging him to a duel because he said he had just become aware that Parnell had been staying with Katie in the O'Shea house unknown to him. When he had gone home to Katie that day he had found Parnell's suitcase in the house. After a furious row with Katie he had gone back to London and written the letter. Some time later O'Shea seems to have accepted Parnell's 'assurances' that there was nothing going on and no more was mentioned of a duel.

Catherine O'Shea eventually married Charles Stewart Parnell and had several children by him.

After a particularly successful Land League convention in 1881, Parnell arrived on the train from Avondale at Harcourt Street station to find there were tens of thousands of people waiting for him. It was dark at the time (8.10 p.m. on Sunday 25 September). As his horse-drawn carriage moved down Harcourt Street to St Stephen's Green the horses were taken from the carriage and teams of men pulled it down Grafton Street to College Green. Outside the Bank of Ireland building (the site of 'Grattan's Parliament') he stopped the procession and imitating (perhaps unconsciously) the action of the other 'Uncrowned King of

Ireland', Daniel O'Connell, fifty years earlier, pointed dramatically to the building declaring, 'It's a place of memories, which no Irishman would ever forget.' The crowd went wild and it took an hour to get to Sackville Street to the Land League offices. There he addressed the enthusiastic crowd, which called for three cheers for the 'Irish Republic'.

Agitation and unrest over the land issue continued unabated. In the last months of the previous year nearly 1,700 outrages were reported. The response of the government was to introduce a policy of coercion but Parnell continued his opposition. In a speech in Wexford he said, 'We won't get anywhere until we remove English misrule.' Afterwards, when he was asked if his speech might lead to his arrest, he replied, 'I think I am likely to be arrested at any time – so are we all.' When one of his fellow-Irish members of parliament asked him if he had any instructions for them if he were to be arrested, he is said to have replied, 'If I am arrested, Captain Moonlight will take my place.'

A few days later, 13 October 1881, the porter at Morrison's Hotel, at the corner of Dawson Street and Nassau Street, where Parnell was staying, told him that two gentlemen were waiting to see him. When Parnell allowed them up to his room they courteously presented him with a warrant for his arrest. He accompanied them to a cab and as they passed the Bank of Ireland in College Green, where he had made his dramatic gesture a fortnight before, a group of Dublin police jumped on two jaunting cars and drove ahead of the cab. An escort of mounted police were waiting as they went down Parliament Street to the quays, and they then proceeded up to Kilmainham Jail.

When they arrived at the jail Parnell refused to allow himself to be searched. He was given a medium-sized room with a table and chairs but no carpet. Parnell seems to have accepted his arrest with resignation and even relief, for he realised that the Land League's effectiveness was coming to an end, now that Gladstone was conceding the 'Three Fs' of Fair Rent, Free Sale and Fixity of Tenure.

However, a succession of arrests of other leaders soon changed the mood. The Land League was proposing a rent strike and Parnell reluctantly came round to the view that there was no other option.

On 18 October 1881 a manifesto was issued by the leaders in Kilmainham Jail calling on all tenants to pay no rents until the government restored the constitutional rights of the Irish people. The manifesto was signed by Parnell, John Dillon, Thomas Sexton, AJ Kettle and Thomas Brennan. The names of Michael Davitt and Patrick Egan were also included. The manifesto was condemned by the Catholic hierarchy and the Land League gradually lost all influence.

Parnell's stay in Kilmainham was by no means too unpleasant. He was moved to a 'beautiful room facing the sun, the best in the prison'. The other leaders were in adjoining rooms and they were free to associate at will. Parnell's room looked out on a small courtyard in which he and his companions could exercise and play handball for up to six hours a day. Food was varied and available from outside the prison. A Dublin locksmith is supposed to have provided Parnell with a set of keys to enable him to walk free if ever there was the threat of moving him to prison in England. (Katie O'Shea claimed later to still have the keys in 1914.)

Whatever the truth of this, Parnell spent six months in Kilmainham Jail. While he was still there Katie gave birth to their first child, a baby girl, on 15 February 1882. Although the child was quite healthy at first, her condition deteriorated later and when Parnell, on parole due to the death of a nephew, visited Katie in Eltham in England, he found the baby seriously ill. He and Katie were alone at the time when the baby died.

On the day of their daughter's funeral Parnell was back in Kilmainham Jail but was released on 2 May along with Dillon and some others. The chief secretary, William Forster, who had ordered the leaders' arrests, resigned in protest. On Forster's way back to England he drove by coach to the boat in Kingstown Harbour instead of going by train from Westland Row. Unknown to him, two members of a secret society, called the Invincibles, were waiting at the railway station to assassinate him. By his change of plans he escaped with his life. With the departure of Forster, Gladstone appointed Lord Frederick Cavendish in his place. The undersecretary, TH Burke, a Catholic but regarded by ultra-nationalists as a 'Castle rat' or traitor, was also on the assassins' list, and was still in Ireland.

On the morning of Saturday 6 May 1882 Cavendish and the new

viceroy, Lord Spencer, went to Dublin Castle to meet their staff. Afterwards Spencer rode off under escort to the Viceregal Lodge in the Phoenix Park, while Cavendish decided he would walk there. On his way Cavendish was overtaken by his undersecretary, Burke, in a horse-drawn cab, who then decided that he would walk the rest of the way with him. It was seven o'clock in the evening and there were a lot of people about, many of whom were watching a polo match.

Meantime Lord Spencer had arrived at the Viceregal Lodge and sat down at an open window towards the front to work on some papers. The next moment he heard a cry that he said later he would never forget. He looked out and saw a man rushing towards the Lodge shouting, 'Mr Burke and Lord Cavendish are killed.'

The two men had been killed by men using twelve-inch-long surgical knives which had been bought in London and smuggled into the country hidden in women's skirts. The assassins then escaped on a sidecar and it was not until the following year that they were arrested and charged with the murder. All the murderers were members of the Invincibles and were of the working class, with the exception of one of them, James Carey. He was a Dublin town councillor and was regarded by his neighbours as a very respectable and religious man. When the trials began in 1883, Carey turned state witness. The four other defendants were convicted and hanged in Kilmainham Jail but Carey was given a free pardon and sent out of the country to South Africa for his own safety. However, he was tracked there by a man called O'Donnell and shot dead.

It emerged from the trial that Burke was the primary target of the assassins and Cavendish was killed simply because he happened to be in Burke's company. After the Phoenix Park murders some Dublin citizens went to the assassination spot and removed blood-stained sods of grass as souvenirs. (A cross cut in the grass opposite Áras an Uachtaráin now marks the spot where the murders took place.)

Parnell was in Eltham with Katie when he read the news of the atrocity in the *Observer* on Sunday 7 May. Katie saw him go suddenly rigid with shock and when he showed the headline to her he said, 'I shall resign.' He made an offer of resignation to Gladstone but his resignation was not accepted.

Richard Pigott was memorably described at the
time by one who knew him:

> He was a shiftless, moon-faced man who
> fell into villainy, not so much because he
> was vicious, as because he was
> incompetent. Generations of mean and
> flabby ancestors must have gone to the
> making of this man, whose capacity for
> crawling servility and obsequious
> defence gave him the right to claim
> spiritual descent from Uriah Heep. His
> big, round head was tangled at its base
> with bushy beard, and his forehead jutted
> out as if it had started on the road of
> nobility but had failed to get there. He
> wore a monocle screwed into his right
> eye, and he had a trick, when in doubt, of
> putting his hand to his mouth and
> holding his lip.   *St John Ervine*

Richard Pigott lived at 7 DeVesci Terrace, Monkstown and had
a photographic business on Eden Quay where he dabbled in
pornography and blackmail.

The month before the Phoenix Park murders took place the leaders in Kilmainham had reached an informal arrangement with Gladstone. They had agreed that, in return for the release of the prisoners, the relaxation of the coercion laws, the amendment of the Land Act and the protection of tenants in arrears of rent, Parnell would use his influence to calm the country and get his followers to accept the new Land Act. This arrangement came to be known as the Kilmainham Treaty. The prison releases took place on 2 May and thus set in motion the chain of events which culminated in the dreadful murders.

After the assassinations the Government immediately rushed through another Coercion Act but Gladstone and Parnell went ahead with the terms of the Kilmainham Treaty. Parnell's outspoken condemnation of the atrocity was a big factor in the continued co-operation. He now strongly opposed the new coercion laws but worked with the government in making the new Land Act effective. The result was that his position as leader was stronger than ever.

The increasing rapport between Parnell and the English liberals greatly annoyed the Conservatives, whose organ was *The Times* newspaper. It had always been virulently anti-Irish and in 1887 it published a series of articles entitled 'Parnellism and Crime'. One of these articles contained what it claimed was a facsimile of a letter by Parnell to a friend, in which he said that his opposition to the Phoenix Park murders was a necessary piece of policy and that Burke had got 'no more than he deserved'. Parnell immediately denounced the letter as a forgery but *The Times* insisted it was genuine and that they had other similar letters.

The source of the letters was a man called Richard Pigott, who was born in 1828 in County Meath. He was a political journalist who owned several newspapers with patriotic titles like *Flag of Ireland, The Irishman* and *The Shamrock*. In 1881 Parnell bought Pigott's newspapers for £3,000 and replaced them with his own newspaper *United Ireland*. It was during this transaction that Pigott acquired samples of Parnell's hand-writing.

In 1885 when he was short of money he proposed writing a pamphlet to be called 'Parnellism Unmasked' which would supposedly prove the connection between Parnell and political crime in Ireland. The project was endorsed and subsidised by

Edward Houston, the secretary of a Unionist association who also had connections with *The Times*. Pigott was finding the task of providing any tangible evidence against Parnell extremely difficult and soon came to the conclusion that his only hope lay in forging some evidence.

In a real 'cloak-and-dagger' operation he summoned Houston to Paris and there handed over 'incriminating' documents for the sum of £605. Houston immediately approached *The Times* with his 'evidence' and that newspaper was so eager to discredit Parnell that on 18 April 1887 it published the 'facsimile'.

When Parnell saw the newspaper article he didn't pay much heed to it and later in the House of Commons he merely dismissed the letter as a forgery. The affair seemed to be about to peter out naturally when one of the Irish MPs decided to sue *The Times* for libel because he too was mentioned in the articles. This seemed to spur the newspaper to increase its campaign and it published another Parnell letter. This was dated 9 January 1882 and was supposedly written by Parnell before the murders, when he was still in Kilmainham.

> Dear E
> What are these fellows waiting for? This inaction is inexcuseable; our best men are in prison and nothing is being done. Let there be an end to this hesitency. Prompt action is called for. You undertook to make it hot for old Forster and co. Let us have some evidence of your power to do so. My health is good, thanks.
> Yours very truly,
> Chas. S. Parnell

The House appointed a special commission to investigate. The commission had a majority of Conservative members and there was little doubt what conclusion they would come to.

Meanwhile Parnell and Katie embarked on a complete study of his handwriting and those of 'possible imitators . . . [and] we made some interesting discoveries'.

On 21 and 22 February 1889 Pigott was called before the commission. He gave a fairly convincing performance until the second day when he was asked to write down certain words. He misspelled 'inexcusable' and 'hesitancy' in the same way as in the letter. With these gaffes Pigott's guilt was blindingly obvious. Parnell's counsel, Sir Charles Russell 'with short sharp questions drove Pigott deeper and deeper into the mire of confusion and self-contradiction.'

When the cross-examination finished Parnell correctly forecast that Pigott would leave the country before the commission met again. Pigott did indeed flee to Spain and registered in a Madrid hotel under the name of Ronald Ponsonby. As luck would have it, he was spotted walking down the street by Willie O'Shea! The police were alerted and were waiting in his room when he returned but before they could arrest him he took a gun from a bag, put it to his mouth and killed himself. (Parnell was later paid £5,000 in damages by *The Times* which also suffered £200,000 in costs.)

After the 'Pigott affair' Parnell seemed to be in an unassailable position but then on Christmas Eve 1889 Willie O'Shea cited him as co-respondent in his divorce case against Catherine. Strangely enough the news of the divorce suit didn't make front-page news at the time. When the *Freeman's Journal* asked Parnell about it he replied that O'Shea had known about the relationship for years and was only now taking action because he was put up to it by *The Times*.

Even more curious is the fact that, during the eleven months between the filing of the action and the start of the court case, there was little reaction from the public, clergy or Parnell's followers. In February 1890 Parnell told Michael Davitt that he would come through 'without a stain on my reputation'.

While Katie was greatly agitated about the case, Parnell himself seemed totally disinterested and refused to defend himself. The one thing he wanted more than anything else was the divorce and the resulting freedom to marry Katie. He told her, 'I have given, and will give, Ireland what is in me to give. That I have vowed to her, but my private life shall never belong to any country, but to one woman.'

The divorce hearing began on 15 November 1890 in the same room where Pigott had been unmasked. Katie's counsel told the court that he intended to produce no witnesses and that he would not cross-examine. The result was, therefore, a foregone conclusion: the jury found for Willie on all counts. The judge then granted him custody of the two youngest girls, who were in fact

Parnell's children. Katie wrote later that when the *decree nisi* was brought to her house by a solicitor, 'We were very happy that evening and Parnell declared he would have the decree framed.'

The Irish leaders continued to support Parnell and in Dublin shortly after the close of the divorce proceedings, on 25 November, Parnell was almost unanimously re-elected as leader of the Home Rule Party. But shortly afterwards Gladstone sent a message that it would be impossible to get the British Parliament to pass a Home Rule Bill for Ireland as long as Parnell was leader. This caused consternation in the party, as they knew that Gladstone was their only hope for Home Rule and at the same time they had overwhelmingly chosen Parnell as their leader. He told his party that he would only quit if Gladstone would introduce the Home Rule Bill immediately. This Gladstone refused to do and things remained as they were until 6 December 1890 when the 'anti-Parnellites' withdrew their support and elected Mr Justin McCarthy as their chairman. The split had happened at last and the anti-Parnellites were in the majority.

The British Parliament closed for the Christmas recess on Tuesday 9 December. On his way back to Ireland Parnell told a reporter that he 'had not the slightest fear of carrying with him the Irish people' and in a message to the people of Ireland he said, 'Tell them I will fight to the end.'

When the train from Kingstown arrived in Westland Row station Parnell was cheered by a large crowd. They removed the horses from his carriage and drew him in triumph through the streets to Rutland Square where he was staying. The same evening there was another triumphant march to the Mansion House in Dawson Street to collect the Lord Mayor, and then with bands and torch-lights the procession wound its way to an enormous crowd at the Rotunda Rooms. The poet Katherine Tynan was there that night and she wrote of the occasion:

> It was nearly 8.30 when we heard the bands coming; then the windows were lit up by the lurid glare of thousands of torches in the street outside. There was a distant roaring like the sea. The great gathering within waited silently with expectation. Then the cheering began, and we craned our necks and looked on eagerly, and there was the tall, slender, distinguished

figure of the Irish leader making his way across the platform. I don't think any words could do justice to his reception. The house rose at him; everywhere around there was a sea of passionate faces, loving, admiring, almost worshipping that silent, pale man. The cheering broke out again and again; there was no quelling it. Mr Parnell bowed from side to side, sweeping the assemblage with his eagle glance. The people were fairly mad with excitement.

In his speech Parnell stated that if the constitutional movement 'is broken, sundered, separated, discredited and forgotten, England will be face to face with that imperishable force which tonight gives me vitality and power . . . and if Ireland leaves this path upon which I have led her . . . I will not for my part say that I will not accompany her further'.

The violence that was hinted at in the speech surfaced the very next day. Before the Rotunda meeting Parnell had dismissed the editor of *United Ireland* because he had defected to the anti-Parnellite side. During the meeting some members of the 'anti' side had occupied the newpaper's offices. When Parnell heard this the following day he drove furiously to the premises and pulled up the horse so suddenly that it fell flat on the ground. Parnell seized a crowbar and smashed down the door. He next appeared at a second storey window of the premises to the cheers of the crowd. He made a short speech and ended with the words, 'I rely on Dublin. Dublin is true. What Dublin says today Ireland will say tomorrow.'

The frantic extrovert behaviour of Parnell in Dublin in those days was so different from his usual aloof, reserved manner that many observers began to suspect that he was actually mad. John Dillon remarked however, 'Men say here that Parnell is mad but it seems to me that his astuteness is absolutely infinite.'

Early in 1891 a by-election in North Kilkenny was fought with unusual bitterness but at the end of the day Parnell's candidate was beaten by nearly two to one, 2,527 votes to 1,362. Many thought that he would now throw in the towel but he was again received back in Dublin by an enthusiastic welcoming multitude. As he passed the old Parliament buildings in College Green he again pointed to it dramatically and the crowd cheered him to the echo.

The following March the Parnellite candidate was defeated in the Sligo election but a more happy event occurred on June 25 when Katie and Parnell were married in a registry office in Steyning in England. The honeymoon was short-lived, however, for Parnell had to return to Ireland to fight another by-election in Carlow in which his candidate again lost. Although Dublin was still solidly behind him he was losing support throughout the rest of the country.

Still he threw himself whole-heartedly into campaigning in the forthcoming general election. He travelled around the country making speech after speech in an effort to regain lost ground.

One Sunday he spoke at a meeting in Cabinteely just south of Dublin and the jostling crowd broke one of the windows of his carriage. The breaking of the window upset him because he had always thought that it was unlucky to break glass. He also got drenched that day for he spoke with his hat off during a downpour.

When he returned to Brighton to Katie he looked worn out and ill. She was thoroughly alarmed, so much so, that Parnell told her he would give up the struggle if she asked him to but she admitted that when she looked into his eyes, 'I knew I could not say it.'

One week later he was back campaigning in Ireland and again he got thoroughly wet when he spoke bareheaded at a meeting in Galway. His last public speech in Dublin was from Costigan's Hotel close to where the Parnell Monument now stands. A few days later, in spite of his doctor's advice not to travel, he went back to England promising, 'I shall come back on Saturday week.'

Under Katie's tender care he improved somewhat but had a restless night that Thursday 1 October 1891. On Saturday he was a bit better but by Sunday he was again unwell and Katie called the local doctor. On Monday he was too weak to leave his bed and had another bad night that night. By Tuesday he was feverish and late that evening he was dozing but suddenly opened his eyes and said, 'Kiss me, sweet wifie, and I will try to sleep a little.'

Katie wrote later:

> I lay down by his side, and kissed the burning lips he
> pressed to mine for the last time. The fire of them,
> fierce beyond any I had ever felt, even in his loving
> moods, startled me, and as I slipped my hand from

under his head he gave a little sigh and became unconscious. The doctor came at once but no remedies prevailed against this sudden failure of the heart's action, and my husband died without regaining consciousness, before his last kiss was cold on my lips.

Charles Stewart Parnell died on 6 October 1891. Katie wanted him buried in Brighton but was prevailed upon to allow him a public funeral in Dublin. His coffin was brought to Ireland via Holyhead. A black cloth was drawn around the coffin as it lay on the lower deck of the ship the *Ireland*. A large green flag was draped over it.

Dublin was waiting to give Parnell a funeral the like of which had not been seen since that of Daniel O'Connell. When the ship docked at Kingstown Harbour a huge crowd stood silent and sombre in the rain, wearing black armbands tied with green ribbons. They watched in silence as the remains were transferred to the train for the short journey to Westland Row station. The coffin was then placed in a hearse, which moved through the streets in a steady downpour. Over a thousand members of the GAA, carrying hurleys tied with black and green ribbons, formed a guard of honour. As the cortege moved through the streets it halted at various points of historical significance along the way.

The first stop was in College Green at the old Irish Parliament building. The next pause was at St Michan's Church in Church Street where the first part of the funeral service was held. Then it moved to the City Hall where the coffin lay in state overnight in front of the statue of his great predecessor, Daniel O'Connell. Wreaths in great profusion were placed around the coffin and prominent among them was one of white lilies and laurel leaves from Catherine bearing the message 'My own true love, best, truest friend, my husband. From his broken-hearted wife.' Thousands of citizens had filed past the coffin before it was brought outside for the final part of its journey, which was attended by over two hundred thousand people.

Again accompanied by GAA members with hurleys, the cortege moved off up past Christchurch to a spot outside St Catherine's Church where Robert Emmet had been executed. Another halt was made at the house where Lord Edward Fitzgerald had been arrested.

From there the funeral proceeded to Glasnevin Cemetery to a plot not far from the grave of Daniel O'Connell. The second part of the funeral service was then read and the burial commenced. When the coffin was lowered into the grave the wreath from Katie was placed on top of it first. Then many mourners dropped flowers on the coffin in tribute.

The whole funeral had taken so long that the October evening was growing dark and a pale moon hung over the scene. And then, remarkably, as recorded by the Dunsink Observatory, a meteor of such brilliance that it lit up the sky like lightning was seen falling through the darkening sky, surely a fitting climax for the interment of 'The Chief'.

In spite of the enormous outpourings of grief and respect for the dead Parnell, his grave was scandalously neglected for many years. It was only in 1940 that a group of his faithful admirers organised the erection over his grave of a massive stone of Wicklow granite bearing the single word 'PARNELL'.

18

◎

THE DAWN OF THE
TWENTIETH CENTURY
1890 – 1916

In 1896 there arrived in Dublin a man who was destined to play a large part in the politics of the next century. James Connolly accepted an invitation to become the paid organiser of the Dublin Socialist Club. He was twenty-eight years old at the time and had already become deeply involved in the socialist movement in his native Scotland.

He was from a very poor family. His father was a carter, employed to remove manure from the streets of Edinburgh at night. At the age of fourteen, James enlisted in the Royal Scots Regiment of the British army where he spent almost seven years. (During his service on Spike Island in Cork harbour he guarded an Irishman the night before his execution. The experience is said to have turned him completely against the British establishment.) Strangely enough, all his army service took place in Ireland and he met his wife (Lillie Reynolds from Co. Wicklow) while he was in Dublin with the army.

Arriving in Dublin to take up his new position with the Socialist Club Connolly set up home with his wife and three daughters in a one-roomed tenement flat in Charlemont Street. Shortly afterwards along with seven like-minded socialists he formed the Irish Socialist Republican Party.

The aim of the new party was 'The establishment of an Irish Socialist Republic based upon the public ownership by the Irish people of the land and instruments of production, distribution and exchange.'

Connolly vigorously engaged in the great cultural revival, which was taking place at the time in Ireland but declared:

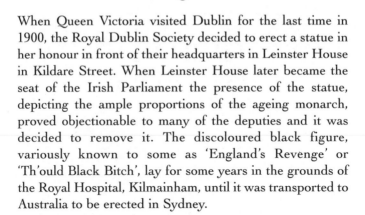

When Queen Victoria visited Dublin for the last time in 1900, the Royal Dublin Society decided to erect a statue in her honour in front of their headquarters in Leinster House in Kildare Street. When Leinster House later became the seat of the Irish Parliament the presence of the statue, depicting the ample proportions of the ageing monarch, proved objectionable to many of the deputies and it was decided to remove it. The discoloured black figure, variously known to some as 'England's Revenge' or 'Th'ould Black Bitch', lay for some years in the grounds of the Royal Hospital, Kilmainham, until it was transported to Australia to be erected in Sydney.

When Queen Victoria died in 1901 there were many manifestations of mourning throughout the city but when a vote of sympathy was proposed at Dublin Corporation it was defeated by 42 to 35 votes. Later a resubmitted motion only succeeded by 30 to 22 with many abstentions.

On Saturday 6 May 1905, a remarkable act of heroism was performed on Burgh Quay by Patrick Sheahan, a member of the Dublin Metropolitan Police. At the corner of Hawkins Street three workmen had been overcome by sewer gas in a deep tunnel beneath the road. With no thought for his own safety the constable descended into the shaft and rescued two of the victims before he himself was overcome. Before the rescue operation had finished one of the workmen and the constable had died and twelve rescuers had been affected by the gas. Medals for bravery were awarded to two firemen and thirty civilians who had taken part in the rescue efforts and a commemorative memorial to the heroism of Patrick Sheahan and the other rescuers was erected by the citizens of Dublin in 1906.

James Connolly was born in Edinburgh and at one time served in the British Army. The IRB military council met in his bedroom in Liberty Hall on Easter Sunday before the Rising.

If you could remove the English army tomorrow and hoist the green flag over Dublin Castle, unless you set about the organisation of the Socialist Republic, your efforts would be in vain. England would still rule you; she would rule you through her capitalists, through her landlords, through her financiers, through her usurers, through the whole array of commercial and individualist institutions she has planted in this country and watered with the tears of our mothers and blood of our martyrs, England would rule you to your ruin even while your lips offered hypocritical homage at the shrine of that freedom whose cause you have betrayed.

While Ireland was growing more and more nationalist Britain was becoming increasingly imperialist. The Golden Jubilee of Queen Victoria in 1897 was celebrated with great enthusiasm in Britain but in Ireland things did not go so smoothly. Anti-jubilee protests were widely held and in Dublin James Connolly led the opposition.

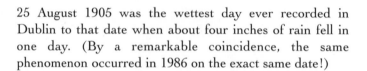

25 August 1905 was the wettest day ever recorded in Dublin to that date when about four inches of rain fell in one day. (By a remarkable coincidence, the same phenomenon occurred in 1986 on the exact same date!)

Well into the 1900s a sickening stench constantly hung over the city from all the back street abattoirs, tripe and offal houses. In 1916 there were still 200 dairies and up to 6,000 cows kept in the city.

In 1901 electric power was introduced to the city but although houses and streets were gradually lit by electricity the use of gas lighting was to last for many decades more.

In 1906 a Dublin coalman by the name of O'Carroll had a fine of ten shillings imposed on him because he did not have his name displayed on his cart in a 'legible' manner. He refused to pay the fine and had a ton of coal confiscated as a result. The fact that his name was clearly displayed in the Irish language carried no weight with the court.

In 1907 Ireland was probably the tenth richest country in Europe. Top salaries were about £2,000, while a labourer earned around £50 a year. Huge numbers were unemployed, however, and up to a quarter of Dublin's population lived in 22,000 single rooms. As many as 13,000 of the single rooms were occupied by three or more people. Rent for single rooms cost as much as three shillings a week.

Prostitution was widespread. In an area between Talbot Street and Amiens Street, known as 'Monto', there were a great number of prostitutes plying their trade. (The district got its name from one of its main streets called Montgomery Street.) The area always enjoyed a brisk trade from the British regiments based in the city but from *Ulysses* and other evidence it seems it was frequented by Dublin's citizens also.

A large screen was erected in the National Club in Parnell Square and it showed eviction scenes and photographs of men who had been executed or died in prison during Victoria's reign. Black flags bearing white inscriptions giving the numbers of those who died in the famine, the numbers of men jailed or forced to emigrate and the numbers of houses destroyed, were displayed by the protesters. The *Daily Mail*, reporting on a meeting of ISRP supporters, described one such flag as having silver-coloured letters showing that 1,500,000 people had starved during the famine, 300,000 had been evicted and over 400,000 forced to emigrate.

A 'jubilee' procession was organised by James Connolly for the next day in which the centrepiece was a big black coffin bearing the words 'British Empire'. The police attacked the procession, and a full-scale riot developed. When the procession reached the Liffey the coffin was thrown into the river to the shouts of 'Here goes the coffin of the British Empire. To hell with the British Empire.' Connolly was arrested and lodged in prison. The same evening the police baton-charged the crowd which was watching the magic lantern show at Parnell Square and a 75-year old woman was killed. The enraged crowd then roamed through the streets smashing the windows of any shop displaying jubilee decorations.

Later in the year republicans began organising commemoration committees to honour the men of '98 for the forthcoming centenary celebrations. The idea was enthusiastically endorsed by constitutional nationalists who managed to take over the main Dublin committee. Right-wing Catholics now began to support the movement.

Among the plans of the committee was the erection of a monument to Wolfe Tone. On 15 August 1898 an enormous crowd of 100,000 people assembled for the procession from Rutland Square to the St Stephen's Green entrance at the top of Grafton Street for the laying of the foundation stone. James Connolly brought out the first edition of his newspaper the *Workers' Republic* in time for the event. It carried the now famous slogan, 'The great appear great to us because we are on our knees.'

In October that year the Boer War broke out. Many Irish people supported the Boers against the British on the principle 'the enemies of Britain are our friends'. At a meeting in Dublin that month a large number people pledged support for the Boers and

———— ◎ ————

In 1907 the magnificent Fusiliers' Arch which stands at the
Grafton Street corner of St Stephen's Green was erected to
commemorate the men of the Royal Dublin Fusiliers who
died in the Boer War. The names of those who died are
inscribed on panels. (Some more nationalistic Dubliners
christened the archway 'Traitors' Gate'.)

The Fusiliers' Arch at the corner of St Stephen's Green at the
top of Grafton Street bears the names of Irishmen who died in
the Boer War.

———— ◎ ————

condemned the idea of Irishmen joining the British army to fight against them.

Later an Irish Transvaal Committee was set up to stop army enlistment. In December 1899 the committee tried to hold a meeting to protest against the visit of Joseph Chamberlain who had resigned from the Liberal Party because of its Home Rule policy. Chamberlain was to be given an honorary degree by Trinity College. The protest meeting was banned and the venue, Beresford Place, near the Customs House, was occupied by a large force of police beforehand. A huge crowd gathered in spite of the ban and when Maud Gonne, James Connolly and Arthur Griffith drove into the area on a horse-drawn brake, the crowd surged forward in welcome. The police dragged the driver off the brake and tried to lead the horses away but Connolly, drawing on his experience as a carter, took over the reins and drove through the police ranks. The cheering crowd then fell in behind the brake and the triumphant procession made its way through the Dublin streets, down O'Connell Street, over the bridge and up to College Green where Trinity College was roundly booed.

Maud Gonne, who was greatly admired for her beauty, became actively involved in the nationalist movement and founded *Inghinidhe na hÉireann* (Daughters of Ireland). She married and later divorced John MacBride who was executed in 1916. After 1922 she lived in Roebuck House, Clonskeagh until her death.

One of the worst ghettos of the poor was the area known as Ormond Market. This was the area on the north side of the Liffey bounded by Chancery Street, Arran Street, Ormond Quay Upper and Charles Street. At one time it was the centre of the retail meat trade but when that trade moved elsewhere the area became a warren of run-down tenements of the poor. The area contained 1,000 families and had only 130 houses to accommodate them. The St Vincent de Paul Society reported in 1912 that the area was unfit even for the stabling of animals. The houses were demolished that year and Dublin Corporation built proper houses for the poor.

In 1904 the speed limit was set at 20 miles an hour. Motor cars had to be registered for a fee of £1. They also had to display number plates. By 1913 the price of petrol rose to the equivalent of about 2p a litre in present day prices.

The first Irish Motor Show was held in the RDS in January 1907. It featured the only Irish-made motorcar, an eight-horsepower machine made by Chambers and Co. in Belfast It was on sale for £182, while other models were a six-horsepower Rover for £130 and a fourteen-horsepower Singer for £295.

In the same year a chauffeur was fined the then large sum of £25, for 'scorching through Grafton Street, College Green and Westmoreland Street at fully fifteen miles an hour'.

It was decided in 1909 to tar the streets of Dublin for the first time ever because of the increasing use of motor cars in the city.

Arthur Griffith was born in 1871 in Dominick Street and later lived at122 St Lawrence Road, Clontarf. He was a keen chess player. In 1904 he founded Sinn Féin (Ourselves Alone) at 6 Harcourt Street. He took part in the Treaty negotiations but died eight months later in 1922.

The campaign against Irishmen joining the British forces was proving very successful and Queen Victoria was now enlisted in the Government's counter-efforts. She first decreed that Irishmen in the army must wear the shamrock on St Patrick's Day. (A far cry from the days when they 'were hanging men and women for the wearing of the green'!) A state visit to Dublin was then arranged and she arrived on 4 April 1900 to be greeted by impromptu protest demonstrations. All copies of the *United Irishman* were seized because they carried an article by Maud Gonne critical of the 'famine queen'.

The authorities next laid on a free party in the Phoenix Park for 5,000 children from various Protestant schools throughout the city to celebrate the queen's visit, so Maud Gonne and her 'daughters' decided to set up a counter-jamboree for all the children who were not invited. Some months later, on Sunday 1 July 1900, over 30,000 children, led by pipe bands, marched to Clonturk Park in Drumcondra in a procession three kilometres long. As they marched along the children carried Irish, Boer and American flags

———— ◎ ————

Over two and three-quarters of a million people visited the Irish International Exhibition held in the fifty-two acres of Herbert Park in 1907. There were stands of over a thousand exhibitors displaying every kind of commercial and industrial product. Irish firms were represented by 583 stands, French stands numbered 278, English firms had 187 and other exhibitors came from Germany, Italy, Holland, Hungary, Japan and many other countries. A special attraction was a Somali village, complete with native villagers carrying spears and shields.

The exhibition was opposed from the start by nationalist organisations because they saw a threat to Irish firms from foreign competitors, particularly British ones. Catering for the event was given to J. Lyons of London and when it was decided to reduce the catering staff because of a fall-off in visitors, 200 Irish workers were sacked but 600 English workers were kept on.

Other bones of contention were some of the paintings on display in the Fine Arts section. One painting depicted the martyrdom of sixteenth-century Protestants by Catholic priests, while also on display was 'a couple of glaringly naked pictures' which shocked the delicate sensibilities of the visitors.

Among the distinguished visitors to the exhibition were King Edward VII and Queen Alexandra. They arrived on the royal yacht in Kingstown Harbour, accompanied by Princess Victoria. They came ashore on July 11 and after receiving an address of welcome from the loyal citizens of the town, made their way to the exhibition. There they proceeded around the exhibits. One of the events planned for the royal visitors was the conferring of a knighthood on William Martin Murphy, but the Lord Lieutenant, Lord Aberdeen, had not been told beforehand so there was no ceremonial sword available. Murphy had not been told either so he declined the honour!

———— ◎ ————

and sang songs such as 'God Save Ireland', 'O'Donnell Abu', and 'The Memory of the Dead'.

The pro-Boer campaign so annoyed the British authorities that over forty prominent nationalists, including eleven MPs were sent to prison for their political activities in 1901 and 1902.

In 1900 the Irish Parliamentary Party, up to now divided into the Parnellite and anti-Parnellite factions was re-united at last under a new leader, John Redmond. Redmond was a Parnellite, an upper-class Catholic and a graduate of Trinity College. Elected MP in 1881, he opposed Irish independence and instead sought Home Rule within the Empire.

In 1905 John Redmond lived at 7 Belvedere Place. His maiden speech in Westminster caused him to be suspended and forcibly removed from the chamber. His brother was killed in action in France during the First World War.

In 1900 a new organisation called *Cumann na nGaedheal* was established. The founders of the new body included Arthur Griffith, Maud Gonne and Major John MacBride, who had fought for the Boers, Tom Clarke, who had been imprisoned for his Fenian activity in England, and John Daly, who was mayor of Limerick. Their aims were to promote Irish economic resources and Irish culture.

———— ◎ ————

In December 1907 the *Freeman's Journal* carried a report on the death of one 'Banker' Patterson, who left £80,000 to charity when he died. 'Banker' made his money by giving loans of single shillings at one penny a week interest. He was illiterate and so miserly that he sat in the dark to save money, wore no trousers in summer, and his only possessions when he died were a cup, a plate and a knife.

———— ◎ ————

The theft of the so-called 'crown jewels' from Dublin Castle in July 1907 (at the time of the visit of Edward VII) is one of the great unsolved mysteries of the last century. The regalia of the Order of St Patrick were placed in the office of the Master of Arms on 15 March. The official in charge, the Ulster Knight of Arms, verified that they were still there on 11 June but when the safe was opened in July they had disappeared. The regalia, including the Grand Master's jewelled star and badge, to the total value of £30,000, had mysteriously vanished and the culprits were never caught.

———— ◎ ————

There was exceptionally bad weather during Horse Show week in 1910. The *Freeman's Journal* reported at the time:

> Rain, rain, rainclouds like dirty blankets, not a vestige of life in the air, underfloor inches of slush, beauty checked, restrained, marred, almost destroyed; not a horse in good humour, horsemen scowling and growling, not a bit of colour or picturesqueness about; nothing but a wearisome, monotonous, merciless downpour.

———— ◎ ————

In 1905 Griffith started a new organisation, which later became known as Sinn Féin. As the name 'Ourselves Alone' implies, its aim was self-reliance in all things. Part of its policy was the withdrawal of Irish MPs from Westminster, the setting up of Irish courts, civil service, stock exchange and central bank. It would also appoint Irishmen to represent Irish interests abroad.

In 1903 when King Edward VII visited Dublin the corporation refused to give him the customary address of welcome. His successor, George V, arrived in Dublin in 1911 to an equally chilly reception from nationalists – although the rest of the inhabitants were very enthusiastic. The various nationalist societies decided that they would erect a large banner across Grafton Street to register their disapproval. An application was made to the Dublin Paving Committee for permission to erect two large poles at the bottom of the street to carry the banner. Without asking what message the banner would display, the committee gave permission and dug the holes for the poles.

The societies prepared the banner carrying in gigantic letters the slogan 'Thou Art Not Conquered Yet, Dear Land'. On the night before the visit they hoisted it between the two poles. Next day when the authorities became aware of the message they dispatched workmen to remove the banner. But by then the damage had been done. Half of Dublin had seen it and the newspapers and photographers had recorded the message.

When Tom Clarke was released from prison in 1898 he had gone to New York and in 1907 he came back to Dublin. He opened a small newsagent's shop and soon attracted young political activists. Together they founded the *Irish Freedom*, a militant newspaper that preached the doctrines of the Irish Republican Brotherhood. The vibrant 'new' IRB recruited members from Sinn Féin, the Gaelic League and the Fianna, (a sort of revolutionary Irish Boy Scout organisation). Along with the growing nationalist movement, the early years of the century saw the intensification of the struggle for workers' rights and the attainment of votes for women.

The arrival of 'Big Jim' Larkin in Dublin greatly boosted the trade union movement. Born in Liverpool of very poor parents Larkin was outspoken in trade union matters from an early age. In 1909 the Irish Transport and General Workers Union was formed and over a thousand workers joined the first day. The ITGWU soon

————— ◎ —————

Larkin did not return to Ireland from America until 1923. He died in January 1947 and after a lying-in-state at the Thomas Ashe Memorial Hall in College Street an immense crowd attended his funeral to Glasnevin Cemetery. In 1980 a wonderfully dramatic statue of him with arms up-raised was erected in O'Connell Street opposite Clery's. One of the quotations inscribed around the base is 'The great appear great because we are on our knees; let us rise.'

James Larkin lived at various addresses in Dublin but died at 41 Wellington Road, Ballsbridge. His union, the Irish Transport and General Workers Union was founded in a tenement room in Townsend Street which had 'a table, a couple of chairs and a candle'.

————— ◎ —————

Tom Clarke was imprisoned for his Fenian activities
and later executed in 1916 for his part in the Rising.

became a force to be reckoned with in Dublin and was to play an
important role in subsequent events.

In 1911 2,000 women working in Jacob's Biscuit factory came
out in sympathy with ninety bakers who were on strike for better
wages and conditions. The success of this strike led to the
formation of the all-women's union, the Irish Women Workers'
Union. The leading spirits in this union were Jim Larkin's sister,
Delia, and Countess Markievicz. The new union soon had over a
thousand members.

The constitutional efforts to achieve Home Rule continued all
this time. The 1886 bill had been defeated in the English House of
Commons; the 1893 bill was passed by the Commons, but defeated
in the Lords. The third attempt at getting the measure passed saw
an enormous increase in tension in Ireland as the loyalists of the
North, with the active backing of the British Tory party, vowed to
resist Home Rule by force of arms if necessary.

In March 1912 a huge demonstration was held by nationalists in
Dublin. O'Connell Street was packed from one end to the other by
thousands who listened to speeches by John Redmond and others.

———— ◎ ————

The staging of John Millington Synge's *The Playboy of the Western World* in the Abbey Theatre in 1907 led to incredible scenes in the theatre. The fact that the play dealt with Irish peasant life, lauded by the Gaelic League as being 'morally' on a higher level than those of other parts of the country, made it a sensitive subject. Douglas Hyde maintained that Irish speakers were cleaner, more virtuous and more religious than others.

The play opened on 24 January and the following day the *Freeman's Journal* in its review said, 'a strong protest must be entered against this unmitigated, protracted libel upon Irish peasant men, and worse still on Irish peasant girlhood' and 'No adequate idea can be given of the barbarous jargon, the elaborate and incessant cursings of these repulsive creatures. Everything is b****y this or b****y that.'

The paper also published a letter from 'A Western Girl' which deplored the use in the play of the word 'shift'. The writer declared that the word, 'indicating an essential item of female attire' was one 'which the lady (Miss Sarah Allgood, who played the part of the Widow Quin) would probably never utter in ordinary circumstances, even to herself'.

The following Monday-night's audience was even more demonstrative. During the part of the play where Pegeen Mike is left alone with Christy Mahon a storm of protest broke out. Booing, shouting, the singing of 'God Save Ireland', shouts of 'Sinn Féin Forever' and banging on the seats with sticks, filled the theatre. One voice was heard to shout, 'Such a thing could not occur in Ireland.' The police were called and things quietened down but at the end of the play the audience started singing patriotic songs such as 'A Nation Once Again' and 'The West's Awake'.

Trinity students attended the next night's performance. When the play started there was such uproar that the police were again called. WB Yeats, who had earlier appealed for calm, ran up and down the aisles, pointing out trouble-makers to the police to get them ejected. One of these was Padraic Colum's father who was later fined forty shillings. Yeats was one of those who gave evidence against him.

The Wednesday performance saw further disturbance but by Thursday night, the more 'objectionable' passages were removed from the play and things quietened down after that. A police presence was maintained in the theatre, however.

———— ◎ ————

Constance Markievicz, the daughter of Sir Henry Gore-Booth, of Lissadell, Co. Sligo, was born in London, presented at Court, married a Polish Count and was sentenced to death for her part in the Easter Rising.

One of the speakers was Pádraig Pearse who gave the prophetic warning to Britain:

> . . . if we are tricked this time there is a party in Ireland . . . that will answer with the strong hand and the sword's edge. Let the *Gall* (English) understand that if we are cheated once more there will be 'red' war in Ireland.

On 11 April 1912 Henry Asquith introduced the third Home Rule Bill to a full House of Commons. The first and second readings were carried by approximately 100 votes each time in spite of the bitter opposition of the Tories. The bill then went to the committee stage when amendments could be considered.

Opposition to the bill came from another, unexpected, direction – the women's movement launched strong attacks on the bill because it did not give them the vote. (The meeting in O'Connell Street in March had been picketed by members of the Irish Women's Franchise League but their placards were torn up and the women were treated roughly by the demonstration's stewards.)

In June 1912 women from all over Ireland met in Dublin to demand equal rights for women. The meetings were addressed by Countess Markievicz and Delia Larkin. The same month eight women activists smashed windows in Government Buildings and were arrested and jailed because they refused to pay their fines. Their campaign did not end there. In July Asquith visited Dublin and two English suffragettes attacked the coach in which he and John Redmond were travelling. A hatchet thrown into the coach slightly injured Redmond in the face. Next the suffragettes started a fire in the Theatre Royal where Asquith was due to speak at a Home Rule meeting the following day.

The actions of these militant women sparked off mob violence against women in general and any respectably dressed woman was liable to be attacked as a suffragette. An open-air rally held by the Women's League to protest at Asquith's visit was surrounded by an angry mob that shouted 'Throw them in the river.' Several of the women, including Countess Markievicz, were injured in the violence which followed.

The two women who had attacked Asquith and Redmond were sentenced to five years' penal servitude in Mountjoy Jail. In August they, and four Irish suffragettes also in prison, went on hunger strike. The authorities resorted to force-feeding the women but after many weeks of the practice the authorities gave in and the two English women were released.

The Irish National Party was totally opposed to the women's movement for equality. Not only that but they supported the so-called 'cat and mouse' policy of the government whereby hunger-striking women-protesters would be released until they recovered their health and then subsequently re-arrested.

Meanwhile the ITGWU went on energetically organising the unskilled workers of the city. Most companies, with varying degrees of co-operation, had been organised but two remained un-recruited. Guinness' brewery workers were so well treated and had such good wages and conditions that there was no hope of recruiting them. The other company outside the 'fold' was the Dublin United Tramway Company owned by William Martin Murphy.

Murphy had made his money constructing tramways and railways in England and further afield. In Ireland he owned not only the Tramway Company, but also the *Irish Independent* newspaper, the Imperial Hotel and the largest department store in Dublin. Although he was not a bad employer he bitterly resented any attempt to organise his workforce. As a counter to the ITGWU he organised the employers of Dublin into the Dublin Employers Federation in 1911.

William Martin Murphy was a good employer but resented the unionising of his employees. He formed the Dublin Employer's Federation as a counter-measure.

He warned his employees not to join Larkin's union and in August 1913 he sacked 100 employees who had disobeyed him in joining the ITGWU. Then on 26 August, the day the Dublin Horse Show was to open, Larkin called out over 700 employees of the Tramway Company. The police reacted violently to the strikers and one man was killed in a melee. Larkin roundly condemned both the employers and the police. He was arrested for his 'seditious' speeches, brought to court and released on bail.

A meeting to be held in O'Connell Street the following Sunday, 30 August 1913, was banned by the authorities. Larkin refused to accept the ban and promised he would speak at the meeting. The police on the other hand were on the alert to arrest him if he showed up.

Larkin spent the Saturday night in the house of Countess Markievicz in Leinster Road, Rathmines and on Sunday morning the countess and some of her theatrical friends disguised Larkin as an elderly clergyman. Because Larkin's strong Liverpool accent would be easily recognised he was to pretend to be stone deaf; his 'niece' (a part played by one of the women) would answer any questions for her deaf 'uncle'. They booked rooms for the 'clergyman' and his 'niece' in the Imperial Hotel. The meeting was to be held in front of the GPO. Shortly after the meeting began Larkin stepped out onto the balcony in the front of the hotel and began to address the meeting to the cheers of the crowd. The police, however, were in the hotel and arrested him before he had a chance to say more than a few words. Other policemen charged the crowd in the street and after ferocious baton charges the crowd was dispersed, leaving over four hundred people injured.

On 2 September 1913 two four-storey tenement houses collapsed in Church Street, killing seven and injuring many more. The collapsed buildings had been occupied by more than forty people. The houses had been inspected a short time before and had been declared safe. An inquiry set up afterwards discovered that 87,305 people lived in similar tenements throughout the city and that most families had only one room each.

The day after the tenement collapse there was an enormous funeral for one of the men killed in the O'Connell Street riot. An inquest later found that he had been killed by a blow from a baton but, although several witnesses identified the policeman responsible, the jury refused to accept the evidence.

A few days later tension in the city increased when the employers, led by William Martin Murphy, organised a lockout of all employees who had joined the ITGWU. All over the city workers found themselves locked out, so that by the end of the week over 25,000 workers were out of work. Women working in Jacob's factory were sacked for refusing to remove their Women's Worker Union badges.

The lockout caused incredible hardship both to the workers and their families. The union headquarters at Liberty Hall was turned into a relief station, providing food and clothing for thousands of families.

The plight of the workers and their families was so desperate that a plan was conceived to send workers' children who were starving to sympathetic homes in England. The Catholic Archbishop of Dublin, Dr Walsh, immediately condemned the plan. In a letter to the Dublin papers he asked the mothers of the children if they had 'abandoned their faith'. He went on:

> I can only put it to them that they can no longer be held worthy of the name of Catholic mothers if they so far forget that duty as to send away their little children to be cared for in a strange land, without security of any kind that those to whom the poor children are to be handed over are Catholics, or indeed are persons of any faith at all.

A number of children were sent to England but on the morning of 22 October 1913 a number of priests and helpers invaded the Corporation Baths where about fifty children were being scrubbed prior to their departure to the boat at Kingstown. The priests managed to prevent thirty children from leaving but the women in charge did manage to set off for the boat with nineteen. They were pursued by the priests who, in the words of one of the number, 'following in the track of the little voyagers, captured ten of the party before the landing stage was reached, and ultimately induced the remaining nine, after they had gone aboard, to come ashore'.

Large numbers of Catholics, led by priests, picketed the evening sailing of the boats from Dublin's North Wall to England. When the last boat had sailed the crowd marched back along the quays singing 'Faith of Our Fathers' and other hymns.

Another attempt by Delia Larkin to take children by train from Amiens' Street station two days later was prevented by a group of priests and a band of young men. She was forced to seek refuge in Liberty Hall, while the priests and helpers continued their picketing along the quays each evening.

James Connolly, who had not been in favour of the scheme to send the children to England, now roundly condemned the archbishop for his attitude. He said that if he was as concerned for the bodies of the children as he was for their souls he would do everything he could to solve the labour dispute. Connolly announced that the scheme was now over, that the food station in Liberty Hall was being closed down and that the people should ask the archbishop and priests to provide for them. The archbishop was forced to appeal for funds and also that the dispute be settled. Connolly then quietly restarted the free meals in Liberty Hall.

The scheme to take starving workers' children to England was seen by many as a major tactical blunder by Larkin. It turned a large section of Catholic opinion against him. But he had other important things on his mind at the time. He was to go on trial on Monday 27 October 1913 for his 'seditious' speeches and he knew he would be sent to jail. He told an open-air meeting in the Phoenix Park that he was prepared for a sentence of anything up to two years' jail. He spoke of his campaign:

> For years and years I have done the work I was born for. I have proved there were 21,000 families living five-in-a-room in Dublin. Call that Catholicism, Christianity! It is something different. I have raised the morals and sobriety of the people. Even Murphy says Larkin has done good, but 'hands off the trams' (laughter). I have taken no man's honour or no woman's honour. I never stood in a public house bar and alcoholic drink never touched my lips. I am careful about my conduct because I know this cause requires clean men.

The next day he was sentenced to seven months in prison and brought to Mountjoy Jail under heavy armed guard. The following Sunday a huge protest meeting was held in London and among the speakers was George Bernard Shaw and James Connolly. In his speech Connolly asked that everyone work and vote against the Liberal Government until Larkin was released. He pointed to the absurdity of jailing Larkin for his 'seditious libel' when Carson and the Unionists were openly preaching treason and drilling a private army. Two by-elections were held shortly afterwards with disastrous results for the Liberals. Two days later Larkin was released from prison, having served only seventeen days of his sentence.

Next Larkin and Connolly appealed to the British TUC to refuse to handle Dublin goods but for tactical reasons the TUC refused their request. This effectively ended the dispute – the workers in Dublin saw no further hope of success and were forced back to work. The strike, however, had given the workers a new awareness of their power and the alliance which grew between workers, nationalists and intellectuals was to have a significant impact on future events.

By 1913 Larkin was the undisputed leader of the Dublin working classes. He lived as one of them. 'He had no property except three sons and a wife, and some sticks of furniture not worth £5.' His salary was two pounds and two shillings a week, which he handed over to his wife. The family lived in a tiny house in Auburn Street in Phibsborough, near the Royal Canal, for which he paid nine shillings a week in rent.

He was generous to a fault with workers who had fallen on hard times. As a teetotaller he frequently spoke of the harm that drink caused to the working classes. He berated those workers whose drinking left their wives and children short. He insisted that the wives and family be looked after first and then the men could have a drink. He also put a stop to the practice of workers being paid their wages in public bars with its obvious temptations.

Larkin regarded his union as something more than an organisation devoted to merely employment matters. With his sister Delia he actively promoted the social and cultural side of things. Choirs, dancing classes, Irish language lessons and dramatic society activities were all organised. He founded a fife-and-drum band and an Irish pipe band.

The greatest achievement in the social side of things was the rental of a house and three acres of land in Clontarf as a recreation centre for the workers and their families. A great day of festivities was held on a Sunday in August 1913 for the opening of Croydon Park. The park and Liberty Hall became the social centres for the workers' families during the lockout.

The defeat of the workers in the lockout did little to diminish the affection which they held for Larkin. They believed that it was the trade unions in England which had let them out. However, the weight of responsibilities finally wore him down. In June 1914 he offered his resignation as General Secretary of the Transport Union and made plans to return to Liverpool. A general meeting of all the membership was held in the Antient Concert Rooms (at the Westland Row end of present-day Pearse Street) to consider the matter. When speaker after speaker spoke of their loyalty and appreciation of him he agreed to withdraw his resignation.

Political activity did not cease, of course, during the years of labour troubles. In the middle of the lockout the ITGWU established the Irish Citizen Army to defend the workers. Another more 'nationally' minded force, the Irish Volunteers, was also founded in 1913. The formation of the Citizen Army was announced by Connolly at a rally to celebrate Larkin's early release from jail. In his speech he said:

> I am going to talk sedition. The next time we are out for a march, I want to be accompanied by four battalions of trained men. I want them to come with their corporals, sergeants and people to form fours. Why should we not drill and train our men in Dublin as they are doing in Ulster? But I don't think you require any training.

Thousands of recruits enrolled, among them, Countess Markievicz. The new army trained regularly in Croydon Park and soon became quite proficient in their defence of the workers against the police and employers. The example of Carson and the Northern Unionists in setting up their own army was a powerful incentive to the nationalists to do the same. The Irish Republican Brotherhood also started drilling in secret in Dublin and began buying a few rifles when funds permitted.

When the nationalists decided to imitate the Unionists they looked for a respectable figure to head-up their organisation. They chose Eoin MacNeill, a history professor at University College Dublin, who readily agreed to their request. On 11 November 1913 a preliminary meeting to establish the Volunteer force was held in Wynn's Hotel, Lower Abbey Street. Among the committee members elected were Roger Casement, Pádraig Pearse, Thomas MacDonagh, Eamonn Ceannt, Con Colbert and Joseph Plunkett – all of whom would be later executed for their part in the 1916 Rising. An enrolment meeting was called for the Rotunda on November 25 and the organisers were overwhelmed by the response. Over 10,000 men attended and signed up. More than 5,000 others had to wait for another day.

In April 1914, the women's organisation, which became known as *Cumann na mBan*, was also inaugurated in Wynn's Hotel. Their first objective was to aid the Volunteers by collecting money for the purchase of arms.

Meanwhile the Unionists in the North were stepping up their campaign for the exclusion of 'Ulster' from any Home Rule arrangement. Under intense pressure, Redmond reluctantly agreed that if one tenth of the voters in any county demanded it, that county would be able to vote itself out of Home Rule for a given number of years.

Redmond's concession dismayed nationalists throughout the country but it only stimulated people like Connolly, Pearse, Clarke and others to more radical solutions. The Irish Citizen Army, which had languished somewhat when the lockout ended, became invigorated. Larkin was elected chairman, Seán O'Casey, the playwright, was secretary and Countess Markievicz, treasurer.

A public meeting was held by the Citizen Army in Liberty Hall in March, which called on all members of the ITGWU to join. A new dark-green uniform and a slouch hat with the brim turned up and fastened with the badge of the ITGWU (which featured a red hand), were on display. The army strength grew till it soon had over a thousand men. Croydon Park proved extremely useful for drilling and rifle training. The 'Starry Plough' banner was adopted at this time.

When Larkin departed for America in 1914 James Connolly took over and from then on he was the dominant figure in the Labour movement.

With the imminent prospect of Home Rule and no agreement on Ulster's right to opt out, the question arose as to what the British army in Ireland would do if they were ordered to proceed against the Ulster Unionists to force them into Home Rule. The officers based in the Curragh Camp in Kildare were asked what their choice would be if they were ordered to move against Ulster or be dismissed. Sixty officers of the Cavalry Brigade led by General Gough said they would choose dismissal. The government backed down in the face of such opposition and the determination of the officers was never put to the test. The 'Curragh Mutiny', as it was called, never actually took place.

The Curragh Mutiny and the open landing of nearly 25,000 rifles and nearly two million rounds of ammunition for the Ulster Volunteer Force, without any interference from the authorities, sparked a surge of recruits to the Irish Volunteers. By the end of May 1914 they numbered nearly 130,000 men. The growth of the Volunteer army alarmed Redmond, who now sought to exert some control over the organisation. When Eoin MacNeill sought Redmond's approval for the Volunteer movement, the latter insisted on representation on the Volunteers' committee, otherwise he would create an alternative Volunteer movement. Eventually, to avoid a split, the Volunteer committee agreed to accept the Redmondite nominees.

The urgent need for guns and ammunition for the Volunteers resulted in a plan to purchase a consignment of 1,500 second-hand Mauser rifles and 45,000 rounds of ammunition in Hamburg. The conveyance of the arms to Ireland was entrusted to Erskine Childers, the son of an English father and Anglo-Irish mother. Childers was an expert sailor and had fought against the Boers in South Africa and his experiences there had changed him from being a Unionist to being a fervent nationalist.

The consignment of arms was brought out of Hamburg harbour on board a tug to a meeting point in the North Sea where Childers' yacht, the *Asgard* and another yacht, the *Kelpie* were waiting. Part of the cargo, 900 rifles, were transferred on board the *Asgard* and the other 600 were transferred to the *Kelpie*. On board the *Asgard* were Childers, his wife Molly, Mary Spring Rice, who was a Gaelic League supporter, an English army officer called Gordon Shepherd and two Donegal fishermen, Patrick McGinley and Charles Duggan.

The *Asgard* then sailed for Howth harbour, while the *Kelpie* sailed to Wales where its cargo was again transferred, this time to the *Chotah*, a steam-yacht which brought its cargo to Kilcoole in Co. Wicklow.

The *Asgard* took four weeks to complete its journey, running the gauntlet of gales and the British navy on the way. On Sunday 26 July the *Asgard* entered Howth Harbour and a body of Volunteers marched out from Dublin to meet it. Apart from some of the officers, they had no idea of the purpose of the march. One of the Volunteers who was not in on the secret was Arthur Griffith. Those who knew included Thomas MacDonagh, Bulmer Hobson and Cathal Brugha.

When the Volunteers realised what was afoot there was great

excitement and they rushed to the quayside so that the officers, who included Eamon de Valera, had great difficulty restraining them. It only took twenty minutes to land the cargo. The ammunition was taken away in motorcars to secret locations and a thousand rifles were handed out to the men. No bullets were issued.

The Volunteers had taken the precaution of cutting the telegraph wires but the authorities soon knew about the landing. The police and a detachment of the King's Own Scottish Borderers were sent to intercept the Volunteers. At Clontarf the marching Volunteers were stopped by the police and soldiers with fixed bayonets. Some of the police refused to obey orders to seize the rifles and were dismissed on the spot. The Volunteer leaders proceeded to parley with the police thus giving time to many of the Volunteers to disappear with their guns to safe hiding places. In all the police only confiscated nineteen rifles.

The news of the successful gunrunning caused great excitement in the city when the news spread. There was also great anger at the behaviour of the authorities when contrasted with the open connivance of the forces of the Crown in the Larne gunrunning in Ulster. The false rumour that some of the Volunteers had been bayoneted added greatly to the tension.

A crowd of men, women and children followed and jeered the Scottish Borderers as they marched back to the Royal (now Collins) Barracks at Arbour Hill. As they passed along Bachelor's Walk and neared the Halfpenny Bridge, stones and verbal abuse were showered on them. The officer in charge brought the troops to a halt. It was claimed later that the officer had intended warning the crowd that unless they stopped harassing his men he would order them to shoot. At the subsequent inquiry Alderman Byrne claimed that there was no stone throwing while an ITGWU official said he had seen more stone throwing at soccer matches in Belfast without interruption of the game. At any rate, the raised hand-signal of the officer in charge, Major Haig, was taken as an order to shoot. Several volleys rang out, leaving three dead and at least thirty-five wounded, fifteen seriously. One of the dead and several of the wounded were subsequently found to have bayonet wounds. An eyewitness claimed a woman had been shot at point-blank range by an officer.

The dead were later given a public funeral. The coffins were followed by Volunteers in military formation and a salute was fired over the grave. Within one month the Scottish soldiers, now scathingly called the 'King's Own Sons o' Bitches' were sent to the front in France and Belgium, where they found themselves, ironically enough, fighting alongside the Munster Fusiliers. Later efforts to erect a memorial to the victims of Bachelor's Walk were expressly forbidden by the chief of HM Forces in Ireland. Another twist to the whole affair was the withdrawal of a previous royal proclamation placing an embargo on the importation of arms. On 5 August 1914 one day after the declaration of the Great War the importation of arms into Ireland was again allowed.

19

◎

'A TERRIBLE BEAUTY IS BORN'
1916

The assassination of the Austrian Archduke Ferdinand in Sarajevo on 28 June 1914 precipitated World War I. When the British Government announced on 3 August that for all practical purposes Great Britain was at war with Germany, John Redmond immediately offered the unqualified support of nationalist Ireland. He said that Britain could safely withdraw every soldier from Ireland, that the country would defend itself against any foreign aggression and that nationalists and Unionists would unite in face of the common threat. (In fact, by the time the war ended over 300,000 Irish men and women had served in the British forces and about 35,000 Irish soldiers had been killed.)

Although Redmond's speech was received with warm applause from both sides of the House of Commons it was not universally approved in Ireland. Most did approve, particularly with the belief that at last Home Rule would be granted, but a section of Irish nationalists adhered to the old principle that 'England's difficulty is Ireland's opportunity'.

James Connolly spelled it out at a commemoration of the three workers killed during the 1913 lockout:

> If you are itching for a rifle, itching to fight, have a country of your own; better to fight for our country than for the robber empire. If you ever shoulder a rifle let it be for Ireland . . . Make up your mind to strike before your opportunity goes.

The Irish Republican Brotherhood (IRB) also saw an opportunity that should not be missed. Its Supreme Council decided that a rising should take place before the war ended – and no one

——— ◎ ———

The GPO in O'Connell Street had been first opened to the public in January 1818. At one time it had been suggested that the site should be used for the new Catholic Cathedral but the authorities did not think it appropriate to allow it in such a prime location.

After the 1916 Rising the GPO had to be practically rebuilt as only the front section was relatively undamaged. (Some bullet holes can still be seen there to this day.)

——— ◎ ———

During the rising in Easter Week various volunteers came forward to join the ranks of the garrison in the GPO and among them were two sailors, a Finn and a Swede, who knew very little English. Declaring that 'they had small nationalities and didn't like England' they asked that they be allowed to join the fight. They were given rifles and they actually took part in the fighting on the roof.

——— ◎ ———

On the afternoon of Easter Monday 1916 a column of elderly part-time soldiers had been out on a route march in the Dublin Mountains. These elderly soldiers were derisively known as the 'Gorgeous Wrecks' from the words 'Georgius Rex' on their belts. They all carried rifles but no ammunition and as they marched back into the city, unaware of what had happened since they had left that morning, they were suddenly shot at and five were killed and eight wounded.

——— ◎ ———

expected that the war would last four years. Tom Clarke and Seán Mac Diarmada (a Belfast tram conductor from Co. Leitrim, who had joined the movement in 1905) were given the responsibility for organising matters.

The following month on 9 September 1914 a special meeting of like-minded nationalists took place in the Gaelic League building in Parnell Square. Among those present were six out of the seven signatories of the proclamation of the Republic which would be issued two years later at Easter 1916: Thomas J Clarke, Seán Mac Diarmada, Pádraig Pearse, Joseph Plunkett, Eamonn Ceannt, and James Connolly. Others present included William O'Brien of the Citizen Army and Seán T O'Kelly who was later to become President of Ireland.

Meanwhile the Home Rule Bill was passed at last, but suspended for one year, or later if the war continued. Redmond accepted the arrangement and urged Irishmen to join the British army. In response, the original committee of the Irish Volunteers, composed mostly of IRB members, expelled the Redmondites from the committee. Tension increased between the two factions. When Redmond declared a public recruiting meeting at the Mansion House in Dawson Street for 25 September, Connolly proposed taking the building by force to prevent the meeting taking place. He had to abandon the plan when British troops armed with machine guns secured the building beforehand.

Pádraig Pearse was born at 27 Great Brunswick Street (now Pearse Street). As leader of the the 1916 Rising he read the Proclamation of Independence outside the GPO.

————— ◎ —————

About 150 women took part in the rising in Dublin; more than 30 served in the GPO. The most famous of course is Countess Markievicz but Maud Gonne, Kathleen Clarke, Nora and Ina Connolly, Áine Ceannt and Muriel MacDonagh all played an important part. The Citizen Army accepted women in its ranks more readily than did the Volunteers but de Valera was the only Volunteer commander who absolutely refused to have any women under his command.

————— ◎ —————

The gunboat *Helga*, which shelled Liberty Hall, had been built in Dublin and later became the Irish fishery protection ship the *Murchú*. During World War Two it served in the Irish Marine Service.

————— ◎ —————

At the execution of the leaders in Kilmainham Jail they were blindfolded and a piece of white paper or cloth was put on each chest as a target. The execution party passed their rifles behind them to be loaded and as one of the rifles was loaded with a blank round none of them knew for certain that they had shot anyone.

————— ◎ —————

Thwarted from the original plan, Connolly, Larkin and Countess Markievicz led several hundred members of the Citizen army from Liberty Hall in a protest march to Dawson Street.

It must not be forgotten, however, that those opposing the Redmond campaign were in a decided minority. Countrywide, over 180,000 members of the Volunteers sided with Redmond and only about 11,000 men opposed him, while in Dublin City the numbers 'for' were 2,375 and 'against' were 1,103.

Next the government introduced draconian methods to suppress any dissent. Civilians could be tried by court-martial for aiding the enemy and could be executed if found guilty. Newspapers, such as Connolly's *Irish Worker* and Griffith's *Sinn Féin* were banned and the printers were warned that any criticism of the government or the recruiting campaign would lead to their arrest and the closure of their premises. The *Freeman's Journal*, however, sided whole-heartedly with the army recruiting campaign. Although a nationalist paper it now vied with the pro-British *Irish Times* in its imperial fervour. To counteract this propaganda the banned newspapers reappeared under such titles as *The Worker*, *Nationality*, *Scissors and Paste*, and so on.

The first anniversary of the outbreak of the war led to a clash between the pro- and anti-war sympathisers. The first week of August 1915 was designated 'Dublin War Week' – a week of intense recruiting for the British army. But that same week the funeral of an old Fenian, Jeremiah O'Donovan Rossa took place. Rossa had suffered greatly in English prisons for his Fenian activities and when he died in America it was decided to bring him home to Ireland for a hero's funeral. The coffin lay in state in Dublin's City Hall and huge crowds gathered to pay homage as the funeral passed through the streets to Glasnevin Cemetery on 1 August 1915. Both Redmond's unarmed National Volunteers and the armed Irish Volunteers led by Pádraig Pearse in full Volunteer uniform and wearing a sword, agreed to marshal the crowds. At the graveside Pearse gave the famous speech which ended with the words:

> The Defenders of this Realm have worked well in secret and in the open. They think that they have pacified Ireland . . . They think that they have foreseen everything, think that they have provided against

everything; but the fools, the fools, the fools! – they
have left us our Fenian dead, and while Ireland holds
these graves, Ireland unfree shall never be at peace.

In September 1,200 armed Irish Volunteers marched through
Dublin in open display. The Citizen Army also engaged in
extraordinary manoeuvres. Led by Countess Markievicz, they
carried out a mock attack on Dublin Castle. Such activities and
various lockouts on the docks led to a great increase in the numbers
joining the Citizen Army. The campaign to recruit men for the
British army continued, however. William Martin Murphy
organised the employers to sack able-bodied men so that they
would be forced to join up or starve. While thousands did enlist in
the British army a steady stream of men also joined the Irish
Volunteers. That same year a large body of emigrant Irishmen in
England returned to Dublin rather than fight for the empire. They
set up a company of Irish Volunteers at a camp in Kimmage under
the name of 'Pearse's Own'.

The dilemma for the British Government continued into 1916.
The Volunteers were openly drilling, holding recruiting meetings,
marching in their green uniforms, or the belts and soft hats which
became a substitute for a uniform. They even carried out a mock
attack on the GPO in O'Connell Street in rehearsal for the real
thing which was to come later. The Volunteer executive issued a
warning that any attempt to disarm the men would be met with
force. At the same time it was important for the government to get
as many as possible to join the British Army. On the other hand the
Irish leaders such as Connolly, Pearse and Clarke were pressing for
bold action to awaken the dormant nationalism which they
believed still existed in the Irish people. Connolly, in fact, insisted
that the Citizen Army would, if necessary, take action on its own.
The great fear of the leaders was that if they delayed too long the
unrivalled intelligence system of the Royal Irish Constabulary
would discover all their plans.

Finally the Supreme Council of the IRB made the fateful
decision to start the rising on Easter Sunday, 23 April. Because of
the absolute necessity for secrecy, and because of the tendency of
Connolly to take precipitate action, the council actually decided to
arrest him and keep him under guard. Only the threat of action

against them by the Citizen Army and Countess Markievicz persuaded them to release him. His enthusiasm for immediate action was undiminished and from then onwards he was taken into the confidence of the Supreme Council of the IRB, even though he was never an IRB man.

The decision was kept such a closely guarded secret that not even men like Arthur Griffith, Bulmer Hobson (secretary of the Volunteers), The O'Rahilly (treasurer), Commandant JJ O'Connell (head of the military sub-committee) or Eoin MacNeill (Chief of Staff) were informed. (They were not told the plans because they maintained that the Volunteers should not take any action except in a defensive capacity.) Next the council appointed Pearse as Commander-in-Chief and Thomas MacDonagh told his adjutant, Eamon de Valera, about the plans.

Easter Sunday, 23 April 1916, was confirmed as the day of action and on 3 April Pearse issued orders for a three-day march and manoeuvres to be held by all the Volunteers for Easter Sunday in three weeks time. MacNeill, Hobson and others were becoming suspicious by this time and MacNeill demanded that no action should be taken without his permission. To preserve the secret the council gave him that assurance because they knew he had the power to wreck the whole enterprise.

On Wednesday 19 April a curious document was published which, it was alleged, had come from the Castle authorities and which showed that they planned to arrest all the leaders of the Volunteers. The document, which became known as the 'Castle Document', had almost certainly been forged by Seán Mac Diarmada and Joseph Mary Plunkett with the intention of providing an excuse for the rising and strengthening the resolve of any waverers among the leadership.

Next some alterations in the Rising plans were made. It was decided that Easter Monday (and not Easter Sunday) would be the day because the Fairyhouse Races on Easter Monday would be sure to take large numbers of English army officers out of the city.

The plans called for a force of about 3,000 men of the Volunteers and the Citizen Army to take immediate action in Dublin. A simultaneous uprising was to take place in the rest of the country. Precise and detailed plans were made for the occupation of strategic buildings and positions throughout the city to contain the

British forces and prevent reinforcements arriving. The plans were daring but impractical in the event, as the numbers required to carry them out successfully were never available.

A week before the planned Rising a Provisional Revolutionary Government of seven men was constituted, and a Proclamation of the Irish Republic was printed. Each of the seven members of the 'Revolutionary Government' signed the proclamation: Thomas Clarke, Pádraig Pearse, Seán Mac Diarmada, Thomas MacDonagh, Eamonn Ceannt, James Connolly and Joseph Plunkett.

By Holy Thursday the suspicions of those leaders not in on the plans led them to confront Pearse with their fears that something more than routine manoeuvres was involved. Pearse told them then that a rising was intended. MacNeill was enraged and told Pearse that he would do everything he could, short of telling the authorities, to stop the rising.

He issued orders giving Bulmer Hobson control of all the Volunteers in the city and cancelling every order not made personally by himself or Hobson. (MacNeill's countermanding order was conveyed to Limerick by The O'Rahilly on Easter Sunday but when he heard that the Rising had started he immediately returned to Dublin to take part.) However, Pearse, MacDonagh and MacDermott managed to persuade MacNeill on Friday morning to countermand his orders because a large shipment of arms was arriving from Germany which would greatly increase their chances of success. Unknown to any of the leaders at the time was the fact that the gunrunning ship, the *Aud*, had already been captured.

By Saturday morning, the Dublin Castle authorities knew of the *Aud*'s capture and later that day the Volunteers leaders heard the bad news. MacNeill once more changed his mind and sent out messages at midnight on Saturday to Volunteers throughout the country that no manoeuvres were to take place. He also asked the *Sunday Independent* to print this message the following day:

> Owing to the very critical position, all orders given to Irish Volunteers for tomorrow, Easter Sunday, are hereby rescinded, and no parades, marches, or other movements of Irish Volunteers will take place. Each individual Volunteer will obey this order strictly in every particular.

The message was read with consternation and anger by Volunteers throughout the city. Early that morning the Military Council met in Liberty Hall and in spite of the setbacks and confusion they decided to go ahead with the original plans. The Rising would take place in Dublin on Easter Monday at noon. Orders were sent out to country units confirming MacNeill's order but Volunteers in Dublin were all ordered to remain in the city.

The following order was conveyed to the Dublin battalions: 'The four City Battalions will parade for inspection and route march at 10.00 a.m. today.' It was signed by Thomas MacDonagh, Brigade Commandant, and countersigned by Pádraig Pearse.

On Easter Monday morning about 1,200 Volunteers and 200 members of the Citizen Army answered the order. They marched through the Dublin streets in small companies, the officers and many of the men wearing the green Volunteer uniform. All carried arms. The sight of marching men was such a common sight that little attention was paid to the companies led by Pearse and Connolly as they marched up O'Connell Street to the GPO. Here they halted and the order was given to take over the building. No opposition was encountered inside the GPO. The few British troops inside surrendered without a fight. The reason became clear when they were called upon to hand over their ammunition – they revealed that they had none!

Next all the corner houses commanding the approach roads to the GPO were taken over by snipers, who were hidden behind sandbags. The four corner houses of Abbey Street were likewise commandeered. Kelly's ammunition shop, which stood at the corner of Bachelor's Walk, and Hopkin's jewellery shop on the corner of Eden Quay were also taken over in the same way.

A green flag bearing the words 'Irish Republic' was hoisted over one corner of the GPO and the Irish tricolour was raised at another. Across the street a flag showing a plough and stars was raised over the Imperial Hotel. (Seán O'Casey's play *The Plough and the Stars*, about the events of Easter Week, was later to be the cause of much controversy.)

Next Pearse went outside the GPO and read the proclamation declaring Ireland to be a republic. All the signatories of the proclamation except Thomas MacDonagh and Eamonn Ceannt were among the occupiers of the GPO.

Inside the GPO the Volunteers made improvised 'sandbags' by stuffing mailbags with paper, rubbish, coal, and anything else they could get their hands on. The windows were smashed to allow the Volunteers to see and fire at their attackers. Some windows were barricaded with wax dummies taken from an exhibition in nearby Henry Street; consequently some of the GPO 'defenders' were King George V, Queen Mary and Lord Kitchener!

The first casualties of the Rising was a party of Lancers riding down O'Connell Street just after the GPO was occupied. They were totally unaware of the occupation of the building until they were suddenly shot at. Four of the Lancers were shot dead

Other buildings throughout the city were also earmarked for occupation. The Citizen Army quietly took over St Stephen's Green, closed the gates and began digging trenches. Later on Tuesday when they came under heavy fire from high houses around the Green they withdrew to the College of Surgeons on Stephen's Green West and Little's public house on the corner of Cuffe Street.

The South Dublin Union in Mount Brown was taken by the Fourth Battalion under Eamonn Ceannt and Cathal Brugha after a stiff fight and the Mendicity Institute on the quays was taken by Seán Heuston and his men. Boland's Mill was occupied by de Valera's battalion to hold the line at the canal and also because it commanded the area from Westland Row to Beggars Bush barracks. His troops also took over the buildings commanding Mount Street Bridge. Jacob's Biscuit Factory in Bishop Street was occupied by Volunteers under Thomas MacDonagh and Major John MacBride, mainly for the large supplies of food it contained. Davy's pub at Portobello Bridge was also occupied. The Volunteers occupying the factory were jeered by hostile crowds waving Union Jacks and calling them cowards for not going to fight in France. The Four Courts was occupied by Commandant Edward Daly. Other places taken over were the railway stations at Harcourt Street and Westland Row.

A group of Volunteers took over the Magazine Fort in the Phoenix Park by the simple ruse of pretending to play a football match beside the fort and when they went to retrieve the football which was 'accidentally' kicked near the sentry, they overpowered him and took over the fort. They failed to get the main store of arms however and an explosion they set off to destroy the fort was only partially successful.

One important position not taken was Dublin Castle. Part of the Citizen Army had been detailed for that task but so few men turned up that it was decided not to occupy it but to try to prevent any soldiers leaving it. Unknown to the insurgents there was only a small group of soldiers under the command of a corporal guarding the Castle and it could have been taken easily. A policeman on duty was shot dead but when the soldiers on guard duty returned fire the attackers were driven off. So instead of taking the Castle the small Citizen Army group occupied the City Hall and some other buildings nearby.

There were about twelve hundred British troops in various barracks in the city at the time and when news of the rising reached England two brigades were sent over to Kingstown so that by Tuesday the British army strength in the city was about five thousand.

Trinity College became a British garrison manned by the students of the College Officers' Training Corps. By Wednesday a line of British army posts stretched from Trinity to Dublin Castle and to Kingsbridge Station. This effectively divided the insurgent army in two.

By Wednesday the British had managed to get the gunboat *Helga* into position on the Liffey near the Customs House and they attempted to shell Liberty Hall. They were unsuccessful at first as the shells only fell on the Loopline Bridge. They then tried further downstream but this time the shells fell in the Phoenix Park. Finally they brought guns to the corner of Tara Street and George's Quay and managed to destroy the building.

Then, together with artillery pieces in the grounds of Trinity College, they started shelling other rebel strongholds. The GPO was badly hit and the upper storey destroyed. Several other buildings in O'Connell Street were also demolished or set on fire with incendiary shells.

Later that same Wednesday evening, battalions of the Sherwood Foresters arrived in Kingstown. One column approached the city by the Stillorgan Road and met little opposition. Another column came in by Ballsbridge and met fierce resistance from de Valera's Third Battalion. He had ordered a flag to be raised on an empty distillery building and the strategy worked in drawing enemy shell-fire. Men were placed in houses in Northumberland Road and houses at the corners of Haddington Road. Seven men occupied Clanwilliam House commanding Lower Mount Street Bridge. As the Foresters approached along the route they were met by devastating fire. By the time they had taken the bridge eighteen officers and two hundred and sixteen other ranks had been killed and wounded. In spite of such spirited resistance the British forces advanced gradually and inexorably on the rebel strongholds.

James Connolly was wounded on Wednesday when he ventured from the GPO into Prince's Street to dispatch a squad to Abbey Street. Almost at once a shot from a sniper shattered his ankle. He was carried back into the GPO and even though he was seriously wounded he later insisted on being brought around on a stretcher to supervise operations.

On Thursday the British troops started to shell O'Connell Street from a nine-pounder gun positioned at Trinity College. Because they were using incendiary shells the effect was devastating. By evening the Imperial Hotel (with Clery's department store on the ground floor), the Royal Hibernian Academy, Elvery's Sports Shop, the offices of the *Freeman's Journal*, and many other buildings were engulfed in flames. The heat was so intense that the windows in the GPO began to scorch and show signs of going on fire. The men inside had to continually douse them with water. Eventually everyone had to be withdrawn from the front of the building except those fighting to prevent the building going up in flames.

By Friday the task was hopeless and by evening the whole building was in flames and no longer capable of being defended. The garrison was called together and told to prepare to evacuate the building. The plan was to dash out a side door into Henry Street, make their way up Moore Street and occupy the Williams and Woods Jam Factory in Parnell Street.

The first group to try the manoeuvre was led by The O'Rahilly. He led a small group out the door and was to report back about conditions in the streets. He never did, for he was shot dead in Moore Lane.

Pearse stood beside the door as the men took turns to leave the burning building. As the last contingent made their way out into Henry Street they came under fire from British troops in Moore

Lane. Plunkett and Mac Diarmada rallied the men and a van was dragged across the opening for some protection. Pearse stumbled as he ran but managed to reach Moore Street unscathed. Connolly was carried out safely on a stretcher.

The group then occupied a house at the end of Moore Street and spent that Friday night breaking down the connecting walls of the houses in an effort to tunnel their way up to Parnell Street but could get no further than Number Sixteen. Here they established their headquarters.

On Saturday morning they held a consultation around Connolly's stretcher and agreed that the situation was hopeless. They sent a message to the British commanding officer that they wished to surrender. A young nurse, Elizabeth O'Farrell, carrying a white flag, brought the message to the British barricade in Parnell Street. She brought back the demand for unconditional surrender. The order she took back to the group was as follows:

> Carrying a white flag, proceed down Moore Street, turn into Moore Lane and Henry Place, out into Henry Street, and around the Pillar to the right hand side of Sackville Street, march up to within a hundred yards of the military drawn up by the Parnell Statue, halt, advance five paces and lay down arms.

At half past three on Saturday afternoon of Easter week Pearse surrendered his sword to Brigadier-General Lowe at the British post in Parnell Street. He also sent Elizabeth O'Farrell with an order of surrender to the other Republican commanders. James Connolly countersigned the order to units of the Citizen Army, as he knew they would obey no one else. The order was dated Saturday 29 April 1916 at 3.45 p.m.

One by one all the rebel positions were surrendered, although the men in Jacob's biscuit factory held out until 3.00 p.m. on Sunday afternoon. The men in the South Dublin Union under Eamonn Ceannt were also reluctant to give in but when he told them that the veteran Tom Clarke was surrendering they agreed to do likewise.

Many of the surrendering Volunteers were taken to the open ground in front of the Rotunda hospital. There Seán Mac Diarmada addressed them and praised them for their courage. The prisoners were kept out in the open all night and the next morning were marched down O'Connell Street to College Green and up Dame Street, Thomas Street and James' Street to Richmond Barracks (Keogh Square) in Kilmainham. The injured Connolly was taken to Dublin Castle.

Once they arrived in the barracks detectives from the Dublin Metropolitan Police (DMP) separated the leaders from the rest of the men. Among the leaders were Tom Clarke, Seán Mac Diarmada, Thomas MacDonagh, Pádraig and Willie Pearse, Eamonn Ceannt, Joseph and George Plunkett and Michael Collins. Generally speaking most of the prisoners were treated with some leniency; only the leaders faced court martial. The rank and file were taken to be interned in various camps in England and Wales. As they were marched to the boats they had to run the gauntlet of abuse from many of Dublin's citizens. 'Shoot the bastards!' and 'Traitors' was a frequent cry. The story is told of one prisoner who, having passed through a mob howling insults at him and his companions, on being asked if he hoped to be released by the military, replied, 'Bejasus, I hope not!'

At the same time there was quite a lot of support for the rebels, particularly among the poor of the city. One woman told a journalist, 'Sure we cheer them. Why shouldn't we? Aren't they our own flesh and blood.'

Wholesale looting occurred in the city during the Rising. With the start of hostilities on Monday the DMP were withdrawn and this was taken as a signal for the poor to descend on O'Connell Street, Henry Street, Grafton Street, Camden Street and other shopping areas. Everything that could be carried was taken away. Clery's was denuded of its stocks. People filled sacks with whatever they could find. Women fought over fur coats, dresses, bales of cloth and furniture. One man donned a dress-suit and walked away carrying a set of golf clubs. An army of children laid siege to Noblett's sweet shop at the corner of North Earl Street. Men and women fought each other for bottles of whiskey and stout from ravaged public houses. One woman offered some of the Volunteers in the GPO bottles of stout. All refused except one and just as he was about to drink, an officer dashed the bottle to pieces and announced that the next man found taking a drink would be shot without warning.

Young boys stole footballs and sporting equipment from Elvery's Sports Shop. A boy was observed in Talbot Street striking a tennis ball with an expensive golf club while wearing a new suit many sizes too big for him. Every so often he would follow the flight of the ball through a fine pair of new binoculars. One woman and her daughter were arrested while carrying two hair mattresses, one pillow, one pair of corsets, eight window curtains, one quilt, one topcoat, two ladies' coats, half a dozen ladies' hats and four chairs! The B and I Steampacket Company suffered the loss of £5,000 worth of goods – a colossal amount in those days.

A well-known and tireless pacifist called Francis Sheehy-Skeffington tried to organise some citizens to prevent the looting. On his way home on Tuesday evening he was arrested by Captain Bowen-Colthurst and taken to Portobello Barracks. Later that night Bowen-Colthurst brought him out with his patrol as a hostage. He was told that if the patrol was shot at, he would be shot dead.

Then Bowen-Colthurst arrested two editors, Thomas Dickson of the *Eye-Opener* and Patrick McIntyre of the *Searchlight* and brought them to Portobello Barracks also. The next morning he ordered that Sheehy-Skeffington and the two journalists be shot. Their bodies were buried in sacks in the yard of the barracks that night. (In May the bodies were reburied in consecrated ground.) Two days later Bowen-Colthurst raided Mrs Sheehy-Skeffington's home and placed herself and her seven-year-old son under arrest. The object of the raid was to find evidence that might justify the murder. (Bowen-Colthurst was later court-martialled in June and found guilty but insane. He was imprisoned in Broadmoor Criminal Mental Asylum but was released in 1922. He emigrated to Canada and died there in 1966.)

The Rising had proved costly. The official figure for those killed or severely wounded was 1,351 people. Many parts of the city, especially O'Connell Street, lay in ruins. Nearly 3,500 men and eight women were arrested. Of these 1,836 men and five women were interned in England and Wales.

Many of the civilian casualties were sustained by people braving the bullets in search of food. Tending the wounded in the streets was also a dangerous activity – a nurse and an ambulance worker were killed. Bodies had to be dug out of the rubble of demolished buildings, only to be buried under equally distressing circumstances. Only one mourner was allowed per coffin and the coffin itself was often subject to searches for hidden arms.

Decomposing carcasses of horses and unburied, or poorly buried, corpses posed a great threat to public health. Many shallowly buried bodies of soldiers were discovered and handed over for reburial to the military authorities. Coffins were so scarce that many bodies were left lying in the city morgue. Over sixty unidentified bodies taken off the streets were taken to pits behind Dublin Castle for burial. Many of these were later claimed by relatives and were given a proper burial.

The Rising interrupted milk and food deliveries, closed shops and cut off gas supplies. The take-over of Boland's Mill by the rebels affected the bread supplies. During the week of the Rising the insurgents tried to distribute loaves but to little effect. After the surrender thousands of loaves still in the bakery were distributed freely among the poor of the district.

For the leaders of the Rising retribution was swift and they were shot one by one. Pádraig Pearse, Thomas MacDonagh and Thomas Clarke were tried by court martial and shot at dawn on Wednesday 3 May in the yard of Kilmainham Jail.

Joseph Plunkett was also sentenced to death and married his sweetheart Grace Gifford in Kilmainham Jail the evening before he was shot. On Thursday 4 May he, Edward Daly, William Pearse (Pádraig's brother) and Michael Hanrahan (MacDonagh's second-in-command at Jacob's factory) were executed; Major MacBride on 5 May; and Eamonn Ceannt, Michael Malin, Con Colbert and Seán Heuston on 8 May.

Countess Markievicz was also sentenced to death but the sentence was commuted to penal servitude for life. Eamon de Valera was one of the last leaders to surrender and he too was sentenced to death on 10 May. But his connections with America and the widespread revulsion and anger at the executions, which spread throughout the country and abroad, led to his sentence being commuted to penal servitude for life. Finally, on Friday 12 May, Seán Mac Diarmada and James Connolly were executed. Connolly, who was being held in Dublin Castle and was dying from his wound which had become infected, was carried on a stretcher to an ambulance and brought to Kilmainham Jail. There he was put sitting on a chair at the opposite end of the stone-breakers yard from where the others had been shot and was executed. In all ninety-four leaders were sentenced to death but only fifteen were executed.

The newspapers and the general public took to calling the rising the 'Sinn Féin Rebellion' because so little was known about the real leaders that connection with the Sinn Féin movement seemed the only explanation. (In fact the Sinn Féin organisation played little part in the Rising and as already stated, Griffith was unaware of the planned rising beforehand.)

Pearse had spoken about a blood sacrifice being needed and the night before he was executed Tom Clarke told his wife that they had struck the first blow for Ireland's freedom but he added prophetically 'Between this moment and freedom, Ireland will go through hell.'

Many of the businesses closed during the Rising reopened by 5 May. Gas supplies were restored by 10 May and trams were running again by 14 May. Cinemas and theatres gradually reopened and the curfew was postponed to midnight by 14 May. The pubs, which had been ordered to close during the executions, were allowed to resume business but had a closing time of 8.00 p.m. on weekdays.

The execution of the leaders of the Rising was a major blunder on the part of the British forces. The attitude of the Dublin populace changed from one of indifference, if not outright hostility, to a tide of sympathy for the insurgents. Picture postcards of the executed leaders were in nearly every shop. A large portrait of Pádraig Pearse in one shop window drew great crowds. Street urchins sold leaflets containing the 'last and inspiring speech by Thomas MacDonagh'.

The Prime Minister, Henry Asquith, visited Dublin on 12 May to assess the situation for himself. He halted the executions and returned to England convinced of the urgent need for a settlement. (There was some evidence that General Maxwell ignored a telegram from Asquith to halt the execution of Connolly.) Roger Casement meanwhile was brought to London and went on trial on June 26 in the Old Bailey. He was found guilty and hanged on 3 August.

Roger Casement, born at 29 Lawson Terrace, Sandycove, spent much of his early life working in Africa and Brazil for the British Consular Service. While there he wrote scathing reports exposing the appalling conditions of workers in the rubber industry and was eventually knighted in 1911.

Returning to Ireland in 1913, Casement espoused the nationalist cause. Before the Easter Rising of 1916 he went to Germany to raise arms for the rebels. Arms were eventually despatched on the *Aud*.

Casement later became convinced that the rising would not be a success and decided to return to Ireland to persuade the leaders to call it off. He landed by German U-boat in Tralee Bay on Good Friday, 21 April 1916. He was captured the next morning and a Berlin railway ticket was found in his pocket. Executed on 3 August 1916 in Pentonville Prison, Casement was the sixteenth man of WB Yeats' famous poem 'Sixteen Dead Men'.

His body was later brought back to Dublin in 1965 and interred in Glasnevin cemetery.

20

◎

AFTER THE RISING
1916 – 1922

The prison camps provided fertile conditions for the development not only of the IRA but also the more secretive Irish Republican Brotherhood (IRB). One of the most active organisers was a young man from Cork named Michael Collins. He had taken part in the Rising and had fought in the GPO.

Michael Collins lived at numerous addresses around Dublin but claimed 1 Brendan Road, Donnybrook, as his main address. In spite of being at the top of the authorities' wanted list he moved freely around the city.

The IRB was also reorganised in Dublin by Kathleen Clarke, widow of the executed leader Thomas Clarke. At Christmas 1916 most of the prisoners were released and the IRB replaced the provisional council with a Supreme Council. Some crucial

In 1918, just before the First World War ended, a German submarine sank the Dublin–Holyhead mailboat, *Leinster*, just outside Dun Laoghaire harbour. The ship was carrying almost 500 British soldiers at the time. The total number of lives lost in the disaster was 501.

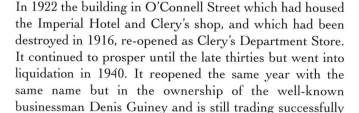

Before the British troops were withdrawn from Ireland an event occurred in April 1920 which became known as the 'Portobello Affray'. About 250 soldiers of the Berkshire Regiment attended a show in the Theatre Royal and afterwards walked along Burgh Quay shouting 'Down with de Valera' and 'Down with Sinn Féin'. They then marched back to Portebello Barracks, annoying and insulting any citizens they met on the way. By the time they reached their barracks a sizeable crowd had gathered and a serious riot developed. Two people were killed and nineteen were injured.

In 1922 the building in O'Connell Street which had housed the Imperial Hotel and Clery's shop, and which had been destroyed in 1916, re-opened as Clery's Department Store. It continued to prosper until the late thirties but went into liquidation in 1940. It reopened the same year with the same name but in the ownership of the well-known businessman Denis Guiney and is still trading successfully today.

by-elections were held in the first half of 1917 and the success of candidates standing for the revitalised Sinn Féin astounded the country and shocked the Redmondites. These victories further helped to influence Irish public opinion, so that when the remaining prisoners were released in July 1917 they were welcomed home by huge crowds waving Republican tricolour flags in the streets of Dublin.

One of the released prisoners was Eamon de Valera and when he stood for election in East Clare he had a resounding victory. Even though the elections were for seats at Westminster the Sinn Féin candidates stood for an abstentionist policy.

The Castle authorities continued to harass the Volunteers and eighty-four men were arrested in August 1917. Among them was Thomas Ashe, who had led a detachment of Volunteers in a battle against armed police in Ashbourne, Co. Meath, during the Easter Rising. He had been later sentenced to death but released with the other Volunteers. On this occasion he was sentenced to one year's hard labour in Mountjoy Jail. In September the Republicans demanded that they be treated as prisoners of war. The demand was refused. The prisoners then went on hunger strike. Ashe was forcibly fed and died as a result on 25 September 1917.

His funeral became the latest in a long line of great public funerals through the streets of Dublin. His body, dressed in Volunteer uniform, lay in state in City Hall. A Volunteer Guard of Honour stood around the coffin as thousands filed past to pay their respects. As the funeral procession passed through the streets countless thousands lined the pavements. The procession was led by armed Volunteers commanded by de Valera, over 200 priests and representatives of every nationalist organisation. 30,000 people followed the hearse. In Glasnevin cemetery three volleys were fired over Ashe's grave and Michael Collins, dressed in full Volunteer uniform, gave the oration.

In March 1918 John Redmond died. His life-long service to his country was largely forgotten, particularly by those who espoused the physical-force method of righting wrongs, but modern Ireland is more inclined to acknowledge the debt it owes to a devoted son.

The Irish Volunteers greatly increased in numbers during the succeeding months and soon were estimated to number between 50,000 and 60,000 throughout the country. But things did not go their way politically all the time. The Sinn Féin party lost three by-elections in a row in early 1918. But then the British made a massive blunder; they announced that conscription would be applied to Ireland. Despite wholesale protest and opposition all over Ireland the bill was passed in the House of Commons on 16 April 1918 by 301 votes to 103. The Home Rule party members walked out in protest. In the event conscription was never introduced in Ireland and Sinn Féin got the credit for that rather than the Home Rule party.

The fury of the protests in Ireland led the authorities to believe another rising might take place. In May 1918 they arrested scores of Sinn Féin leaders, including Eamon de Valera, Countess Markievicz, Arthur Griffith and Kathleen Clarke. They were deported to England and interned. To appease American opinion the authorities claimed to have discovered a 'German plot'.

A general election took place on 14 November 1918 for the first time in eight years. The Sinn Féin candidates had an overwhelming victory, helped immeasurably by impersonation and vote rigging by their supporters it must be said. The old Home Rule party was practically wiped out. Sinn Féin won nearly three-quarters of the seats: Sinn Féin 73 seats, Unionists 25 seats, and the Home Rule party 6 seats. Those successful Sinn Féin candidates not in jail met in Dublin in the Mansion House in Dawson Street on 7 January 1919. Twenty-six elected candidates were present. They decided to convene *Dáil Éireann* (Assembly of Ireland), 'an Irish Parliament for a sovereign independent Irish Republic'.

The first Dáil met amid great excitement in the Mansion House on the afternoon of 21 January. The house was packed and the deputies were cheered as they arrived. When the role call was made the constant refrain in answer was 'In a foreign prison'. In the case of the Unionists the response was simply 'Absent'.

On that very first day of the new Dáil Éireann, nine Volunteers, led by Dan Breen and Seán Tracey, shot dead two policemen, Constables Mac Donnell and O'Connell, who were guarding a cart carrying gelignite to a quarry at Soloheadbeg in Co. Tipperary. Both constables were Catholics and one was a widower with four children. The terrorist action had not been ordered by the leadership but it proved to be the beginning of a bitter two-and-a-half-year guerrilla war.

In February de Valera escaped from Lincoln Prison in England and at the Dáil meeting in April he was elected president.

In March 1919 Volunteers of the Dublin Brigade attacked Collinstown Aerodrome (now the headquarters of Aer Rianta) and seized a large amount of arms and ammunition. More incidents occurred, month after month, throughout the country in which men were killed on both sides. Martial law was declared in various parts of the country, so that Ireland was approaching a state of war.

The guerrilla campaign, led by Michael Collins and Cathal Brugha, became highly organised and run on military lines. Police barracks all over the country came under attack. In Dublin Collins concentrated on eliminating a key part of the British intelligence system. He organised a group of hit men, known as 'The Squad' to kill members of the Dublin Metropolitan Police 'G' Division, the heart of the authorities' information gathering. The first member to be shot was Patrick Smith on 31 July 1919. (He was unarmed at the time but was shot in the back five times. He died some weeks later, leaving a wife and seven children.)

Following a series of similar incidents Dáil Éireann was declared a dangerous association and suppressed on 10 September. The banning of all Republican newspapers followed on 20 September. The Republicans responded by launching a stencilled information sheet called the *Bulletin*, which carried accounts of atrocities perpetrated by the Crown forces. Secret and incriminating information obtained by the Republicans during raids on British mail, or supplied by well-placed informers inside Dublin Castle or Government offices, were also frequently published in the *Bulletin* to the embarrassment of the authorities.

The RIC were being stretched to the limit, so the British forces were augmented by large numbers of men brought over from England. These recruits were so numerous that there were not enough proper uniforms for all of them, so they were dressed in khaki coats with black trousers and caps. They promptly got the name of 'Black and Tans' – after a well-known pack of foxhounds. Yet another armed force, named the Auxiliary Division, made up of British ex-army officers, was sent to aid the RIC. These 'Auxiliaries', who were paid £1 a day, had no pension rights, were not under military discipline and were not subject to trial by the civil courts.

As 1920 passed, the Black and Tans and the Auxiliaries quickly established a pattern of ruthlessness that was to continue till the end of 1921. When the IRA shot a policeman or soldier the 'Tans' and 'Auxies' took revenge by burning houses or whole villages; prisoners were murdered while 'trying to escape', property was stolen or destroyed; passers-by were shot dead.

Seán Treacy, who along with Dan Breen had fired the opening shots in the war, was cornered in a security sweep in Talbot Street in 1920. In the ensuing gun-battle Treacy and a British Intelligence Officer named Price were shot dead. A newsagent and a young boy were also killed by flying bullets.

The IRA, under the direction of Michael Collins, fought fire with fire. He was a man who was utterly ruthless, completely fearless and although sought by the authorities from 1919 onwards he seldom bothered to adopt a disguise, cycling openly through the streets of Dublin, depending on his Squad and intelligence network to protect him. As the year wore on, atrocity followed atrocity. Both sides engaged in shootings, burnings and reprisals of all kinds.

In November 1920 an eighteen-year-old medical student named Kevin Barry who lived at 8 Fleet Street in Dublin, was captured after an IRA attack on a British army lorry in Church Street. Three soldiers, one of whom was also aged eighteen, were killed in the attack and the British soldiers were in no mood for kid-glove treatment. Barry was repeatedly beaten in an effort to get him to reveal the names of his companions. He was sentenced to death even though it was quite clear that his gun had never been fired and he was hanged in Mountjoy jail on 1 November 1920.

Another traumatic event occurred at the end of the same month. On Sunday 21 November, members of Collins' Squad entered various hotels throughout the city and shot dead fourteen people, including eleven British Intelligence officers (some in front of their wives) and wounded several more. The IRA claimed that they were all undercover agents for the Crown but one was an innocent veterinary officer shot dead in bed in the Gresham Hotel as he was reading a newspaper.

That same afternoon there was an important Gaelic football match at Croke Park between Dublin and Tipperary. The military surrounded the grounds and proceeded to search for IRA men.

Kevin Barry was hanged in Mountjoy Jail in 1920 for his part in
an attack on a military lorry in which three soldiers were killed.

The Auxiliaries suddenly opened fire without warning, killing
twelve men and women and wounding sixty more. (One Tipperary
player called Michael Hogan was among the dead and the Hogan
Stand was later named after him.)

Later in the evening three prisoners in Dublin Castle (Peader
Clancy, Dick McKee and Conor Clune) were shot dead 'while
trying to escape'. Contrary to some accounts, they were not
tortured beforehand. One observer of the bodies, a Dr
MacLysaght, stated categorically that they were not tortured.
However, a medical doctor who examined Conor Clune's body
found thirteen bullet holes in his chest. This day became known as
'Bloody Sunday'.

The funerals of Clancy, McKee and Clune were huge events in
the tradition of Irish public funerals. In spite of the constant efforts
of the authorities to capture Michael Collins, he went to the Pro-
Cathedral for the funeral service and helped to carry the coffins.
He later appeared openly at the graveside, without disguise, to lay
a wreath on the graves. A woman bystander was so surprised to see
him that she blurted out, 'Look! There's Mick Collins'. Collins'
reaction was to mutter in disgust, 'You bloody bitch!'

On 14 March six prisoners were hanged in Mountjoy Jail for
'high treason'. Two of them were accused of taking part in the

Bloody Sunday shootings. The day of the executions was a day of public mourning in the city. Businesses were closed and a crowd of 20,000 gathered outside Mountjoy Jail. When the bells tolled for the executions the crowds fell to their knees in prayer.

A state of war existed in Dublin. Collins' men carried out ambushes and the military replied with raids and shootings. An 8.00 p.m. curfew was imposed and military lorries roared through the streets every night carrying raiding parties all over the city. A colossal reward of £10,000 was offered for the arrest of Collins.

The military took to raiding hospitals in the search for wounded IRA men. Doctors and nurses were ordered to report all cases of bullet wounds. They refused to obey. Because of this new threat the Volunteers stopped taking wounded comrades to the public hospitals. One Volunteer who was wounded in an ambush on Auxiliaries in Pearse Street was taken to Mercers Hospital where his leg was amputated. A short time later his commanding officer in the ambush, Seán MacBride, and three comrades went to the hospital, took away the wounded man and brought him to the house of Mrs Darrell Figgis who kept him until he had recovered.

It is estimated that, over the first two months of 1921, 317 Volunteers and civilians were killed and 285 were wounded. The Crown forces suffered 174 killed and 288 wounded. During the following months the mayhem continued.

On 25 May 1921 120 men of the Dublin Brigade of the IRA, at the instigation of de Valera, attacked the Customs House on the docks. It housed nine departments of the British Administration and its destruction would be a severe blow to the authorities. The men entered the building and forced the staff to leave. They then set fire to the building but before they could escape the place was surrounded by British forces. Five of the Volunteers were shot dead and seventy were captured. The next day only the walls of the once beautiful building were left standing. Incalculable amounts of historic Irish documents and civic records were destroyed along with the building. The operation had been at the same time a great success and a great disaster for the IRA. Collins was furious with de Valera for his lack of understanding of proper guerrilla tactics.

During 1921, however, the first tentative moves were made to come to some agreement between the British Government and the Irish Executive.

The destruction of the Customs House in 1921 resulted in the terrible loss of historic Irish documents and civic records. The beautiful building was designed by James Gandon in 1781. There were many objections from merchants, home-owners and dockers to its construction. There were even riots at the time, led in some cases by Napper Tandy.

Elections for separate parliaments for 'Northern Ireland' and 'Southern Ireland' took place in May 1921. There were 128 seats to be contested in the 'South' and fifty two in the 'North'. Sinn Féin was the only party to contest the elections in the 'South', except for the four Trinity College seats, where the candidates were also unopposed. Sinn Féin 'won' the 124 seats to the great shock of the British cabinet who had been led to believe that many of the seats would be strongly contested. (In actual fact no voting took place in the 'South' for any of the seats and all the nominees were deemed elected. In the 'North', all the seats were contested.)

On 28 June 1921 the 'Parliament of Southern Ireland' had its first meeting. It was held in the Council Room of the Department of Agriculture and Technical Instruction. It was all over in minutes – the only persons present were the Lord Lieutenant, nominated senators and the four lower-house members for Trinity College. On 13 July it met once more and then adjourned, never to meet again.

The tentative feelers for peace eventually bore fruit. Hostilities ended on 11 July 1921. The truce was signed in the Mansion House by General Macready and Assistant Secretary Cope acting for the Crown, and Commandant Robert Barton TD and Commandant Edmund Duggan TD acting for the Army of the Republic. The next day de Valera and a group of other Republicans, not including Collins, travelled to London to meet Prime Minister Lloyd George.

Real negotiations did not begin until 11 October 1921. After very difficult and sometimes deadlocked negotiations the Anglo-Irish Treaty was signed in London on 6 December 1921. The leaders of the Irish delegation this time were Michael Collins and Arthur Griffith. The British cabinet were satisfied that at last the age-old problem was solved but Collins took a more realistic point of view. He is reported as saying after he signed, 'I have signed my death warrant.'

The Dáil debate on the Treaty began on 14 December and it soon became apparent that the deputies were split down the middle in their attitude to it. De Valera, having refused to lead the delegation in London, now strongly opposed the Treaty. His stance was supported by deputies Cathal Brugha, Austin Stack, Rory O'Connor, Erskine Childers and others, including nearly all of the women delegates. Collins defended the agreement as the best that could be achieved. He had strong support from Kevin O'Higgins, Richard Mulcahy, Eoin O'Duffy, William Cosgrave and others. The Dáil went into recess for the Christmas period and when it reconvened on 3 January 1922 the arguments continued. Finally in a vote taken on 7 January 1922 the Dáil split over the treaty – 64 voted for and 57 voted against

De Valera then resigned as president and stood against Griffith in the hope that he would be re-elected, thus enabling him to sack those members of the cabinet who were pro-Treaty. However, Griffith won by 60 votes to 58.

Negotiations between the Irish authorities, led by Collins, and the British Army culminated in the Lord Lieutenant surrendering Dublin Castle to Michael Collins in mid-January and a provisional government being installed. (Much of the negotiations were held in the Gresham Hotel.) The first of the British regiments marched to the boats, led by their army bands. The Auxiliaries and Black and Tans were returned to England and the disbanding of the RIC began. A new unarmed police force, the Garda Síochána (Civic Guards), was established. As the British forces began to withdraw their troop from barracks all over the country many were taken over by anti-Treaty forces.

In June there was a general election in which de Valera got only thirty-six seats out of a total of 128. It was plain that most of the Irish people favoured the Treaty.

The anti-Treaty Republican Army Council decided to set up its headquarters in the Four Courts on the quays. The Dublin Brigade entered the building on the night of 13 April 1922 and barricaded the windows with sandbags. They also started an escape tunnel just in case. Later strategic buildings such as the Ballast Office, Lever Brothers building on Essex Quay, the Masonic Hall in Molesworth Street and the Kildare Street Club were all occupied.

One of the Republicans in the Four Courts garrison was Seán Lemass, later to become leader of Fianna Fáil (Soldiers of Destiny)

Seán Lemass's lack of fluency in the Irish language was frequently a target for criticism by Fine Gael. On one occasion James Dillon bitingly said that Lemass 'couldn't bid a dog "good day" in the language'. On another occasion Lemass sent a note to TK Whitaker, secretary to the Department of Finance, saying, 'Dev wants me to brush up on the language – please send me books on economics and finance'!

and Taoiseach after Eamon de Valera. In the Four Courts it was his function to issue passes to men who wished to leave the building. As an added touch, he added the seal of the Lord Chief Justice of Ireland to each pass.

The British cabinet then told Collins that unless he acted against the Four Courts they would regard the Treaty as being abrogated and early on 28 June the Free State Army attacked the Four Courts. Collins had given the occupants twenty minutes to surrender and when they refused, he gave the order to start shelling the building. Two field guns, borrowed from the British, were in position on the quays on the other side of the Liffey from the Four Courts. They first shelled from a position near Winetavern Street and later from the quay at Bridge Street. The Irish Civil War had started.

21

◎

THE CIVIL WAR
AND THE HUNGRY THIRTIES
1922 – 1939

Churchill and Lloyd George were delighted with the commencement of hostilities between the pro-Treaty and anti-Treaty supporters. When the attack on the anti-Treaty forces holding the Four Courts was largely ineffectual due to the lack of proper high-explosive shells (shrapnel shells were all they had), Lloyd George threatened to use British troops if Collins was not able to dislodge them. The provisional government resisted any such moves and by 30 June had forced the Four Courts garrison to march out of the blazing building in surrender. (Many invaluable historical documents and records were destroyed in the fire.)

The 'Irregulars', as the anti-Treaty side became known, had also occupied the Grenville and Hamman Hotels in O'Connell Street but these troops were easily removed. On Monday 3 July 1922 Eamon de Valera, Austin Stack and Oscar Traynor left the Hamman Hotel and passed unrecognised down the street and over O'Connell Bridge to safety. On Wednesday Cathal Brugha darted out of the blazing Hamman building with a gun in his hand. When ordered to surrender he refused and was shot several times. He died two days later.

The fighting in Dublin lasted for eight days and at the end of it O'Connell Street once more lay in ruins. Sixty people had been killed and over 300 wounded.

The war continued in the rest of the country. On 12 August 1922 Arthur Griffith died, probably from stress and overwork. His death was a great shock to the people of Ireland but an even greater shock was to come ten days later when Michael Collins was shot dead in an ambush by Irregulars at Béal na mBláth in Co. Cork.

———— ◎ ————

In 1924 the name of Dublin's principal street was changed from Sackville Street to O'Connell Street. A previous attempt by Dublin Corporation in 1885 to change the name to honour O'Connell had been prevented by Hedges Eyre Chatterton, the vice chancellor of Ireland, getting an injunction against the move. The citizens of Dublin started using the new name, however, and the corporation allowed the old street name-plates to deteriorate in the meantime. When Chatterton prevented Dublin Corporation from changing the name of Sackville Street it threatened to give the name 'Chatterton Street' to the lower part of Temple Street which had a most unsavoury reputation. It is now called Hill Street (off Parnell Street).

———— ◎ ————

In the late 1920s The Irish Hospital Sweepstakes were set up by Joe McGrath, Richard Duggan and Spencer Freeman. The first sweep was based on the November Handicap of 1930 but subsequent sweepstakes were based on the English Grand National and Derby. Tickets cost ten shillings each (about £20 in today's money). The ticket gave the punter two chances of winning big money: if you drew a horse in the first draw, or raffle, you were assured of a big prize, and then if your horse went on to win or be placed in the race you won an even bigger sum.

The sweepstakes proved to be an enormous success. The organisers hoped for sales of about £125,000 – in fact the actual sales were nearly six times greater! A large proportion of these were sold (illegally) in the United States. Sales of tickets topped eight million in 1932. At the beginning there could be only one winner of the biggest prize but when the prize money reached huge amounts it was decided to divide the receipts into units of £100,000 each to spread the winnings around.

———— ◎ ————

Collins' body was first brought to Cork City where it was received with scenes of great distress and mourning. From Cork it was brought by sea to Dublin on the *Classic*. (A moving tribute to the dead leader was paid by the British navy in Cobh Harbour as the *Classic* passed down on its way to the sea. The navy ships were all drawn up in line-astern with their sailors lining the decks in salute as the Last Post was sounded.) From Friday to Sunday the body lay in state in Dublin City Hall flanked by a guard of honour, including members of the Squad. The funeral on Sunday was the greatest since that of Parnell, with thousands marching behind the coffin which was carried on a gun carriage, and which, ironically, had been used in the shelling of the Four Courts. At the graveside in Glasnevin Cemetery Richard Mulcahy, Collins' Chief of Staff, made a short speech and old comrades fired a volley over the grave.

After the death of Collins the new leaders of the Free State side were William Cosgrave, who had fought in 1916, Kevin O'Higgins, who had been elected to the Dáil in 1918, Ernest Blythe, a Northern Presbyterian who had been a supporter of Arthur Griffith, and Richard Mulcahy. These men were determined to consolidate the Free State.

William Cosgrave, leader of the pro-Treaty side after the death of Collins, was a staunch supporter of democracy. He was born in James' Street but lived most of his life in Beechpark, Templeogue.

———— ◎ ————

The sweepstakes were not welcomed by everyone. The Protestant Archbishop of Dublin, Dr Gregg, condemned the whole thing and the *Catholic Bulletin* thundered, 'The sweep is a great international scandal, a malignant menace, a putrid pool, a giant evil.'

———— ◎ ————

Although the Irish Hospital Sweepstakes proved to be extremely successful for over forty years, by the 1980s it had declined to almost insignificance. Where once the capital expenditure on hospitals had been funded by up to fifty-five per cent by the sweepstakes it was now down to two per cent. State lotteries in the United States were becoming commonplace, thus removing the greatest source of income for the Irish sweeps.

In 1987 the Hospital Sweep closed, making 160 workers redundant. Those with up to forty years service got a miserly £3,300 redundancy payment and when the Labour Court decided that they should get an additional £10,000 they were told that the Irish Hospital Trust was in liquidation and there was no money to pay them. The building and site of the Hospital Sweepstakes in Ballsbridge were later sold for £6.6 million. (In July 2000 each surviving worker and the families of deceased workers were given a once-off payment of £20,000 in compensation.)

———— ◎ ————

Not everyone embraced the new Irish Free State with enthusiasm. It is reported that during the 1926 Horse Show at the RDS grounds, Ballsbridge, the appearance of the British jumping team was greeted by the crowd singing 'God Save The King', while the Irish Army jumping team was received in silence.

———— ◎ ————

The loss of Collins was a severe blow to the government side. Discipline suffered and various acts of terror were carried out without authority or approval. Some loyal followers of Collins known as the 'Oriel House Gang' gained an unsavoury reputation for torture and the ill-treatment of prisoners. (They got their name from Oriel House near Amiens Street, the building from which they operated.) The official title of the 'gang' was the Criminal Investigation Department (CID). They operated in plain clothes and generally were given a free hand.

In October 1922 the Republicans decided to form a 'national government' with Eamon de Valera as president and Austin Stack, Seán T O'Kelly, Liam Mellows and others as ministers. Erskine Childers was appointed as Minister for Publicity. Childers had been on the run in Cork and Kerry and was now asked to come back to Dublin. On his way he was arrested on 10 November by Free State troops in Wicklow and was found to be in possession of a revolver. This was a capital offence under new government legislation. (The revolver was an ornamental one which had been given to him sometime before by Michael Collins.) He was tried secretly in a military court on 17 November, found guilty and executed seven days later in Beggars Bush Barracks.

Childers was not the first to be executed under the new powers, however. On the same day as his trial, four other young men who had been found in possession of guns were shot. On 30 November three more prisoners were executed. They had been captured near the notorious Oriel House immediately after an attempt had been made to blow up the building.

The Irish Free State officially came into existence on 6 December 1922, having got the Royal Assent the day before. The man appointed to represent British interests as governor general was Timothy Healy, who had done so much to blacken Parnell's character at the end of his career. Healy now took up residence in the viceregal Lodge in the Phoenix Park.

On 27 November Liam Lynch, the Irregulars' Chief of Staff, stated that all TDs who had voted for the emergency powers and the military courts, would be shot on sight. On 8 December four more Republican prisoners, Rory O'Connor (former secretary to Kevin O'Higgins and best man at his wedding), Liam Mellows, Joseph McKelvey and Richard Barrett, who had surrendered in the

———— ◎ ————

For years after the Treaty the Council of the Irish Rugby Union flew the Union Jack over the grounds at Lansdowne Road and refused to fly the tricolour but after intervention by the Taoiseach, Mr Cosgrave, in 1932 they finally relented.

———— ◎ ————

An even more obvious symbol of British rule was the office of the governor general and after the success of Fianna Fáil in the 1932 election a campaign of harassment was begun against James MacNeill, the then holder of the office. It started in April when government ministers Seán T O'Kelly and Frank Aiken walked out of a social event when MacNeill walked in. MacNeill demanded an apology from Taoiseach de Valera but he refused to give one and asked MacNeill to let him have a list of other functions he intended visiting so that there would be no repetition.

In May MacNeill was refused permission to invite foreign Catholics to stay in his Phoenix Park residence during the great Eucharistic Congress to be held that year. The army band was not allowed to attend any function at which he was present. Eventually after a continuing 'war of attrition' MacNeill resigned. The government then appointed an Irish speaker, Donal O'Buachalla, as governor general, a move that was criticised by the Gaelic League on the grounds that it was an insult to the language to appoint any Irish speaker to be a servant to King George.

———— ◎ ————

In 1932 the first Irish film censor was appointed. He was James Montgomery, who was famous for his wit. On being asked what his task was he replied that he wanted to protect Irish audiences from the 'Californication' of American films. He was also reported as referring to the Gate Theatre, with its gay connections, and the Abbey Theatre with its strong rural Irish tradition, as 'Sodom and Begorrah'!

———— ◎ ————

Four Courts, were executed as a reprisal for the shooting dead, near the Ormond Hotel on the quays, of a Free State officer and TD named Seán Hales. There had been no trial and the reason given for the executions was that they were a warning to others.

The shooting of Dáil TDs ceased but the Republicans then started a campaign against the property of supporters of the government. Houses, offices, business premises, even a passenger train, were all destroyed. On 13 January Beechpark, the home of William Cosgrave, was burned to the ground. The government side replied in kind. A supporter of de Valera, called Fintan Lalor, was taken from his lodgings and his body was later found near Milltown Golf Club in South Dublin.

Finally on 24 May 1923 the Republican leadership gave the order to cease fire and dump arms, but they still did not accept the legitimacy of the Free State. The civil war had cost the state enormous amounts of money and hundreds of deaths. (A figure of 4,000 to 5,000 military deaths has been estimated for the combined pro- and anti-Treaty forces. The seventy-seven Republicans executed by the Free State forces were later to loom large in the pantheon of heroes for Fianna Fáil supporters.)

A general election was held in August 1923 in spite of the extremely unsettled state of the country. The newly founded Cumann na nGaedheal party led by William Cosgrave, which represented the pro-Treaty side, got 63 seats. The anti-Treaty side led by Eamon de Valera gained 44 seats and Labour won 14 seats.

When the Dáil convened after the general election the successful Republican candidates refused to take their seats because to do so would mean they would have to take the oath of allegiance to 'HM King George V, his heirs and successors'.

In 1926 de Valera founded the new political party, Fianna Fáil. The inaugural meeting was held in the La Scala Theatre in Prince's Street, off O'Connell Street. In the general election the following year the party had quite a successful debut. They won 44 seats, while the Cumann na nGaedheal party only did marginally better with 47 seats. Although Fianna Fáil's number of seats was only equal to that of the Republican successes of the 1923 election, it was a good showing, considering that many of their supporters had deserted them because of their abstentionist policy. Many of these voters had voted for the Labour Party purely out of frustration.

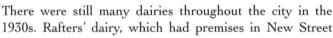

The Eucharistic Congress in 1932 was a major event in the life of the city. Thousands of pilgrims poured in from every part of the country. Special camps were set up in school grounds at Marino, Artane and other places. Many pilgrims stayed in the numerous boats anchored in Dublin Bay for the purpose. When the papal legate arrived in Dun Laoghaire he was greeted by over 50,000 people, headed by de Valera and his government ministers.

Dublin went wild with Catholic fervour. One Dutch commentator wrote of 'Dublin the kneeling city, the city of millions of candles, the worshipping town, Dublin the heart of the Catholic world'. The congress ended with a huge open-air Mass in the Phoenix Park with an attendance of about 500,000 people. After the Mass the Blessed Sacrament was carried in a four-hour procession from the park to O'Connell Bridge. The order of the procession was 'a detachment of cavalry', followed by '60,000 men by parish' and then listed 'Reverend Brothers' and classes of clergy and dignitaries, and finally 'Female Singers' and 'Women'!

There were still many dairies throughout the city in the 1930s. Rafters' dairy, which had premises in New Street near St Patrick's Cathedral, housed over 150 cows.

One of the most famous Lord Mayors of Dublin, Alfred (Alfie) Byrne, was first elected in 1930. He was elected as mayor ten times. Noted for his dapper appearance he always wore a bowler hat and a gold watch-chain.

In the 1930s the poor of inner city Dublin lived in appalling conditions. In 1934 eleven families with fifty-three members were found to be living in one tenement in Townsend Street. Two years later a report spoke of five families with twenty-five members living in six rooms in a tenement in Marrowbone Lane and another with thirty-three people living in the same number of rooms.

De Valera now set about devising some way of taking up seats in the Dáil. Three constitutional lawyers said that Fianna Fáil deputies could take their seats without the oath before the president was elected. De Valera and the other successful candidates went to the Dáil building and demanded entrance to the chamber. They were told that they could do so only if they took the oath. When they refused to do this, the doors to the chamber were locked and they walked out on to the street again. There, de Valera addressed the large crowd that had gathered and explained how taking the 'false' oath would be a betrayal of the Irish people.

Next de Valera announced that they would start a campaign to force the government to hold a referendum to abolish the oath. But then on 10 July 1927 Kevin O'Higgins, Minister for Home Affairs, was assassinated as he walked to Mass in Booterstown. He had no bodyguard and was unarmed. At first de Valera's supporters were suspected as being the perpetrators but he denounced the killers in the strongest language and it later emerged that the attackers were IRA men who were driving to a GAA match in Wexford. They had noticed that O'Higgins had no bodyguard and availed of the opportunity presented to them to publicise their cause. The IRA command had not ordered the killing.

The government reacted by proposing a new Public Safety Bill and an Electoral Amendment Act, which would require every candidate in subsequent elections to swear an affidavit that he or she would take the Oath of Allegiance. Cosgrave also proposed to hold an election for the seats held by the abstentionists.

The bills were passed on 4 August 1927 after an all-night sitting of the Dáil. A week later the Fianna Fáil members again went to the Dáil. Again they said they would not take the oath but de Valera removed the Bible from the table and signed his name in the book, which contained the names of those who had taken the oath. By this 'sleight of hand' it was deemed that the necessary formalities had been fulfilled.

As soon as the new session began Fianna Fáil proposed a motion of no confidence in the government. The crucial vote was set for 16 August 1927. Before that date Labour, led by Tom Johnson and the National Progressive Democratic Party (led by William Redmond, son of John) came to an agreement to support a coalition government which did not include Fianna Fáil. On

———— ◎ ————

The early decades of the twentieth century saw the flourishing of some of Ireland's greatest literary figures. No fewer than three Nobel prizewinners, James Joyce, George Bernard Shaw and Samuel Beckett, were born in the city.

James Joyce was born on 2 February 1882 at 41 Brighton Square, Rathgar. His family constantly changed addresses in Dublin so that he claimed to have lived in nearly twenty different houses throughout the city. It was his proud boast that if Dublin was destroyed it could be reconstructed from a study of his writings. Even so, he spent thirty-six out of his fifty-eight years living in Italy, France and Switzerland.

His best-known Dublin address is 7 Eccles Street, Phibsborough. It was from there that Leopold Bloom set out on 16 June 1904 on his fictional journey through Dublin as described in *Ulysses*. (That date has become known ever since as Bloom's Day.)

James Joyce, author of *Ulysses*, claimed that if Dublin was destroyed it could faithfully be reconstructed by reference to his writings.

———— ◎ ————

Kevin O'Higgins

13 August Johnson, William O'Brien of the Irish Transport and General Workers Union, and RJP Mortished, another trade union activist, held a secret meeting in Powerscourt Arms Hotel in Enniskerry, Co. Wicklow. During the meeting they discussed who would be the ministers in the coalition government. The list of names was eventually agreed but at the end of the meeting the list was torn up and thrown into the waste paper basket in the room. As the three men then left to make their way back to the city by bus, RM Wylie of the *Irish Times* noticed the three men standing at the bus stop. He made some enquiries and discovered the venue for the meeting. He then went back to the hotel, searched the room and found the list in the wastepaper basket. The next day he published the list of proposed cabinet members in the paper.

On August 16 there was high drama in the Dáil chamber when the motion of no confidence was debated for four hours. When the vote was taken there was a tie at 71 votes each for the government and opposition. One Labour deputy was in Canada and Johnson had forgotten to request his return home. Another deputy, John Jinks from Sligo, was not in the House. The Ceann Comhairle (Speaker) gave his casting vote to the government. (There were rumours afterwards that some Cumann na nGaedheal supporters

George Bernard Shaw was born at 33 Synge Street in 1856.
He did not have a happy childhood – his father was a
drunkard and his mother was more interested in her music
than in her son.

He attended the Central Model School in Marlborough
Street and then Wesley College but he claimed later that he
was mostly self-educated. He became intensely interested in
the theatre and later wrote a string of highly successful
plays including *Mrs Warren's Profession, John Bull's Other
Island, Man and Superman, Pygmalion, Heartbreak House* and
Saint Joan.

A bronze statue of Shaw today stands outside the
National Art Gallery in Merrion Square, a site chosen by
Shaw himself because of the important part the gallery
played in his education as a boy.

George Bernard Shaw retained his Dublin accent till he died.
A prolific playwright, he was self-educated.

Eamon de Valera was the longest living surviving leader of the 1916 Rising. After many years as Taoiseach he became President of Ireland and died in 1975 at Talbot Lodge, Blackrock.

had got Jinks drunk and put him on the train home to Sligo. One newspaper correspondent wrote of 'High Jinks in the Dáil!')

In the general election of 1932 Fianna Fáil was more successful but still ended up some seats short of an overall majority. (There were widespread accusations of vote-rigging, impersonation and intimidation in connection with the Fianna Fáil victory. Many 'dead' people cast their votes and some people are reputed to have voted fifty times!) After consultations with Labour, and an agreement to introduce some social legislation, Fianna Fáil and Labour agreed to form a coalition government. On 9 March 1932 Fianna Fáil took office for the first time, with the support of Labour. They had a combined overall majority of 13.

There were various 'scares' at the time that Cumann na nGaedheal would try to prevent Fianna Fáil taking power. When the Fianna Fáil deputies entered the Dáil for the first time after the election they were carrying revolvers which had been issued to them beforehand. However, there was certainly no threat from William Cosgrave; he had too much respect for the institutions of the state.

In February 1932, one month before Fianna Fáil took office, the Army Comrades Association was formed. Its elected leader was

———— ◎ ————

Samuel Beckett was born in 1906 at Cooldrinagh, Brighton Road, Rathgar. He was educated at various schools, including Portora Royal School, Enniskillen. Later he read Modern Irish Literature at Trinity College and after that spent two years as an exchange lecturer in Paris. (By a strange coincidence he acted as secretary to James Joyce for a time while he was there.)

He returned to Dublin in 1932 and became an assistant lecturer in French in Trinity College. He had limited success as a dramatist and novelist before the outbreak of World War II, during which he was a member of the French resistance.

When the war ended he produced a number of works, again with only limited success until he made the big breakthrough with *Waiting For Godot* in 1953. Everything he wrote subsequently was a great success and in 1969 he was awarded the Nobel Prize for Literature. He died in Paris on 22 December 1989.

Samuel Beckett

———— ◎ ————

Dr TF O'Higgins (brother of the murdered Kevin). Irish army ex-servicemen flocked to join and in a few months it had about 3,000 members.

The growth of the association was seen as a threat by the IRA, which had begun to exhibit left-wing tendencies at the time and who now wholeheartedly supported Fianna Fáil. The tough attitude of the Cumann na nGaedheal government to the IRA had provoked bitter enmity. They had celebrated the Fianna Fáil victory with reference to 'the downfall of the Cosgrave murder gang' also stating that 'The IRA stood firm and defeated Cosgrave and coercianism'. The Army Comrades and the IRA clashed frequently, particularly when the Comrades were acting as guards during Cumann na nGaedheal meetings. The IRA tried to prevent the meetings taking place, using the slogan 'No free speech for traitors' as justification.

The growth of fascism in Catholic countries like Italy and Spain inspired many in Ireland to follow the same path. When Eoin O'Duffy was sacked as Garda Commissioner by de Valera on 22 February 1933 he was free to devote his energies to the Army Comrades Association. In July of the same year he was elected leader. The association was then renamed the National Guard. The members chose a blue shirt as their uniform and the flag of St Patrick as their banner. O'Duffy saw himself as an Irish Mussolini but at the same time he did not aspire to be a dictator nor did he have the necessary qualities to become one.

Nevertheless he threatened to lead a march on the Dáil on 13 August 1933 – the day of commemoration of Arthur Griffith and Michael Collins. In reply, the Government banned the march, placed an armed guard on Leinster House and raided homes of known 'Blueshirts' in the search for arms. In August the National Guard was banned. Military tribunals were set up and the full force of the Offences against the State Act was brought to bear on all offenders.

The three opposition parties, Cumann na nGaedheal, the National Centre Party and the National Guard, then came together to form a single party, the United Ireland Party (or Fine Gael) with Eoin O'Duffy as leader but since he was not a member of parliament, William Cosgrave was elected leader of the parliamentary party.

For several months after the formation of Fine Gael there were violent clashes between Blueshirts and IRA supporters. Then on 30 November 1933 police raided the homes of hundreds of Fine Gael supporters and also the party headquarters. Next the government introduced a bill making it illegal to wear uniforms and badges or use military titles in support of a political party. The carrying of weapons, even sticks, was forbidden at public meetings.

The bill was passed in the Dáil but the Seanad (Senate) rejected it. A week later the government introduced a bill to abolish the Seanad itself. In September O'Duffy was manoeuvred into resigning and although he tried (unsuccessfully) to regain power later, it effectively ended his role in Irish politics.

With the demise of the Blueshirt threat de Valera was able to turn his attention to the IRA. He was becoming increasingly annoyed with their activities. When he was giving a radio broadcast after an army march-past on St Patrick's Day 1936 the IRA managed to jam the broadcast. Most of the speech could not be heard and at one time a voice was heard to say, 'Hello comrades. For the last half-hour we have just witnessed a very fine display of English militarism.'

In June that year de Valera declared the IRA an illegal organisation and banned the Wolfe Tone commemoration at Bodenstown. Maurice Twomey, a leading IRA figure was arrested and jailed for membership of an illegal organisation. The rift between Fianna Fáil and the IRA was complete when a government ammunition dump, the Magazine Fort in the Phoenix Park, was raided by the IRA on 23 December 1939. They stole thirteen lorry-loads of ammunition, almost the entire Irish army's stock. In all there were over a million rounds stolen.

These and other acts forced de Valera to crack down hard on the IRA. Many were arrested and sent to detention camps, and some were executed by firing squad.

22

◎

FROM THE EMERGENCY
TO THE HAUGHEY ERA
1939 – 1990

Even though the country was neutral in World War II it did not escape entirely the horrors of war. In January 1941 German bombs fell in Terenure and Harold's Cross but there were no casualties and little damage was caused. On the night of 31 May 1941 more serious incidents occurred when several parts of Dublin were again bombed by German planes. One bomb fell in the Phoenix Park near the zoo. It only caused minor damage, including the windows of Áras an Uachtaráin, but created consternation and panic among the zoo animals. Much more serious damage was caused in the North Strand area where many houses were demolished. Other bombs fell on the North Circular Road, Ballybough, and at Summerhill Parade near O'Connell Schools. The final casualty list had 32 dead and over 80 injured. (After the war the British Air Ministry confirmed in 1946 that they had diverted the wireless beam used by the Germans who then thought they were over Britain when they released their bombs. The Irish Government was later paid £327,000 in the 1950s in compensation by the Germans.)

In February 1942 the government announced that due to grain shortages, in future bread would be made from 100% wheaten flour. This produced a much darker loaf than before, in other words, the famous 'black' bread of the war years.

Rationing was introduced in May of that year. Every household was issued with ration books containing different-coloured numbered coupons. At first the clothing allowance for a year was 52 coupons but as 40 coupons were needed for a man's suit there were such strong protests that the allowance was increased to 78

————— ◎ —————

By the 1930s the *Irish Press* declared that Dublin 'had the worst slums in Europe'. An inquiry into working class housing in 1939–43 found that 112,000 people lived in over 6,000 tenements.

The conditions in which they lived were absolutely appalling. Up to 100 people occupied a single house, with as many as twenty members of the same family to one room. Sanitation was non-existent and there was no running water in most cases. A single water tap and primitive toilet in the back yard was as much as most tenements had. Some of the toilets were no more than large holes in the ground surrounded with a rough wooden fence. Many had no water supply at all. 'Slop' buckets were used to cater for the needs of the families at night-time. These were frequently emptied along hallways and backyards.

Naturally enough, contagious diseases spread extremely rapidly throughout the tenements. Tuberculosis, diphtheria, pneumonia, whooping cough and other diseases were endemic among the inhabitants. Their death rate was double that of suburban neighbourhoods. Infant mortality was extremely high – 116 per thousand in the 1920s.

Eventually the newspapers, such as the *Daily Nation* at the turn of the century and particularly the *Irish Press* in 1936, succeeded in focussing attention on the problem. Their campaigning eventually bore fruit. Various housing acts were passed in the Dáil in the 1930s and slum clearance at last got under way. Tenements in the worst areas were pulled down and new schemes of flats were erected on the cleared sites.

The process continued into the 1940s and 1950s with new housing estates in places like Ballyfermot, Crumlin, Cabra, Donnycarney, Inchicore, Marino and Glasnevin taking large numbers of families from the inner city. Some neglected areas remained into the 1970s however, in places like Mountjoy Square and North Great George's Street. Thankfully none exist at the present day.

————— ◎ —————

for the year. Other items rationed were tea (half an ounce, about fifteen grams, per person per week), footwear, sugar and butter.

During the war the fuel situation in Dublin became acute. Coal supplies were extremely low and while at first the allowance of coal per household for the months of February and March 1942 was two bags, by April this was cut to zero – all coal was needed for industry. More and more the citizens had to rely on turf. In October that year the Turf Controller (there was such an official!) announced that there were 500,000 to 600,000 tons of turf available but that there was no place to store it. The solution was simple. The Phoenix Park provided ample space and soon huge stacks of turf along the roads through the park became a familiar sight. In fact they remained there long after the war had ended.

Another scarcity plagued the people of Dublin during those years. In 1942 gas rationing was introduced and the use of gas was restricted to certain hours each day. The cute Dubliners discovered that there was a 'glimmer' of gas left in the pipes after the supply was cut off. They realised that the 'glimmer' was enough to boil the odd kettle of water for their tea during these 'forbidden' hours. This gave rise to the introduction by the Gas Company of an official to detect the culprits. The people immediately christened him the 'Glimmer Man'. Where he suspected that the gas was being used after the permitted time he would enter the premises and by the simple method of feeling the gas rings he could determine if the gas had been recently used.

The political scene in the 1930s and '40s was dominated to a large extent by de Valera, and when he retired by Seán Lemass. The emergence of Dr John Charles McQuaid as the Catholic Archbishop of Dublin added another powerful presence to life in the city.

In March 1946 the Dublin members of the Irish National Teachers Organisation, after months of fruitless negotiations with the Fianna Fáil government, went on strike for higher salaries. Surprisingly enough Dr McQuaid supported the teachers in their demands but his offer to mediate in the dispute was rejected by the government. The strike lasted until the end of October and it involved the closure of 140 city schools and 40,000 children being without teachers. Over 1,200 teachers withdrew their services but the religious orders kept their schools open.

———— ◎ ————

In the early months of 1940 Dublin's municipal services –
water supplies, street cleaning, bin collection and fire
fighting were severely disrupted by a strike by the Irish
Municipal Employees Trade Union. The workers were
seeking an increase of eight shillings (40p) per week. On
instructions from the government the corporation offered
an increase of two shillings (10p) per week. The offer was
refused and a strike began in March. Eventually the strike
ended due to the government standing firm.

———— ◎ ————

The heroism of those Irish seamen who lost their lives
during World War II in their efforts to maintain essential
supplies to their country is commemorated by a monument
unveiled by President Hillery on City Quay in May 1990.
It consists of a column of granite bearing the names of the
seamen and the ships on which they sailed. A large bronze
sea-anchor stands against the column.

———— ◎ ————

Dr John Charles McQuaid, Archbishop of Dublin for thirty years from the 1940s was the last of the authoritarian leaders of the Catholic Church in Ireland.

The striking teachers staged a dramatic protest during the All-Ireland Football Final in Croke Park in September knowing that Taoiseach de Valera would be present. By queuing from early in the morning they succeeded in getting side-line tickets and they brought their protest banners into the grounds by the trick of rolling them up and pushing them down the legs of their trousers.

At the half-time interval the teachers got onto the pitch and paraded their banners in front of the Taoiseach. The gardaí waded into the strikers and their actions served to gain more sympathy for the teachers. By the end of October the government conceded and brought in new salary scales which were accepted by the teachers who called off the strike.

The political situation in Northern Ireland had begun to intrude more and more into life in the Republic in the 1960s. At the end of 1968 the Taoiseach, Jack Lynch, was shocked when told that arms had reached the North through the activities of some of his ministers. In the subsequent Arms Trial all of the accused including Charles Haughey were found 'Not Guilty'. The result was greeted ecstatically by Haughey's supporters who gathered outside the courthouse and inside the Four Courts Hotel on the quays. They shouted 'We want Charlie' and 'Lynch must go'.

———— ◎ ————

The last tram journey on Dublin's streets took place on 10 July 1949 when the tram from Nelson's Pillar to Dalkey made its final journey.

———— ◎ ————

The world-famous Abbey Theatre caught fire and was completely destroyed in 1951. It did not re-open until 1966. In the meantime 'the show went on' in the Queen's Theatre in Pearse Street.

———— ◎ ————

In 1955 relations between the Government Coalition and the Archbishop of Dublin, John Charles McQuaid, became rather strained when he called for the abandonment of an international soccer match between the Republic of Ireland and Yugoslavia in Dalymount Park on October 19. Catholic organisations in the city supported the ban in protest against the imprisonment of Archbishop Stepinac by the Yugoslav leader, Tito. The Football Association refused to back down, however, even when President Seán T O'Kelly announced he would not attend the match. This was followed by the news that the Number One Army Band would not be allowed to attend and the team trainer, a member of the Garda Síochána, had withdrawn his services. In spite of the objections the match went ahead in front of a capacity crowd of over 21,000 spectators.

———— ◎ ————

In 1957 the last remaining equestrian statue in the city, that of Lord Gough in the Phoenix Park, was blown up by 'persons unknown'. The magnificent bronze horse on which the lord sat was the subject of some controversy as many maintained that the positioning of the horse's legs meant the horse would fall over if it attempted the gait in real life.

———— ◎ ————

Haughey himself called for Lynch's resignation. But Jack Lynch was made of stern stuff. He called for a vote of confidence in the Dáil in November. Haughey and Kevin Boland had threatened to vote against the government but in the end neither of them did so.

'Honest' Jack Lynch concealed a 'fist of steel in a velvet glove' as Charles Haughey and others learned to their cost.

In the meantime things were deteriorating in Northern Ireland. In August 1971 internment without trial was introduced and on 'Bloody Sunday', 30 January 1972, British paratroopers shot dead 13 people in a civil rights march in Derry. Three days later on 2 February a large crowd marched on the British embassy in Merrion Square in Dublin with sections of the crowd chanting 'Burn, Burn, Burn'. The embassy windows were first of all smashed by a man wielding a hammer. Fire bombs were then hurled in through the smashed windows, setting the building on fire.

The IRA had gained control of the march and although it was supposedly organised by the Dublin Trade Unions, they were not sufficiently strong to maintain control. It was quite evident that the IRA had planned the whole thing.

Because of the increasing IRA activity the Lynch government introduced an Offences against the State (Amendment) Bill in the Dáil. It gave sweeping powers to the police against the IRA.

In 1957 when Dublin staged an international theatre festival one of the plays produced was *The Rose Tattoo* by Tennessee Williams. Even before the play was staged, Deputy Seán Brady, TD had requested the Minister for Justice to get the play banned because it was 'unquestionably indecent'.

On 23 May, Alan Simpson, the producer of the play, was arrested for producing 'an indecent or profane performance'. The cause of all the trouble was a scene in the play where one of the characters is supposed to accidentally drop a condom on the floor and is berated by a female character for his 'immoral' intentions. Simpson's co-director Carolyn Swift, in a letter to the *Irish Times* on 4 November 1999, wrote 'In fact no condom was used. Nor was any prop in the likeness of a condom. This was acknowledged by one of the witnesses when asked if a condom had been dropped. "No," Garda Martin had replied, "but I'm sure it was a condom that was not dropped!" '

The court proceedings dragged on for nearly a year but in the end the judge threw out the case. However, the damage was done and the Pike Theatre never recovered.

In 1958 the Archbishop of Dublin, Dr John Charles McQuaid, would not allow Catholic services to inaugurate the festival known as *An Tóstal* because plays by James Joyce and Seán O'Casey were to be performed. O'Casey replied by banning all performances of his plays in Dublin until further notice.

In 1963 Dublin barmen threatened to go on strike in protest at a plan to serve cooked meals in the pubs. They said they were prepared to serve soup, snacks or sandwiches, but no 'heavy' meals.

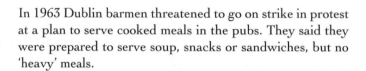

Both Fine Gael and Labour opposed the bill and when the final debate began on Friday 1 December 1972, the government side was facing defeat.

That same day two bombs exploded in Dublin, one in Sackville Place behind Clery's and the other on Eden Quay outside Liberty Hall. Two people were killed and 127 others were injured. Immediately Fine Gael announced that they would no longer oppose the bill and it was carried by 69 votes to 22.

On Friday 27 May 1974 the whole country was shocked when twenty-three people (fifteen women, six men and two baby girls) were killed and over 100 injured in bomb explosions in Dublin and five people were killed and twenty-eight injured in Monaghan. The Dublin bombs went off in Parnell Street, Talbot Street and South Leinster Street at 5.30 p.m.

The bomb in Parnell Street was in a car parked outside the Westbrook Garage near the junction of Marlborough Street. The bomb which exploded in the crowded Talbot Street was in a car parked within 20 metres of the Gardiner Street junction. The South Leinster Street bomb was in a white Austin 1800 about 50 to 75 metres from the Lincoln Place junction. Two men were seen locking the car and calmly walking away from it. Two of the three cars had been hijacked in Belfast the day before.

The 'Troubles' continued to affect Dublin during 1976. In July the British Ambassador, Christopher Ewart-Biggs was killed when his car was blown up just outside his residence near Stepaside. In September a pub and a cinema in Lower Abbey Street were bombed in protest against the government's introduction of the legislation which would allow suspects to be detained for seven days without trial.

After the general election of February 1982 Charles Haughey, now leader of Fianna Fáil, succeeded in wooing the independents who held the deciding hand. One of them was Tony Gregory, who represented a North Dublin inner city constituency. Haughey offered him an £80m deal, including the building of 440 new houses in his constituency and the development of a 27 acre site at Dublin Port. The wheeling and dealing to gain the support of the fringe deputies led to a bizarre scene in Leinster House when the division bell for the crucial vote was sounded on 9 March 1982. Three Workers' Party deputies, Joe Sherlock, Paddy

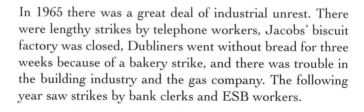

One of the most sensational murder cases to shock the city occurred in 1963. The murder victim was a sixteen-year-old girl, named Hazel Mullen. She had fallen in love with a South African medical student named Shan Mohangi and had become engaged to him. Mohangi worked part-time as a chef in the Green Tureen restaurant in Harcourt Street and it was there that Hazel called to speak to him on 17 August 1963. She told him that the engagement was off as she had started seeing someone else. Mohangi flew into a rage and strangled her on the premises. When Hazel was reported missing he pretended to search for her but meanwhile he dismembered her body in the basement of the restaurant. Later he made the mistake of trying to burn the remains but created such a smell that the fire brigade was called to investigate. Mohangi was later tried for murder and was eventually convicted of manslaughter.

In 1965 there was a great deal of industrial unrest. There were lengthy strikes by telephone workers, Jacobs' biscuit factory was closed, Dubliners went without bread for three weeks because of a bakery strike, and there was trouble in the building industry and the gas company. The following year saw strikes by bank clerks and ESB workers.

One of the most controversial developments in Dublin's history was the total destruction by the ESB of almost one complete side of Lower Fitzwilliam Street to make way for the erection of new offices in 1965. Sixteen houses, comprising one of the finest stretches of Georgian houses anywhere, were knocked down to make way for a new office block.

Charles Haughey

Gallagher and Proinsias de Rossa, had promised to vote for Haughey but found themselves outside the chamber of the House when the vital vote was to be taken. Undeterred, they burst into the press gallery, climbed into the distinguished visitors' gallery and then jumped down to the floor of the house just in time to vote!

In July 1982 an extraordinary sequence of events began to unfold. First a young nurse named Bridie Gargan was attacked in the Phoenix Park as she was sunbathing beside her car. She later died in hospital from the horrendous wounds inflicted. Some days later an Offaly farmer named Donal Dunne was callously shot dead with his own shotgun by a man who pretended to buy the gun from him. An intensive police hunt for the killer finally ended in Pilot View, Bullock Harbour near Dalkey at the flat of the Attorney General, Patrick Connolly, where the killer, Malcolm MacArthur, was staying while Mr Connolly was in America on holiday. The whole affair was described by Haughey as 'Grotesque, Unbelievable, Bizarre and Unprecedented'. Conor Cruise O'Brien seized on the initials GUBU and so the 'GUBU factor' entered the lexicon of Irish life.

Meanwhile the Minister for Justice, Seán Doherty authorised the police to tap the phones of two prominent journalists in

On Tuesday 8 March 1966 at 2.00 a.m. Nelson's Pillar in the middle of O'Connell Street was destroyed by an explosion. The forty metre high column which had been erected in 1808 was split half way up and the four-metre statue of Nelson was blown to the ground. No one was injured in the blast

Dublin Corporation later called in the army to have the whole column removed and their demolition of the remaining portion by explosives resulted in more damage than the original blast. The rubble was brought to St Anne's Park in Raheny but Nelson's head can still be seen at the Dublin Civic Museum in South William Street.

The following notice will be remembered by many who have climbed the Pillar. It hung beside the entrance for many years:

> Admission 6d
> Erected in 1808
> 166 steps
> 120 ft to platform
> One price only

Nelson's Pillar was erected in 1808 by a committee of traders and bankers after the Battle of Trafalgar. Originally the entrance to the monument was underground but an entrance at street level was added in 1894.

Dublin, Bruce Arnold and Geraldine Kennedy. Doherty claimed later that the phone tap was requested by the cabinet. The journalists were subsequently awarded substantial damages in the High Court action they brought against the state.

———— ◎ ————

In January 1972 Dr McQuaid retired after thirty years as archbishop and died a year later in 1973. His great friend Eamon de Valera retired that year as President of Ireland and died two years later in 1975.

———— ◎ ————

In November 1972 the new Archbishop of Dublin, Dr Dermot Ryan, attended a service in Christchurch Cathedral, the first Catholic bishop to do so since the Reformation.

———— ◎ ————

The worst storm to hit Dublin in seventy-one years occurred on Saturday 12 January 1974. Two people were killed in the city. Wind speeds of up to 180 kilometres per hour were recorded. Great numbers of trees were blown down in the Phoenix Park and many enterprising citizens chopped them up for firewood.

———— ◎ ————

The 1970s saw the bitter controversy over Dublin Corporation's plans to build civic offices on Wood Quay. The quay is probably Dublin's oldest and is believed to have got its name from the fact that the original quay was built of wood. An archaeological dig on the site in 1969 uncovered proof that a Viking settlement had existed there. Four years later when only a small portion of the site had been investigated the Corporation ordered the dig to stop as they wished to build offices on the site. There was such a public outcry against this plan that the government intervened and ordered further investigation but then in February 1974 it gave the go-ahead for four office blocks on the site. Again there were large-scale protests and in 1976 an organisation called The Friends of Medieval Dublin, led by an Augustinian priest named Father FX Martin, managed to get the Irish High Court to declare Wood Quay a national monument. Work went ahead however in spite of huge protest marches and eventually the battle was lost and the four office blocks were built.

———— ◎ ————

———— ◎ ————

In March 1974 the Corporation decided to erect seven sets of traffic lights for the first time in O'Connell Street.

———— ◎ ————

The strike of Dublin binmen which began in February 1974 finally ended several weeks later on 21 April. The strike was caused by maintenance men refusing to repair collection machinery.

———— ◎ ————

In 1978 the Matt Talbot Memorial Bridge, downstream of the Customs House, was opened to southbound traffic and at the same time traffic across Butt Bridge was made one-way northbound. The bridge was the first to be constructed of pre-stressed concrete. It is named in honour of Matt Talbot (1856–1925), an ordinary Dublin workingman of great virtue, who worked for a time for Dublin Port and Docks Board and later in T and C Martin's timber yard on the North Wall.

The Talbot Memorial Bridge was opened in 1978. As well as honouring Matt Talbot it also commemorates all the sailors from Dublin who died at sea.

———— ◎ ————

———— ◎ ————

On the 16 February 1981 a dreadful fire in the Stardust ballroom in Artane claimed the lives of forty-five young people. The ballroom was packed with youngsters who were celebrating Valentine's Night.

Eyewitnesses later gave evidence that they saw two seats on fire on a closed balcony at 1.45 a.m. The balcony was empty at the time and the blaze was behind a hanging fire-proof screen. When staff lifted the screen to deal with the fire it spread rapidly with the consequent loss of life. It was later established that the fire had been started deliberately.

———— ◎ ————

In 1982 a new bridge was built across the Liffey just downstream of Seán Heuston Bridge near Heuston Station. It is a three span concrete structure and is named after a well-known city politician, Frank Sherwin.

Frank Sherwin Bridge commemorates a popular city councillor who died in 1981. It cost £1.5 million to build.

———— ◎ ————

In October 1984 the East Link tollbridge was first opened to traffic. The Dublin industrialist Tom Roche was allowed to build the bridge on condition that ships would still have access to the city quays. The bridge has a single cantilever leaf which can be raised or lowered in one minute.

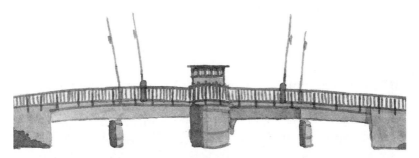

The East Link Bridge over the Liffey caters for two-way traffic and can open to allow boats to pass through.

In 1985 Frank McDonald, a fearless defender of Dublin's architectural heritage, wrote a book entitled *The Destruction of Dublin*. It was an attempt to make Dublin's citizens aware of the threat to the city from unscrupulous developers and particularly the threat to many gracious Georgian houses.

The huge spread of Dublin City that we know today really took off in the 1950s when many inner-city tenements were knocked down and vast new housing estates were built for the displaced tenants in Crumlin, Drimnagh and Ballyfermot, south of the Liffey and Cabra West on the northside. The expansion continued in the 1960s in Walkinstown, Ballymun and Finglas; in the 1970s in Irishtown, City Quay and the Coombe and in the 1980s in Tallaght, Clondalkin and Blanchardstown. Today the population of the city and its satellite towns numbers well over one million people.

23

◎

THE END OF THE
SECOND MILLENNIUM
1991 – 1999

In February 1991 the Irish Family Planning Association lost an appeal against a prosecution for selling condoms in the Virgin Megastore on Aston Quay. The government promised a review but the Catholic Archbishops of Dublin and Armagh warned of the 'dire consequences' which would follow any lifting of the ban. Eventually anyone over seventeen years was allowed to purchase them and today they are freely available and no one passes the slightest heed.

In September of that year the sale of the old bakery building of Johnston, Mooney and O'Brien in Ballsbridge provoked great controversy. Telecom Éireann (Eircom) bought the premises for £9.4 million but it emerged that the seller Dermot Desmond of National City Brokers had earlier bought the premises for £4.5 million and Michael Smurfit, chairman of Telecom, owned ten per cent of NCB. The Taoiseach, Charles Haughey, suggested that certain people should 'step aside' and they did so.

Another major controversy concerned the purchase of Carysfort College by University College Dublin. It was claimed that UCD was pressurised by Fianna Fáil to pay £8 million to a party supporter, Pino Harris, who had previously bought Carysfort for £6.5 million. A further row developed when it became known that a sewage scheme was pushed through Haughey's land at Kinsealy, thereby greatly enhancing its value, and a confidential report on Aer Lingus helicopters found its way to Celtic Helicopters managed by Haughey's son, Ciaran.

Haughey managed to cling on to power for two more years in spite of rumours and allegations of business irregularities involving

Larry Goodman's meat empire, the privatisation of the Irish Sugar Company and his son's helicopter company.

In November 1991 the Finance Minister, Albert Reynolds, supported a motion of no-confidence in Haughey as leader of Fianna Fáil. Haughey replied by sacking Reynolds and insisting on an open vote for the confidence motion. He won by the astonishing margin of 55 to 22.

And then the whole edifice came tumbling down around his ears. Seán Doherty publicly admitted that Haughey had been fully aware of the tapping of the phones of the two newspaper correspondents, Geraldine Kennedy and Bruce Arnold in 1982. Haughey at first denied the charge but on 30 January 1992 he announced his retirement from politics after the Progressive Democrats withdrew their support from his coalition government. On January 22 they had said that either Haughey should go or they would go.

On 11 February 1992 Albert Reynolds was elected Taoiseach to succeed Haughey. His first act was to sack eight of the previous ministers and only Bertie Ahern was left in the same ministry as before. Reynolds had chosen to make his plans in the Berkeley Court Hotel beforehand and most of the appointees were only told of their appointments just before Reynolds began his speech in the Dáil.

On 7 February 1997 a special tribunal of inquiry was set up in Dublin Castle with Mr Justice McCracken in the chair to inquire into allegations of payments by Ben Dunne of Dunnes Stores to Charlie Haughey and Fine Gael TD, Michael Lowry.

The tribunal managed to trace money transfers from Dublin to London, to and from the Cayman Islands and money accounts in the now famous 'Ansbacher Deposits' where wealthy Irish businessmen hid large sums of money away from the prying eyes of the Revenue Commissioners. The McCracken Tribunal did excellent work and took the matter as far as it could.

Another tribunal under Judge Michael Moriarty was set up to continue the inquiry. The tribunal started hearing witnesses on 28 January 1999. It investigated the Ansbacher accounts and discovered millions of pounds were salted away by many prominent Dublin businessmen. Large payments from Ben Dunne to Charles Haughey, not previously discovered by the McCracken

———— ◎ ————

Severe storms battered the country at the first weekend of 1991, and caused the deaths of 14 people and over £15,000,000 worth of damage. Two of the dead were Dublin men who were killed by falling trees. Electricity and phone lines were badly damaged and all ferry services were cancelled.

———— ◎ ————

In April 1991 the ESB went on strike, resulting in the disruption of electricity supplies all over the country. Dublin was badly affected and the Ballymun Towers were without lifts and lighting for long periods.

———— ◎ ————

In 1997 December just two months after her election as President of Ireland, Mary McAleese caused controversy by accepting communion at a Church of Ireland ceremony in St Patrick's Cathedral. She was roundly condemned by right-wing Catholic churchmen but most ordinary people regarded the act as a welcome gesture of ecumenism and evidence of her genuine desire to 'build bridges' between communities.

———— ◎ ————

In 1999 a report on housing policies and future population trends was published which forecast that Dublin's population would rise by 250,000 to 1.65 million in 2011.

———— ◎ ————

tribunal, also came to light. In addition the tribunal uncovered the extraordinary leniency with which Allied Irish Banks treated Haughey while at the same time dealing much more firmly with ordinary customers.

Between the two tribunals already mentioned, another tribunal was set up in 1998 under the chairmanship of Mr Justice Fergus Flood to investigate planning irregularities in north County Dublin but due to legal manoeuvring it only heard its first witness in January 1999. The elderly witness, James Gogarty, proved to be so cantankerous, irascible and quick-witted that the Dublin Castle tribunal soon became 'the hottest show in town'.

Gogarty alleged that he paid £30,000 to Ray Burke, who held various ministries in successive Fianna Fáil governments and who was also a member of Dublin County Council. Gogarty was acting for a large building company called JMSE and he claimed that on one occasion himself and Michael Bailey of Bovale Developments gave Burke £80,000. Gogarty alleged that he was paying Burke a bribe on behalf of JMSE but Burke and JMSE both denied this. These matters and alleged payments to Padraig Flynn, TD, are still being investigated by the tribunal.

Another figure gradually drawn into the inquiry was George Redmond, assistant city and county manager for Dublin for many years. On Friday, 19 January 1999 he was arrested at Dublin airport and found to have £300,000 in his possession on his return from the Isle of Man. Over twenty different bank accounts were found to be under his control and these and other related matters are still being investigated at the time of publication of this book.

Dublin's celebrations for the new millennium got off to a bad start as the Millennium Clock in the Liffey at O'Connell Bridge fell victim to the polluted waters of the river. The 'Chime in the Slime', as Dubliners called it, weighed six tonnes and was supposed to count down the minutes from 1996 but no one could read the green neon digits displayed just under the surface of the water. Various efforts to rectify the matter failed, until in the end the clock was removed altogether.

A more successful venture was the construction of the Millennium Bridge, just west of the Halfpenny Bridge. It was constructed by Price and Meyers to designs by architects Howley Harrington and was opened to pedestrians in December 1999.

Later bollards were erected at each end to deter cavalier motorists who might consider driving across it.

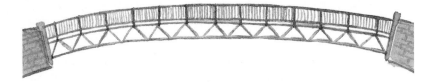

The Millennium Bridge.

Another proposal to erect a monument to replace Nelson's Pillar in O'Connell Street came to grief due to a legal challenge from a Dublin citizen. The proposed 'Monument of Light' was a 125-metre high steel 'spike' with a light on top.

The population of Dublin City and the surrounding area is growing at a very fast rate at the start of the new millennium. It is estimated that if this rate of increase continues that more than half the population of Ireland will be living in the Dublin area by 2047. The increase in population is already causing traffic chaos in the city. The building of new roads is unlikely to solve the problem. New and imaginative remedies are required which will have to involve suburban and underground railways, tunnels and maybe new work practices and patterns.

Apart from the traffic problems and the related housing crisis the future has never looked brighter for this ancient city. The city of Strongbow, Laurence O'Toole, Swift, Grattan, Emmet, O'Connell, Pearse, Joyce and others is strong, vibrant, prosperous and confident as it enters the Third Millennium. One can be sure that the Town of the Hurdle Ford will continue to captivate and endear itself to all who come to know it, just as it has always done in the past.

———— ◎ ————

Many Dublin streets underwent name changes over the centuries. Some changes were made to honour various famous people but a lot of them were made to remove embarrassing or unpleasant names. Here are some of the name-changes:

Crooked Staff	Ardee Street
Pudding Lane	Lincoln Lane
Elbow Lane	Bow Lane
Dunghill Lane	Island Street
Cuckold's Row	Brabazon Street
Gallows Road	Baggot Street Lower
Dirty Lane	Bridgefoot Street
Murdering Lane	Old Kilmainham
Cutthroat Lane	Brookfield Road
Lazar's (Lazy) Hill	Townsend Street
Watery Lane (1)	Brookfield Avenue
Hoggen (Hog) Hill	St Andrews Street
Watery Lane (2)	Lansdowne Road
Cabbage Garden Lane	Cathedral Lane
Dog and Duck Yard	Usher's Lane
Skinners' Row	Christchurch Place
Goat Alley	Digges Lane
Gibbet Meadow	Mespil Road
Hangman's Lane	Hammond Lane
Coldblow Lane	Belmont Avenue

———— ◎ ————

294

Bibliography

Aalen, F H A and Whelan, K: *Dublin City and Country from Pre-History to Present* (1992)

Andrews, C S: *Dublin Made Me* (1979)

Bennett, D: *Encyclopaedia of Dublin* (1991)

Brooke, R: *The Brimming River* (1961)

Clarke, H B: *Medieval Dublin: The Living City* (1990)

Chevevix Trench, C: *The Great Dan* (1984)

Craig, M: *Dublin 1660-1860* (1980)

Curtis, L: *The Cause of Ireland* (1994)

F E R: *Historical Reminiscences of Dublin Castle* (1899)

Foster, R F: *Modern Ireland 1600-1972* (1988)

Gwynn, A: *The Black Death in Dublin* (Studies 1935)

Gwynn, S: *Dublin Old and New* (1938)

Healy, E: *The Wolfhound Guide to Dublin Monuments* (1998)

Hervey, J: *Dublin* (1949)

Horgan, J: *Lemass* (1997)

Kearns, K: *Dublin Street Life* (1991)

Kearns, K: *Dublin Tenement Life: An Oral History* (1994)

Kee, R: *Ireland: A History* (1980)

Kee, R: *The Laurel and the Ivy* (1993)

Kelly, W: *Me Darlin Dublin's Dead and Gone* (1983)

Lalor, B: *The Ultimate Dublin Guide* (1991)

Larkin, E: *James Larkin* (1965)

Liddy, P: *Dublin Today* (1984)

Longford, C: *The Story of Dublin* (1936)

Lyons, F S L: *Ireland Since the Famine* (1973)

MacLoughlan: *A Guide to Historic Dublin* (1979)

McDowell, R B: *Social Life in Ireland 1800-1845* (1970)

Maxwell, C: *Dublin under the Georges* (1936)

Middleton Murray, J: *Jonathan Swift* (1954)

Mitchell, F: *Vanishing Dublin* (1966)

Neeson, E: *Birth of a Republic* (1998)

O'Donnell, E E: *The Annals of Dublin: Fair City* (1987)

Redmond: *The Story of Dublin City and County* (1927)

Robertson, O: *Dublin Phoenix* (1957)

Ryan, D: *The Rising* (1949)

Somerville-Large, P: *Dublin the Fair City* (1996)

Warburton and Whitelaw: *History of the City of Dublin* (1818)

Index

Abbey Street 233, 236
Abbey Theatre 212, 260, 276
Aberdeen, Lord 206
Act of Renunciation 103
Act of Union 131, 143
Adam and Eve, Church of 111
Ahern, Bertie 289
Aiken, Frank 260
Albert, Prince 168
Alfred, Prince 168
All Hallows, Priory of 19, 53, 60
Allen, Archbishop 49
Allgood, Sarah 212
Allied Irish Banks 291
Amiens Street 200
An Tostal 278
Anatomy Act 156
Ansbacher Deposits 289
Antient Concert Rooms 219
Áras an Uachtaráin 187, 271
Arbour Hill 223
Arms Trial 275
Army Comrades Association 267, 269
Arnold, Bruce 283, 289
Arran Street 204
Artane 286
Artillery Barracks 133
Asgard 222
Ashbourne 245
Ashe, Thomas 245
Asquith, Henry 213, 214, 241
Aston Quay 96, 288
Áth Cliath 3, 5, 13
Atmospheric Railway 152
Aud 232
Auxiliaries 247, 248, 249, 252
Avondale 172

Bachall Íosa 7, 30, 46, 52
Bachelor's Walk 140, 224, 233
Back Lane 66, 92, 107
Back-Lane Parliament 108, 109
Baggot Street, Upper 73
Baggotrath 73
Baile Átha Cliath 2
Bailey Lighthouse 164
Bailey, Michael 291
Balfe, Michael William 134
Ballast Board 96
Ballast Office 253
Ballinamuck 118
Ballsbridge 128, 235, 258
Ballyboghill 7
Ballybough 13, 271
Ballyfermot 272, 287
Ballymun 287
Ballymun Towers 290
Bank of Ireland 185
Bannow Bay 25
Bantry Bay 117
Barrett, Richard 259
Barrington, Sir Jonah 104, 122, 129
Barry, Kevin 248, 249
Barton, Commandant Robert 252
Becket, Thomas a' 29
Beckett, Samuel 264, 268
Beggars Bush 234
Beggars Bush Barracks 259
Beresford Place 203
Berkeley Court Hotel 289
Bermingham Tower 34, 57
Big Wind, The 148
Biggar, Joseph 179, 181
Birmingham 149
Bishop Street 234

Black and Tans 247, 248, 252
Black Death, The 40, 41
Black Monday 34
Black Rent 43
Blackpitts 40, 154
Blackrock 115, 171
Blanchardstown 287
Bloody Sunday 249, 250, 277
Blueshirts 269, 270
Blythe, Ernest 257
Bodenstown 124, 270
Body Snatchers 156
Boer War 201, 202
Bohemian Girl, The 134
Boland, Kevin 277
Boland's Mill 234, 240
Bompart, Admiral Jean
    Baptiste 123
Bond, Oliver 117, 122
Book of Common Prayer 55, 56
Book of Kells 158
Booterstown 44, 263
Borlase, Sir John 69, 70
Boru, Brian 13, 15, 17, 18
Borumborad, Dr Achmet 114
Bowen-Colthurst, Captain JC
    239
Boyne River 81, 83, 84
Bray 25
Brazen Head 117
Breen, Dan 246, 248
Brennan, Thomas 186
Bride Street 66
Bridge Gate 56
Bridge Street 3, 62, 254
Bridgefoot Street 133
Brighton Road 268
Brock, Thomas 150
Brodir 15, 17
Broombridge 153

Browne, George, Archbishop
    of Dublin 52, 53, 54
Bruce, Edward 39
Bruce, Robert 37, 39
Brugha, Cathal 222, 234, 247,
    252, 255
Brunel, Isambard Kingdom 152
Buckinghamshire, John
    Hobart, Lord 101
Bulletin 247
Bullock Harbour 281
Bully's Acre 156
Burgh Quay 198, 244
Burke, Edmund 91, 108
Burke, Ray 291
Burke, TH 186, 187
Butler, James 71
Butlers, Earls of Ormond 41,
    45, 46, 47, 48, 72, 73
Butt Bridge 178, 285
Butt, Isaac 175
Butterfield House 133
Byrne, Alfred 262
Cabinteely 194
Cabra 13, 153, 176, 272
Cabra West 287
Camden Street 238
Camden, John Jeffreys, Lord
    102, 113
Capel Street 3, 18, 48, 80, 81,
    82
Capel, Henry, Lord Lieutenant
    87
Carey, James 187
Carlisle Bridge 98, 154, 179
Carrickmines Castle 69
Carysfort College 288
Case's Tower 56
Casement, Roger 220, 241, 242
Castle Street 9, 33, 62, 75
Castleknock 22, 27, 29, 39, 72

Castlereagh, Robert Stewart, Lord 127
Catholic Association 143
Catholic Bulletin 258
Cavendish, Lord Frederick 186, 187
Ceannt, Áine 228
Ceannt, Eamonn 220, 227, 232, 233, 234, 237, 238, 240
Celtic Helicopters 288
Central Model School 266
Chamberlain, Joseph 203
Chancery Place 130
Chancery Street 204
Chapelizod 13
Charlemont Street 197
Charles I 65, 66
Charles II 38, 72, 76, 77
Charles Street 204
Chatterton, Hedges Eyre 256
Chichester, Arthur 63, 65
Childers, Erskine 222, 252, 259
Chotah 222
Christchurch Cathedral 15, 16, 28, 30, 32, 38, 42, 45, 46, 54, 62, 68, 195
Christchurch Place 9, 52, 58
Church Lane 11
Church Street 3, 20, 216, 248
Churchill, Winston 255
Citizen Army *see* Irish Citizen Army
City Hall 126, 150, 195, 229, 235, 245, 257
City Quay 274, 287
Civic Guards *see* Garda Síochána
Clancy, Peadar 249
Clanwilliam House 236
Clarence, Duke of 178
Clarke, Kathleen 228, 243, 246

Clarke, Thomas 207, 209, 211, 221, 227, 230, 232, 237, 238, 240, 241
Classic 257
Clery's Department Store 181, 210, 236, 244, 279
Clondalkin 11, 22, 25, 123, 287
Clonkeen 20
Clontarf 20, 122, 223
Clontarf, Battle of 13, 15
Clune, Conor 249
Cobh Harbour 257
Cockayne, John 109, 111
Coercian Act 189
Colbert, Con 220, 240
College Green 11, 60, 68, 86, 90, 91, 101, 127, 129, 130, 146, 147, 148, 151, 184, 185, 193, 195, 203, 204, 238
College Park 80
College Street 210
Collins, Michael 238, 243, 245, 247, 248, 249, 250, 252, 254, 255, 257, 259, 269
Collins' Museum 118
Collinstown Aerodrome 247
Colum, Padraic 212
Connolly, Ina 228
Connolly, James 197, 199, 201, 203, 217, 218, 220, 221, 225, 227, 229, 230, 232, 236, 237, 240, 241
Connolly, Nora 228
Connolly, Patrick 281
Convention Act 108
Conyngham Road 176
Cook Street 62, 66
Coombe, The 35, 40, 122, 287
Coote, Sir Charles 70
Cope Street 108
Cope, AW 252

Copper Alley 14
Cork Hill 35
Cornmarket 5, 64
Cornwallis, Charles, Lord
    Lieutenant 123, 127
Corporation Baths 217
Corry, Isaac 128
Cosgrave, William 252, 257,
    260, 261, 263
Costigan's Hotel 194
Crampton, Sir William 151
Croke Park 248, 275
Cromer, Archbishop George 49
Cromwell, Oliver 74, 75
Croppies 119
Croppies Acre 118, 157, 159
Crown jewels 208
Croydon Park 219, 220, 221
Crumlin 11, 60, 123, 272, 287
Crumlin Road 5
Cuffe Street 234
Cullenswood 34
Cumann na mBan 220
Cumann na nGaedheal 207,
    261, 265, 269
Curragh Camp 221
Curragh Mutiny 221
Curran, John Philpott 104,
    105, 107, 109, 111, 124, 135,
    146
Curran, Sarah 135
Customs House 151, 203, 235,
    250, 251, 285
D'Esterre, John 140
Dáil Éireann 246, 247, 261,
    263, 265, 267, 270, 272, 277
Daily Mail 201
Daily Nation 272
Dalkey 14, 20, 22, 41, 152, 276,
    281
Dalkey Island 90

Daly, Edward 234, 240
Daly, John 207
Dalymount Park 276
Dame Street 90, 101, 150, 238
Dames Gate 26, 45, 49, 56
Dargan, William 166, 168
Davis, Sir William 80
Davis, Thomas 86, 161
Davitt, Michael 171, 181, 186,
    191
Dawson Street 185, 192, 227,
    229, 246
de Barri *see* Geraldines
de Burgos 41
de Clare, Richard *see*
    Strongbow
de Cogan, Milo 27, 29
de Grey, Thomas Philip, Lord
    Lieutenant 145
de Londres, Henry 33
de Rossa, Proinsias 281
de Valera, Eamon 106, 153,
    223, 228, 231, 235, 240, 245,
    246, 247, 250, 252, 253, 254,
    255, 259, 261, 262, 263, 267,
    269, 270, 273, 275, 284
Defenders 107
Desmond, Dermot 288
Destruction of Dublin, The 287
Devlin, Anne 133, 135
Devoy, John 169
Dickson, Thomas 239
Dillon, James 253
Dillon, John 186, 193
Dodder River 22, 72
Doherty, Seán 281, 283
Domville, Sir Compton 100
Donnelly, Dan 156
Donnybrook Fair 36
Donnycarney 272
Dorset Street 5, 13

Drapier Letters 95, 97
Drimnagh 22, 287
Drogheda 41, 92
Drumcondra 5, 13, 176
Drumcondra Road 13
Dubh Linn 2, 3, 5
Dubhghaill 16
Dublin Bay 92, 126
Dublin Brigade 247, 250, 253
Dublin Castle 1, 9, 33, 34, 49,
   57, 58, 65, 79, 101, 117, 123,
   132, 133, 141, 147, 160, 168,
   173, 175, 178, 187, 208, 231,
   232, 235, 238, 240, 247, 249,
   289, 291
Dublin Chronicle 102
Dublin City Hall 35
Dublin County Council 291
Dublin Horse Show 215
Dublin Metropolitan Police
   107, 198, 238
Dublin Port 285
Dublin Sanitary Association
   158
Dublin Socialist Club 197
Dublin Trade Unions 277
Dublin United Tramway
   Company 214
Dublin, Battle of 11
Duchess of Kent 149
Duggan, Charles 222
Duggan, Commandant
   Edmund 252
Duggan, Richard 256
Dun Laoghaire 144, 262
Dun Laoghaire Harbour 144,
   244
Dundrum 170
Dunne, Ben 289
Dunne, Donal 281
Dunsink Observatory 96, 196

Dwyer, Michael 133
East Link Bridge 287
Easter Rising 1916 225–42
Eccles Street 122, 264
Eden Quay 233, 279
Edward II 39
Edward IV 45
Edward VI 45, 47, 55, 95
Edward VII 178, 206, 208, 209
Egan, Patrick 186
Elizabeth I 55, 58, 60, 158
Elvery's Sports Shop 236, 239
Emmet, Robert 106, 132–5,
   195, 292
Enniskerry 25, 265
ESB 280
Essex Bridge 3
Essex Quay 253
Eucharistic Congress 262
Eustace Street 139
Ewart-Biggs, Christopher 279
Falkland, Henry Cary, Lord
   Deputy 65
Fr Mathew Bridge 3, 32
Fenians 167, 170, 173, 177, 181
Fianna Fáil 253, 260, 261, 263,
   269, 279, 288, 289
Figgis, Mrs Darrell 250
Fine Gael 269, 270, 279
Finglas 287
Fionnghaill 16
Fishamble Street 62, 56, 100
FitzGerald *see* Geraldines
Fitzgerald, Lord Edward 114,
   115, 117, 119–23, 141, 195
Fitzgerald, Maurice 25
Fitzgerald, William Vesey 143
Fitzgibbon, Black Jack 110,
   112
Fitzgibbon, John, Lord Clare
   127

FitzHenry *see* Geraldines
Fitzhenry, Meiler 33
FitzOsmund 28
Fitzstephen, Robert 25
Fitzwilliam Square 166
Fitzwilliam, Earl of 112, 113
Fitzwilliam, Sir William 57
Fleet Street 248
Flood, Henry 91, 99, 105, 107
Flood, Mr Justice Fergus 291
Flynn, Padraig 291
Foley, John Henry 150
Football Association 276
Forster, William 186
Forty Foot 146
Forty-Shilling Freeholders, The
    108
Foster, John 129
Four Courts 32, 52, 234, 253,
    254, 255, 257, 261
Four Courts Hotel 275
Francis Street 5, 20, 113
Free State 257
Free Trade Acts 101
Freeman, Spencer 256
Freeman's Journal 120, 149, 160,
    191, 208, 212, 229, 236
Frescati House 114, 119
Friars Preachers, Priory of 52
Friends of Medieval Dublin,
    The 284
Fusiliers' Arch 202
Fyan's Tower 56
Gaelic League 212
Gallagher, Paddy 281
Gallows Hill 106
Gandon, James 98
Garda Síochána 107, 253, 276
Gardiner Street 128, 279
Gargan, Bridie 281
Garret Mór 47

Garret Óg 47, 48
Gas Company 273
Gate Theatre 260
George II 99
George III 108, 139, 142
George IV 138, 144
George V 209, 234
George, Lloyd 252, 255
George's Quay 235
Georgian houses 280
Georgius Rex 226
Geraldines, Earls of Kildare 21,
    25, 41, 45, 46, 47, 48
German plot 246
Gibson, Lieutenant Colonel 69
Gifford, Grace 240
Gladstone, William Ewart 183,
    187, 189, 192
Glasnevin 11, 171, 176, 272
Glasnevin Cemetery 149, 156,
    196, 210, 245, 257
Glencree 25
Glencullen 170
Glendalough 25
Glimmer Man 273
Goatstown 166
Gogarty, James 291
Golden Lane 178
Gonne, Maud 203, 205, 207,
    228
Goodman, Larry 289
Gore-Booth, Sir Henry 213
Gormund's Gate 56
Gough, Lord 276
GPO 226, 233, 234, 235, 236,
    238
Grafton Street 184, 201, 202,
    204, 209, 238
Grand Canal 102
Grand Canal Hotel 141
Grangegorman 147

Grattan Bridge 80, 82
Grattan, Henry 91, 93, 99, 100, 101, 103, 105, 107, 117, 127, 128, 129, 292
Grattan's Parliament 100, 184
Great Dublin Industrial Exhibition 168
Great Famine, The 155–60
Green Street 109
Green Street Courthouse 114, 135
Green Tureen 280
Gregg, Dr 258
Gregory, Tony 279
Grenville Hotel 255
Gresham Hotel 248, 252
Grey, Lord Leonard 50, 53
Griffith, Arthur 203, 205, 207, 209, 231, 241, 246, 252, 255, 257, 269
Guiney, Denis 244
Guinness, Sir Arthur 86, 162
Gunn, Michael 174
Gunpowder Act 108
Gunpowder Tower 33
Haddington Road 92, 236
Haig, Major 223
Hales, Seán 261
Halfpenny Bridge 136, 223, 291
Hallows, Priory of All 19, 60
Hamilton, William Rowan 153
Hamman Hotel 255
Handel, George Frederick 100
Hanrahan, Michael 240
Harcourt Street 84, 184, 234, 280
Harcourt, Sir Simon 69
Harold's Cross 5, 18, 122, 271
Harris, Pino 288
Haughey, Charles 271, 275, 277, 279, 281, 288, 289, 291
Hawkins Street 151, 198
Healy, Timothy 259
Helga 228, 235
Henrietta Street 128
Henry II 21, 27, 29, 33
Henry III 32, 33, 37
Henry IV 45
Henry Place 237
Henry Street 234, 236, 237, 238
Henry VII 45, 47
Henry VIII 47, 48, 51, 52, 55, 58
Herbert Park 206
Heuston Bridge 138, 159, 286
Heuston Station 286
Heuston, Seán 138, 234, 240
Higgins, Francis 'Sham Squire' 120, 121, 141
High Street 9, 22, 38, 62, 90, 107, 124
Hill Street 256
Hillery, President Patrick 274
Hobson, Bulmer 222, 231, 232
Hoche, General Lazare 117
Hogan, Michael 249
Hoggen Green 11, 19, 22, 27, 29, 36, 60
Home Rule 175, 203, 211, 214, 221, 225, 246
Home Rule Bill 192, 213, 227
Home Rule League 177
Horse Show 208
Houses of Parliament 103
Houston, Edward 190
Howley Harrington 291
Howth 20, 41, 164
Howth Head 164
Hugh Lane 136
Huguenots 84

Humbert, General Joseph
Amable 118
Imperial Hotel 181, 182, 183,
215, 216, 233, 236, 244
Inchicore 5, 13, 272
Ireland 195
Ireland's Eye 14
Irish Citizen Army 220, 221,
229, 230, 231, 233, 234, 235,
237
Irish Family Planning
Association 288
Irish Free State 258, 259
Irish Freedom 209
Irish Hospital Sweepstakes
256, 258
Irish Independent 215
Irish International Exhibition
206
Irish Motor Show 204
Irish Municipal Employees
Trade Union 274
Irish National Land League 182
Irish National Party 214
Irish National Teachers
Organisation 273
Irish Parliament 103
Irish Parliamentary Party 207
Irish People 167
Irish Press 272
Irish Republican Brotherhood
165, 220, 225, 243
Irish Rugby Union 260
Irish Seamen 274
Irish Sugar Company 289
Irish Times 168, 229, 265, 278
Irish Volunteers (eighteenth
century) 99, 101, 105, 109
Irish Volunteers 220, 222, 223,
224, 230, 232, 233, 234, 238,
245, 250

Irish Worker 229
Irishtown 287
Irregulars 255
Islandbridge 9, 11, 104
Jackson, Henry 122
Jackson, William 109, 111, 112
Jacob's Biscuit Factory 211,
216, 234, 237, 280
James II 38, 76, 77, 79, 83, 115
James Street 5, 102, 141, 238
Jameson's distillery 148
Jinks, John 265
John Tayleur 164
Johnston, Mooney and
O'Brien 288
Johnston, Tom 263, 265
Jones, Colonel 72, 73
Joyce, James 264, 278, 292
Joyce, Patrick 114
Kavanagh, Art 57
Kelpie 222
Kennedy, Geraldine 283, 289
Keogh Square 238
Kettle, AJ 186
Khyber Pass 172
Kilcoole 222
Kildare Street 198
Kildare, Earl of *see* Geraldines
Kilkenny People 163
Killiney 165
Kilmainham 5, 11, 13, 50, 156,
189, 190, 238
Kilmainham Jail 106, 114, 135,
185, 186, 187, 228, 240
Kilmainham Treaty 189
Kilwarden, Arthur Wolfe, Lord
133
Kimmage 74, 230
King John 33, 34, 37
King's Own Scottish Borderers
223

Kingsbridge 94, 138, 153, 159, 176
Kingsbridge Station 235
Kingstown 144, 152, 166, 192, 217, 235
Kingstown Harbour 186, 195, 206
Kingstown Temperance Hall 177
Kirwan, John 170
Kitchener, Lord Horatio Herbert 234
La Scala Theatre 261
Labour Party 279
Lake, General Gerard 119
Lalor, Fintan 261
Lambay Island 14, 164
Lancaster, House of 45
Land Act 189
Land League 183, 184, 185, 186
Land Question 175
Larkin, Delia 211, 214, 217
Larkin, James 209, 210, 215, 216, 218, 219, 220, 221, 229
Laudabiliter 29
le Gros, Raymond 27, 28, 29
Leinster 244
Leinster House 114, 119, 126, 198
Leinster Lawn 168
Leinster, Duke of 126
Lemass, Seán 253, 254, 273
Lever Brothers 253
Liberal Party 203
Liberties 35, 154
Liberty Hall 216, 217, 218, 219, 221, 228, 229, 233, 235, 279
Liffey Bridge 44, 136
Liffey Quay 140

Liffey River 1, 2, 3, 9, 13, 20, 32, 40, 73, 78, 82, 102, 104, 122, 178, 204, 287, 291
Liffey Viaduct 176
Limerick 85
Lincoln Place 279
Lincoln Prison 247
Lincoln's Inn 139
Linn Dubh 1
Lombard Street 165
Longphort 9
Loopline Bridge 178, 235
Loughlinstown 122
Lower Abbey Street 279
Lower Fitzwilliam Street 280
Lower Mount Street Bridge 236
Lowry, Michael 289
Lucas, Charles 91, 99
Lynch, Jack 275, 277
Lynch, Liam 259
Mac Diarmada, Seán 227, 231, 232, 237, 238, 240
Mac Murrough Kavanagh, Art 43
Mac Murrough, Dermot 19, 25, 27
Mac Torkill, Asculph 27
MacArthur, Malcolm 281
MacBride, Major John 207, 234, 240, 250
MacBride, Seán 250
MacDonagh, Muriel 228
MacDonagh, Thomas 220, 222, 231, 232, 233, 234, 238, 240, 241
MacManus, Terence Bellew 167
MacNeill, Eoin 220, 231, 232, 233
MacNeill, James 260

Macready, General Sir Nevil 252

MacSwiney, Peter Paul 179

Magazine Fort 234, 270

Malachy, King of Tara 13

Malin, Michael 240

Mansion House 192, 227, 246, 252

Maolmordha, King of Leinster 13, 15, 18

Marino 272

Marino Casino 96

Marino Crescent 96

Markievicz, Countess Constance 211, 213, 214, 216, 220, 221, 228, 229, 230, 231, 240, 246

Marlborough Street 266, 279

Marrowbone Lane 262

Martello Towers 134

Martin, Father FX 284

Martin, T and C 285

Martyrs' Plot 171

Mary Street 148

Mary's Lane Chapel 54

Masonic Hall 253

Mathew, Father Theobald 151

Matt Talbot Memorial Bridge 285

Maxwell, General Sir John Grenfell 241

Maynooth 49

McAleese, Mary 290

McCarthy, Mr Justin 192

McCormack O'Connor, Connor 58

McCracken Tribunal 289, 291

McCracken, Mr Justice Brian 289

McDonald, Frank 287

McGinley, Patrick 222

McGrath, Joe 256

McIntyre, Patrick 239

McKee, Dick 249

McKelvey, Joseph 259

McNally, Leonard 111, 135

McQuaid, Dr John Charles, Archbishop of Dublin, 273, 275, 276, 278, 284,

Meagher, Thomas Francis 163

Mellifont Abbey 21

Mellowes, Liam 82, 259

Mendicity Institute 234

Mercers Hospital 250

Merchant's Quay 39, 49, 56, 62, 111

Merrion Row 84

Merrion Square 102, 141, 145, 147, 168, 266, 277

Merrion Street 84

Messiah 100

Millennium Bridge 291, 292

Millennium Clock 291

Mitchel, John 163

Mohangi, Shan 280

Molesworth Street 253

Molyneux, William 91, 93

Monroe, General Robert 71

Montgomery Street 200

Montgomery, James 260

Monto, The 200

Monument of Light 292

Moore Lane 236

Moore Street 236, 237

Moran, Michael 154

Moriarty, Michael 289

Morrison's Hotel 185

Mortished, RJP 265

Motte-and-baileys 22

Mount Anville 166

Mount Brown 234

Mount Drummond Avenue 135

Mount Street 73, 234
Mount Street Bridge 234
Mountjoy Jail 214, 218, 248, 249, 250
Mountjoy Square 128, 272
Mountjoy, John Charles Blount 60, 61, 63
Mulcahy, Richard 252, 257
Mullen, Hazel 280
Murchú 228
Murphy, Nicholas 119
Murphy, William Martin 206, 214, 215, 216, 230
Murray, Dr 155
Naas, Lord 175
Nagle, Pierce 167
Nassau Street 80, 185
National Art Gallery 266
National Centre Party 269
National Club 201
National Guard 269
National Volunteers 229
Neilson, Samuel 121, 122
Nelson's Pillar 174, 276, 282, 292
New Gate 26, 56
Newgate Prison 109, 114, 121, 122, 124
Newmarket 122
News Letter 156
Nicholas of Down 38
Nicholas Street 9, 107
Noblett's Sweet Shop 238
Norbury, Lord *see* Toler
Norfolk, Duke of 142
North Circular Road 271
North Earl Street 238
North Great George's Street 272
North Strand 271
North Wall 217

North Wall Quay 102
Northumberland Road 236
O'Brien, Conor Cruise 281
O'Brien, William 227, 265
O'Buachalla, Donal 260
O'Byrne, Hugh 59, 133
O'Casey, Seán 221, 233, 278
O'Connell Bridge 3, 98, 179, 255, 262, 291
O'Connell Schools 271
O'Connell Street 203, 210, 211, 213, 215, 216, 226, 230, 233, 234, 236, 238, 239, 244, 255, 256, 261, 282, 285, 292
O'Connell Street, Upper 13
O'Connell, Commandant JJ 231
O'Connell, Daniel 98, 139–54, 161, 167, 179, 185, 195, 196, 292
O'Connor, Rory 19, 21, 25, 27, 29, 252, 259
O'Donnell, Red Hugh 57, 65
O'Donnell, Sir Hugh 57
O'Donovan Rossa Bridge 82, 130
O'Donovan Rossa, Jeremiah 229
O'Duffy, Eoin 252, 269, 270
O'Farrell, Elizabeth 237
O'Higgins, Kevin 252, 257, 263, 265
O'Higgins, TF 269
O'Kelly, Seán T 227, 259, 260, 276
O'Mahony, John 167
O'More, Rory 69, 70, 78
O'Neill, Hugh 59, 61, 63, 65
O'Neill, Owen Roe 70, 71, 72
O'Rahilly, The 231, 232, 236
O'Rourke, Tiernan 21

O'Shea, Captain William (Willie) 182, 183, 184, 191
O'Shea, Catherine (Katie) 182, 183, 184, 186, 190, 191, 194
O'Toole, St Laurence, Archbishop of Dublin 21, 25, 28, 30, 54, 292
O'Toole, Phelim 59
Observer 187
Offences against the State Bill 277
Old Bridge 22
Omnibus 164
Oriel House Gang 259
Ormond Hotel 261
Ormond Market 204
Ormond Quay Upper 204
Ormond, Earl of *see* Butlers
Ormonde Bridge 82
Ormonde, Duke of 89
Ostmantown 31
Our Lady of Dublin 54
Ouzel 88
Oxmantown 31, 68
Pale, The 41, 48, 49, 70
Parliament Street 40, 82, 167, 180, 185
Parnell Square 105, 201, 227
Parnell Street 180, 236, 237, 279
Parnell, Charles Stewart 106, 173–96, 259
Parnell, John 172, 175
Parsons, Sir William 69, 70
Patrick Street 133
Patriot Party 91, 99
Patterson, Banker 208
Pearse Street 213, 219, 221, 227, 229, 230, 231, 232, 233, 236, 237, 238, 240, 241, 250, 276, 292

Pearse, Pádraig 213, 220, 221, 227, 229–33, 237, 238, 240, 241
Pearse, William (Willie) 238, 240
Peel, Sir Robert 155
Peep-o-Day Boys 107
Penal Laws 87
Perrott, Sir John 57
Phibsborough 13, 219, 264
Phibsborough Church 148
Phoenix Park 13, 58, 137, 144, 151, 176, 187, 189, 218, 234, 235, 259, 262, 270, 271, 273, 276, 281, 284
Phoenix Park Murders 187, 189
Pigeon House 92, 133
Pigott, Richard 188, 189, 191
Pike Theatre 278
Pitt, William 105, 112, 125, 127
Plunkett, George 238
Plunkett, Joseph Mary 220, 227, 231, 232, 237, 238, 240
Poddle River 1, 5, 6, 22, 33, 49, 56
Pole Gate 26, 56
Poolbeg 90
Pope Adrian IV 29
Popish Plot 76
Portobello 119
Portobello Affray 244
Portobello Barracks 239, 244
Portobello Bridge 102, 174, 234
Powerscourt Arms Hotel 265
Poyning's Law 101
Poynings, Sir Edward 41, 47
Preston, Colonel Thomas 70, 71
Price and Meyers 291
Prickett's Tower 56

Prince of Wales 146
Prince's Street 236, 261
Progressive Democrats 289
Purcell, Major-General 73
Queen Alexandra 206
Queen Victoria 110, 151, 158,
  164, 168, 198, 199, 205
Queen's Theatre 276
Raheny 1, 282
Rathcoole 123
Rathfarnham 1, 25, 74, 123,
  133, 135
Rathfarnham Castle 73
Rathgar 174, 264, 268
Rathgar Castle 74
Rathmines 1, 72, 174
Rathmines Castle 74
Rathmines, Battle of 68
Record Tower 34
Redmond, George 291
Redmond, John 170, 180, 207,
  211, 214, 221, 225, 227, 229,
  245
Redmond, William 263
Repeal Association 145
Republican Army Council 253
Reynolds, Albert 289
Reynolds, Lillie 197
Reynolds, Thomas 117
Richard II, 43, 44, 79
Richard III 45
Richmond Barracks 238
Richmond Bridewell 147
Richmond Bridge 130
Richmond Gate 153
Richmond Jail 167, 169
Right Boys 107
Ringsend 44, 74, 122, 146
Rochdale 146
Roche, Tom 287
Rory O'More Bridge 78

Rose Tattoo, The 278
Rotunda Hospital 105, 164,
  193
Rotunda Rooms 181, 192
Rowan, Archibald Hamilton
  108, 109, 110, 111, 112
Royal Barracks 118, 159, 223
Royal Canal 102, 153, 219
Royal College of Surgeons 154,
  234
Royal Collins Barracks 138
Royal Dublin Fusiliers 202
Royal Dublin Society 126, 198,
  204, 258
Royal Exchange 40, 126
Royal Hibernian Academy 236
Royal Hospital Kilmainham
  138, 153, 198
Royal Irish Constabulary 230
Royal Zoological Society 151
Russell, Sir Charles 191
Rutland Square 201
Rutland, Charles Manners,
  Lord Lieutenant 125
Ryan, Dr Dermot 284
Sack-em-ups *see* Body
  Snatchers
Sackville Place 279
Sackville Street 96, 98, 112,
  181, 237, 256
St Anne's Park 282
St Audoen's Arch 26
St Audoen's Church 7, 28
St Augustine Street 5
St Begnet 5
St Brigid's Church 5
St Catherine's Church 135, 195
St Colum Cille 5
St Fintan 5
St Germans, Earl of 168
St James's Gate 79

St James's Gate Brewery 86
St John's Hospital 35, 39
St Leger, Sir Anthony 55
St Mac Táil 5
St Martin 5
St Mary del Dam, Church of 35, 39, 45, 52
St Mary's Abbey 18, 35, 38, 48, 80
St Michael's Lane 62
St Michan's Church 17, 30, 68, 121, 195
St Mo Lua 5
St Nicholas Gate 26, 56
St Patrick 5, 6, 7
St Patrick's Cathedral 5, 6, 9, 30, 38, 46, 52, 58, 65, 83, 95, 141, 148, 262, 290
St Saviour's Priory 22, 32
St Stephen's Green 68, 84, 90, 93, 100, 114, 132, 134, 162, 184, 201, 202, 234
St Werburgh's Church 28, 35, 120
Sally Gap 1
Sandford Road 34
Sandycove 134, 146
Sandymount 146
Santry 92, 116
Santry, Lord 100
Sarah Bridge 104
Sarsfield Bridge 138
Sarsfield, Patrick 79, 85
Scalp 25
Seanad 270
Sedan chairs 116
Sexton, Thomas 186
Shankill 11
Shaw, George Bernard 218, 264, 266
Sheahan, Patrick 198

Sheares, Henry 121
Sheares, John 121
Sheehy-Skeffington, Francis 239
Sheil, Richard Lalor 143
Shepherd, Gordon 222
Sherlock, Joe 279
Sherwin, Frank 286
Sherwood Foresters 235, 236
Sidney, Henry, Lord Lieutenant 87
Silken Thomas 48, 49, 50, 53
Silkenbeard, Sitric 15, 18
Simnel, Lambert 45, 47, 52
Simpson, Alan 278
Sinn Féin 205, 209, 241, 245, 246, 251
Sinn Féin 229
Sirr, Major Henry Charles 120, 121, 135, 141
Sixth of George I, the 95, 101, 103
Skeffington, Sir William 48, 49, 50
Smith O'Brien, William 163
Smith, Patrick 247
Smithfield 122, 123
Smurfit, Michael 288
Society of the United Irishmen 107, 108, 109, 110, 111, 113, 117, 121, 123, 132, 141
Soloheadbeg 246
Soup Kitchen Act 157, 159
South Circular Road 106
South Dublin Union 234, 237
South Leinster Street 279
South Wall 102
Soyer, Alexis 159
Speed, John 62
Spencer, Lord 187
Spike Island 197

Spring Rice, Mary 222
Squad, The 247
Stack, Austin 252, 255, 259
Stafford Street 107
Stardust 286
Starry Plough 221
Stepaside 170, 279
Stephens, James 163, 165, 167,
    169, 170, 171
Stephenson 152
Steyne 10, 12, 80
Stillorgan Road 235
Stoneybatter 31, 44
Strongbow 21, 25, 27, 28, 29,
    30, 292
Suffolk Street 11
Summerhill 128
Summerhill Parade 271
Sunday Independent 232
Sutton 134, 170
Swan, Major 117, 121
Swift, Carolyn 278
Swift, Jonathan 91, 94, 95, 97,
    292
Swords 11, 116
Synge Street 266
Synge, John Millington 212
Tailor's Hall 92, 107, 109
Talbot Street 200, 239, 279
Talbot, Peter, Archbishop of
    Dublin 76
Talbot, Richard 77, 79, 81, 83
Tallaght 11, 74, 123, 170, 287
Tandy, Napper 107, 251
Tara 145
Tara Hotel 146
Tara Street 235
Telecom Éireann (Eircom) 288
Temple Bar 14
Temple Street 173, 175, 256
Templeogue 100, 170

Terenure 170, 177, 271
The Playboy of the Western World
    212
The Plough and the Stars 233
The Times 190, 191
Theatre Royal 244
Thingmote 11, 29, 80
Tholsel 38, 40, 58
Thomas Street 5, 20, 22, 119,
    120, 121, 133, 135, 238
Tinnahinch House 103
Toler, John, Lord Norbury
    144, 146
Tolka River 13
Tomar's Wood 13
Tone, Theobald Wolfe 107,
    108, 111, 113, 117, 123, 124,
    201, 270
Townsend Street 156, 262
Tracey, Seán 246, 248
Tralee Bay 242
Tramway Company 215
Traynor, Oscar 255
Treaty of Limerick, The 85, 87
Trevelyan, Charles 157, 159
Trinity College 19, 53, 60, 64,
    86, 90, 108, 158, 203, 207,
    235, 236, 251, 268
Tudor, Mary 55, 234
Tudors 45
Tuite, Thomas 156
Twiss, Richard 110
Twomey, Maurice 270
Tynan, Katherine 192
Ulysses 134, 200, 264
United Ireland 189, 193
United Irishman 205
University College Dublin 288
Upper Castle Yard 33, 170
Victoria 164
Victoria, Princess 206

Walkinstown 287

Walsh, Dr William 217

Warbeck, Perkin 47

Waterloo Road 73

Watling Street Bridge 78, 153

Wellington Bridge 136

Wellington Monument 137

Wellington, Duke of 143

Wentworth, Thomas 65, 67, 68, 69

Werburgh Street 68, 75, 178

Wesley College 266

Westland Row 165, 166, 192, 195, 234

Westmoreland Street 204, 96, 98

Whaley, Thomas 'Buck' 110, 114, 120

Whitaker, TK 253

Whitefriar Street Church 54

Wicklow Mountains 133

William of Orange 77, 79, 81, 84, 86, 101, 115

Williams, Tennessee 278

Windgates 25

Winetavern Street 9, 62, 130, 254

Women's League 214

Wood Quay 9, 39, 62, 284

Wood's Halfpence 95, 97

Workers Party 279

Workers' Republic 201

Workhouses 157

Wylie, RM 265

Wynn's Hotel 220

Yeats, WB 212, 242

York, House of 45

Zozimus 154